THE BORDERS OF DOMINICANIDAD

THE BORDERS OF
DOMINICANIDAD

Race, Nation, and Archives of Contradiction

LORGIA GARCÍA-PEÑA

Duke University Press
Durham and London
2016

Typeset in Garamond Premier Pro
by Graphic Composition, Inc.,
Bogart, Georgia

Library of Congress Cataloging-in-Publication Data
Names: García-Peña, Lorgia, [date] author.
Title: The borders of Dominicanidad : race, nation, and archives
of contradiction / Lorgia García-Peña.
Description: Durham : Duke University Press, 2016. | Includes
bibliographical references and index.
Identifiers: LCCN 2016021424 (print)
LCCN 2016023796 (ebook)
ISBN 9780822362470 (hardcover : alk. paper)
ISBN 9780822362623 (pbk. : alk. paper)
ISBN 9780822373667 (e-book)
Subjects: LCSH: Dominican Americans–Race identity. | Blacks–
Race identity–Dominican Republic. | Immigrants–United States–
Social conditions. | Race in mass media. | Dominican Republic–
Relations–Haiti. | Haiti–Relations–Dominican Republic. |
United States—Foreign relations–Dominican Republic–History. |
Dominican Republic—Foreign relations–United States–History.
Classification: LCC E184.D6 G36 2016 (print) | LCC E184.D6
(ebook) | DDC 327.7307293–dc23
LC record available at https://lccn.loc.gov/2016021424

Cover art: Pepe Coronado, *US/DR en relación*, 2016

A MIS PADRES,

DOÑA MARITZA PEÑA Y DON TULIO GARCÍA,

Y A MIS HOMBRES,

JOHN GALLAGHER Y SEBASTIÁN GALLAGHER-GARCÍA.

GRACIAS POR DÁRMELO TODO. AQUÍ LES DEVUELVO UN CHIN.

CONTENTS

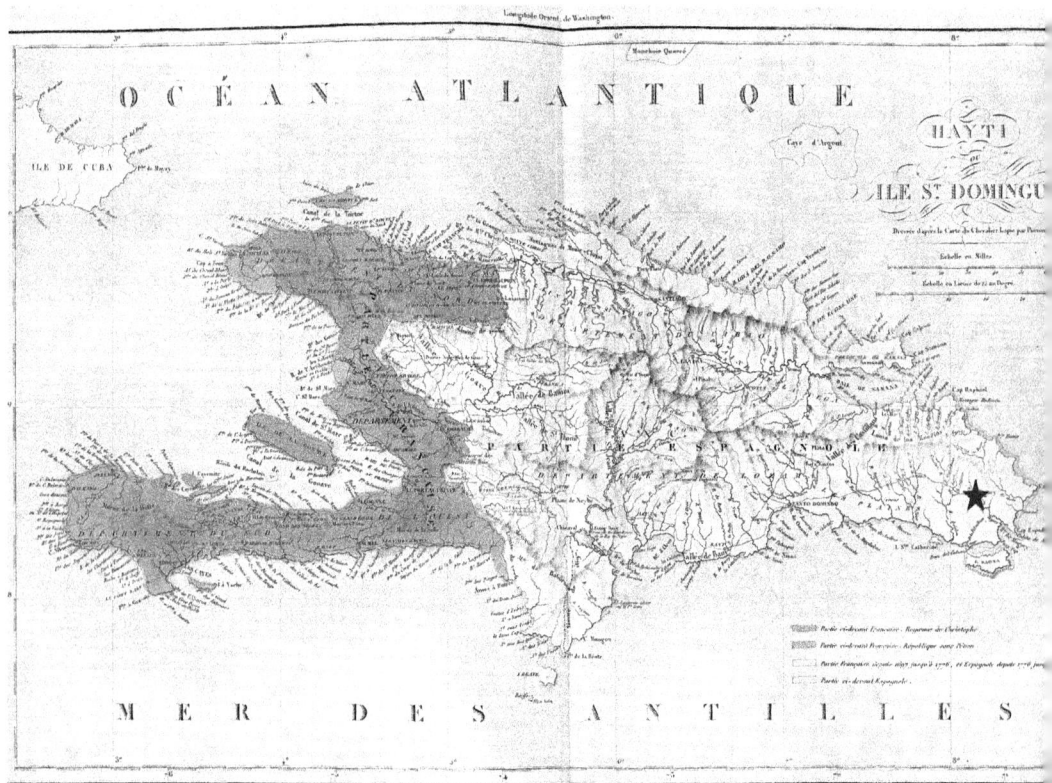

0.1 Map of the unified island of Hispaniola, 1822. Archivo General de la República, Santo Domingo.

NOTE ON TERMINOLOGY

The terms I use to label race and ethnicity of groups and individuals are incredibly complex given their specific meanings across historical moments and geographical spaces. The following is a list of some of the main identity terms I use throughout the book and a short explanation of how I use them:

black: I use "black" as a global category for naming peoples and cultures of African ancestry, recognizing that different nations and cultural groups utilize a diversity of terms to name their race.

criollo: Descendants of the Spanish colonial caste whose ancestry is white European.

dominicanidad: I employ the term as a theoretical category that refers to both the people who embrace the label "Dominican" whether or not they are considered Dominican citizens by the state (such as diasporic Dominicans and ethnic Haitians) and the history, cultures, and institutions associated with them. I opt to keep the Spanish-language spelling to avoid confusion with capitalized Dominicanidad, which refers to hegemonic and official institutions of state control.

Dominicanyork: Working-class Dominican migrants and their descendants who live in United States urban Dominican enclaves.

ethnic Haitian: A person of Haitian ancestry born in the Dominican Republic.

Latina/o: A term that describes people of Latin American descent living in the United States.

mulato: Refers to a mixed-race Dominican of light, medium, or dark brown skin. In the nineteenth century *mulato* was a category of privilege. I opted to keep the Spanish terminology because of its sociohistorical specificity.

rayano: A person from the geographical area of the Haitian-Dominican borderland also known as the Línea Fronteriza.

ACKNOWLEDGMENTS

This book is the result of a long, deeply personal and incredibly rewarding journey. Like many first books, it began long ago as part of my doctoral training, and it has grown with me. I am thankful to see it mature and go out into the world, after many years of dedication and work. But of course, getting to this point required the support of many, including some of the people whose lives and work inform the chapters. My eternal gratitude and appreciation go first to Josefina Báez, whose performance work and writing kindled my curiosity way back when I was a college student at Rutgers University. My interest in her work was the seed that eventually grew into this book. Her friendship has been the most amazing reward. Gracias, mi hermana por tanta luz. The inventiveness of Rita Indiana Hernández; the *acciones* of David "Karmadavis" Pérez; and the literary gifts of Junot Díaz, Rey Andújar, Nelly Rosario, Loida Maritza Pérez, and Aurora Arias provided a road map for translating *dominicanidad* beyond the island and across a vast temporal span. The intellectual legacy of Juan Bosch served as a bridge between the often slippery here and there my book connects. It is my most sincere hope that the archive I created in this book honors their lives and the lives of Olivorio Mateo, Dominga Alcántara, the Andújar family, Sonia Marmolejos, and the many other actors who inform the stories and histories my book memorializes.

This project began while I was a doctoral student in the American Culture Program at the University of Michigan. Lawrence La Fountain-Stokes was incredibly supportive. Yolanda Martínez-San Miguel was an instrumental mentor and advisor. Jesse Hoffnung-Garskof and Richard Turits provided guidance as I began to explore the tensions between history and literature. The mentorship of Jossianna Arroyo, Mary Kelley, Carol Smith Rosenberg, and Julie Ellison and the tireless diligence of Marlene Moore made Michigan a nurturing place for me to grow intellectually and humanly. My friends Afia Ofori-Mensa, Brian Chung, Chris Finley, Danny Méndez, Dean Saranillo,

Heijin Lee, Lee Ann Wang, Kelly Sisson, Rachel Afi Queen, Sam Erman, and Tyler Cornelius gave me feedback and encouragement, pushing me to think about my project across disciplinary fields. Their love and support carried me during difficult times.

I am forever grateful for the guidance of historians Quisqueya Lora, Elizabeth Manley, and Raymundo González, who shared their knowledge and passion for Dominican history with me and taught me the nuts and bolts of conducting research in the Dominican National Archives. Mil gracias por su apoyo, amistad y generosidad.

I had incredible support for the various technical aspects of the manuscript preparation. Juleyka Lantigua and Megan Bayles cut many long sentences in two, supplied multiple commas, erased extra ones, and gave me fair doses of "what is this?" that ultimately made the manuscript more accessible to readers. I am grateful for their editorial support. Kilia Llano made the maps and illustrations. Pepe Coronado took my argument to heart and turned it into a beautiful cover image, and Achy Obejas checked many of the translations. I would simply not have been able to complete this enormous task without the tireless assistance of Chantell Smith Limerick, whose incredible availability, careful edits, diligence, and overall kindness made me feel accompanied through the often lonesome process of writing. I am sure she is in tears reading these words as I am while I write them.

A Ford Foundation dissertation fellowship allowed me to spend a year conducting research at the Dominican National Archive in Santo Domingo. A Future of Minority Studies postdoctoral fellowship was instrumental in beginning the revisions for the book. The Willson Center Research Fellowship at the University of Georgia allowed me to have time to complete a first draft of the manuscript, and the Milton Grant at Harvard University provided me with financial support to conduct the final research trips to Santo Domingo, Washington, DC, and New York.

Along the way I have found incredibly generous mentors who have read the book carefully and provided valuable feedback and guidance. Nicole Guidotti-Hernández and Silvio Torres-Saillant went above and beyond reading several versions of the manuscript, meeting with me on multiple occasions in multiple locations, and providing both intellectual and moral support every step of the way. To the two of them I am forever indebted. Hay un poco de ustedes dos en este libro. My friend Dana Bultman was the first to read a very early draft of the manuscript. She patiently asked important questions and suggested edits and revisions that really pushed me in the right direction. Her enthusiasm for my work carried me at a moment when I most needed it. Laura Gutiérrez was instrumental in pushing me to think about the body as site of intellectual inquiry. Chandra Talpade-Mohanty made a home for me at Syracuse University during the early stages of writing. Along with Linda Carty, Myrna García Calderón, and Silvio Torres-Saillant, she provided an intellectually stimulating forum for exchanges and discussions. It was during those weeks that I was able to draft a blueprint for the book.

My colleagues in the Department of Romance Languages and Literatures at the University of Georgia hosted a presentation that generated important questions informing chapters 3 and 4. Pam Voekel, Betina Kaplan, Jan Pendergrass, Kelly Happy, Lesley Feracho, Judith Ortiz-Cofer, and Nicolás Lucero encouraged my writing amidst the life juggles of my first academic position. I am indebted also to my friends and colleagues at Harvard University—Genevieve Clutario, Lauren Kaminsky, Kirsten Weld, Robin Bernstein, Mariano Siskind, Mayra Rivera Rivera, Alejandro de la Fuente, Mary Gaylord, Kay Shelemay, Joe Blackmore, Jill Lepore, and Ju Yon Kim. Thanks to the scholars and staff at the Dominican Studies Institute, particularly Sarah Aponte, Anthony Stevens, Jacqueline Jiménez Polanco, and Ramona Hernández, and to transnational Hispaniola scholars April Mayes, Raj Chetty, Maya Horn, Arturo Victoriano, Carlos Decena, Néstor Rodríguez, and Ginetta Candelario, who all provided key advise and expertise. Special thanks to the Duke University Press anonymous reviewers for the insightful comments and to Courtney Berger for believing in this project and seeing it to fruition.

The support of my Latino/a studies and ethnic studies community across the United States was crucial throughout the years. Their feedback, questions, letters, and hugs gave this book and me a home in the field of inquiry that had nurtured my scholarship. Gracias Irene Mata, Ondine Chavoya, Arlene Dávila, Lourdes Torres, Josie Saldaña, Adriana Zavala, Deborah Pacini Hernández, Camila Stevens, Vanessa Pérez-Rosario, Marisel Moreno, Ben Sifuentes-Jáuregui, Lisa Lowe, Patricia Herrera, George Lipsitz, Christen Smith, Barbara Ransby, Frances Aparicio and Israel Reyes for being on my side.

I could have never completed this book without the love and support of my mujeres: Nuna Marcano, Josefina Báez, Eric Gómez, Daryelin Torres, Adnaloy Espinosa, Nimsi Guzmán, Indhira García, María Scharbay, Laura Catelli, and Afia Ofori-Mensa. And my dear friends and biggest supporters Junot Díaz, David Tábora, Julie Tábora, Alex Guerrero, and the rest of you who will be angry I forgot to mention your name but will celebrate with me just the same. Ustedes saben que el resto es la selva.

My family may have not always completely understood what I was doing or why, but they were supportive just the same in more ways than words can ever describe. Thank you to my brothers, Albin García Peña and Kerwin García Peña, for taking care of me, for working so I could read, for often carrying a heavier burden so I did not have to. Thank you to my sister, Vashti Nicolas, por añoñarme toda la vida. To my nieces and nephews for their love and laughter. To my cousins in the Dominican Republic—Eliezer, Abel, and Iván Doñé—for chasing after books for me and coming to see my talks, in often hostile environments. Gracias por nunca juzgarme. To my aunts Dorcas and Sarah Peña for the right doses of *moros* and bachatas, particularly on those frustrating days of long blackouts that made my research impossible, and to my dearest uncle, Claudio Doñé, por quererme tanto.

Thank you to my parents for giving me all they had, for having faith in me, and for encouraging me, even when our worlds seem opposite and strange, to keep going forward in a direction that often took me away from them and closer to myself. Your unconditional, absolute love and support is all anyone could ever need. My father, Don Tulio García, introduced me to books and taught me to love words and language. My mother, Doña Maritza Peña, taught me the true meaning of the phrase "sí se puede." She modeled how to stand up for what was right and how to talk back, particularly when everyone is trying to silence us. Gracias por tu valor, mami.

But my deepest and eternal gratitude is for my partner in all adventures, John Paul Gallagher, and our beautiful son, Sebastián. John made me coffee every morning, ran out to buy ink, chased away imaginary and real demons, and clapped in cheer every time I read him a new chapter, a new page, a new paragraph. Sebastián grounded me and opened a new world of that which is possible. With him in my arms, I began to write this book. I finished it to the beat of his bouncing ball in the backyard. I am grateful I sacrificed nothing of you to write this book. I am grateful I always put you first. John and Sebastián, it is because of you two that I am. And this book, as you both know, I wrote with and for you.

My last words of gratitude are for my students across the multiple institutions I have been part of over the last ten years, but most important, my Freedom University students, who challenged me and gave me a home when I most needed one. Gomabseubnida. Gracias. Thank you.

Dominicanidad in Contra*diction*

During my first semester of graduate school at the University of Michigan, I attended a gathering aimed at connecting graduate students of color with university resources. Upon hearing me speak Spanish to a friend, a professor asked where I was from. Understanding he was not interested in my New Jersey upbringing, but rather in figuring out the origins of my ethnicity and Spanish-speaking abilities, I told him I was born in the Dominican Republic. The professor smiled and said to me: "Ah, *dominicana*! I love your country! Good rum and cheap whores!" I excused myself and abandoned the gathering.

As I walked home that night my body shook with a combination of anger, indignation, and confusion. Why did the professor think it appropriate to refer to my birth country in such aggressive terms? What logic made it possible for him to associate me, a doctoral student, with his hedonistic escapades to the tropics? The dynamics at play in the professor's diction are foundational to some of the basic questions this book raises.

Given my scholarly training and my preoccupation with the production of dominicanidad at home and abroad, the encounter with the professor prompted a more urgent questioning of the multiple ways in which silences and repetitions operate in the erasure of racialized Dominican subjects from the nation and its archive. Those silences, as my encounter with the professor shows, are then filled with fantasies that reflect colonial desires and fears.[1] Through a colonizing gaze, the professor replaced my (Dominican) subjectivity with the symbolic tropes of colonial desire: "good rum and cheap whores." Yet as I reflect on what is still a very troubling encounter, I recognize that my body, by its mere positioning within the academic space, also interrupted the professor's "knowledge" of dominicanidad.

In many ways, this book is a project of recovering and historicizing knowledge interruptions through what I call contra*dictions*, "dictions"—stories, narratives, and speech acts—that go against the hegemonic version of national identity and against the mode of analysis we tend to value as historically accurate or what most people call truth. *The Borders of Dominicanidad* is concerned with the ways in which dictions are projected and performed on racialized bodies to sustain the exclusionary borders of the nation. Such acts of violent nation bordering are historically determined; yet they also require the complicity of citizens in the violent policing and erasure of racialized bodies. The professor's diction—"good rum and cheap whores"—summoned the historical nexus that has marked the relationship between my birth country, the Dominican Republic, and my adopted one, the United States. His diction encapsulates the unequal dynamics through which racialized immigrant and ethnic minority subjects are marked as perpetual others, becoming the carriers of two nations' exclusion—the one associated with their ethnicity and the one in which they reside.

Literary scholar Silvio Torres-Saillant argues that emigration for Dominicans is always a form of exile because the emigrants are forced to leave their homeland due to poverty and disenfranchisement: "Emigra quien no puede quedarse. . . . Nuestra emigración es una expatriación" (Those who emigrate do so because they cannot stay. . . . Our emigration is the same as expatriation).[2] I take Torres-Saillant's argument further by insisting that black Dominican migrants are exiles at home and abroad. They are symbolically and physically expunged from their home nation because they are black and poor, yet they remain unadmitted into their host nation for the same reasons. While "black" does not exist as an ethnically distinguished category in the Dominican Republic the way it does in the United States, being black (*prieto*, Haitian, or *rayano*) there inhibits social mobility through civic, political, and economic exclusion. A poor prieto, someone with dark brown skin, can easily be assigned the category of foreigner (*haitiano*). A poor prieto who migrates to the United States then becomes a Dominicanyork, her body doubly marked as black and foreign. The multiple geopolitical borders of dominicanidad—Haiti, the Dominican Republic, and the United States—become visible through the body of the racialized Dominican Latino/a. This dynamic made it possible for the professor to see in me his fantasy of dominicanidad despite my subject position as a US national.

The long and unequal relationship between the United States and the Dominican Republic has been relegated to the often unread margins of the US archive. Historians of American Empire, for instance, rarely include the Dominican Republic in their study of the nineteenth-century expansion that led to the Louisiana Purchase (1803); the Annexation of Texas (1845); and the colonization of Puerto Rico, Cuba, and Guam after the Spanish-American War (1898). This omission exists despite the fact that the United States attempted to purchase Dominican territories between 1824 and 1884 and established unofficial military bases in the Dominican southwest region during the US military occupations of 1916–24.[3]

This Dominican "footnote condition," which writer Junot Díaz allegorizes in his acclaimed novel *The Brief Wondrous Life of Oscar Wao* (2007), extends well beyond the historical archive of nineteenth-century US expansionism. In 2000, for instance, Dominicans became the fastest-growing ethnic group in New York City.[4] Yet the media and advertisement industry rarely portrays Dominicans as exemplary of US Latinidad. Dominican blackness does not fit the colonial fantasy that makes the light-skinned version of Latino/a *mestizaje* marketable in the United States (as exemplified in actors Salma Hayek, Benicio del Toro, Antonio Banderas, and "The Most Interesting Man in the World"). The diversity of Latino/a ethnicities, languages, and cultures are thus replaced with the "repackaged" Latino/a—a concoction of stereotypes, fantasies, and historical figures associated with Spain and Mexico (bullfights and Cinco de Mayo)—that fulfills colonial desire for the foreign and exotic.[5] Amidst such abysmal inequalities, my encounter with the professor, though incredibly enraging, is not surprising.

The Borders of Dominicanidad brings dominicanidad from the footnote to the center of the page, insisting on the impact of dictions on the national and racial identity of a people. The stories and histories upheld by nations and their dominant archive create marginality through acts of exclusion, violence, and silencing. Though these official stories of exclusion are influential in bordering the nation and shaping national identity, this book also shows they are always contested, negotiated, and even redefined through contra-*dictions*.

I see dominicanidad as a category that emerges out of the historical events that placed the Dominican Republic in a geographic and symbolic border between the United States and Haiti since its birth in 1844.[6] Dominicanidad is thus inclusive of subjects as well as the dictions that produce them. It also encompasses multiple territories and ethnoracial identifications: Dominicanyork, *rayano*, *dominicano*, Afro-Dominican. Those, in turn, make up Dominican subjectivities across national spaces.[7]

Living in El Nié

In the United States, the Dominicanyork can be read as African American until the person's accent or ability to speak Spanish sets the individual apart as an *other* black. The Dominicanyork thus inhabits a space of dual marginality belonging to neither nation, a space artist Josefina Báez allegorizes as the "flagless nation" of "El Nié": neither here nor there.[8] But the ambivalence of El Nié is not unique to the Dominican diasporic experience. Gloria Anzaldúa writing in 1987, for instance, described her Tejana condition as one of such discomfort it could be equated to living on barbwire.[9] Speaking about Puerto Rican transnationalism, novelist and critic Luis Rafael Sánchez in his seminal essay "La guagua aérea" (1994) called Puerto Rico a "flying bus."[10] Similarly, scholar Gustavo Pérez Firmat, also writing in 1994, theorized the Cuban American condition as "living on the hyphen."[11] While highlighting the inherent discomfort of their particular liminalities, Anzaldúa, Sánchez, and Pérez Firmat hinted at an advantage awarded to the border-immigrant-transnational subject: They can serve as a bridge between two geographical, historical, and linguistic borders, contesting, as Anzaldúa would argue, "the unnatural historical boundaries" that prohibit human bodies from freely crossing between here and there.[12]

But the specificity of Dominican alterity allegorized through Báez's Nié—which also means, in its most vulgar sense, the "taint"—queers both the hegemonic narrative of the nation-state(s) and the very location of in-betweenness inhabited by Anzaldúa, Sánchez, and Pérez Firmat: "We all live in the same building. El Nié. My mother, my grandmother, la comadre—mi madrina, el ejemplo, la quiero a morir [my comadre—my godmother, the role model, I love her to death]."[13] Through a diction that embodies and projects the very liminal experiences of the black Dominican and Dominicanyork subject the nation seeks to contain, Báez's Nié becomes a trans-historical location where the stories of exclusion can be recovered and preserved. El Nié signifies not the border space that the subject inhabits—Anzaldúa's the barbwire—but rather the body that carries the violent borders that deter them from entering the nation, from access to full citizenship and from public, cultural, historical, and political representation. Such act of border embodiment is a manifestation of Afro Dominican spirituality.

M. Jacqui Alexander's groundbreaking work *Pedagogies of Crossing* meditates on the role of the sacred Afro-religious traditions in the process of uncovering historical silences that produce oppression. She argues that the body of the Afro-religious devotee can become a vessel from which the past, in the form of the dead, can come back offering truths.[14] El Nié functions as an embodiment of past through present knowledge. It bridges Hispaniola colonial and diasporic experiences through the very body of the Dominican-york exile subject. Studies about transnationalism and migration typically look across national borders in order to propose subjects as ethnic minorities or unwanted foreigners, immigrants or emigrants, defining people through nations and in so doing, through a nation-bordering chronology. The symbolic space of El Nié expands our understanding of borders; it displaces the location and polarity of the nation-border, instead proposing the body as the location that contains and reflects national exclusion (borders) across history and generations.

The Borders of Dominicanidad investigates how individuals who inhabit El Nié grapple with the multiplicity of dictions, racial paradigms, and economic disparities sustained by the dominant narratives of the nation. This book asks: How does the Dominican racialized exile subject—the rayano; the exoticized, sexualized brown-skinned *dominicana*; the Dominicanyork; and the Dominican migrant—contra*dict* the hyphenated histories and stories that violently continue to silence them from the archives of the two nations it is charged with bridging? The intellectual impulse guiding my investigation derives from a preoccupation with the footnote condition that mutes Dominican plurality, silencing stories and histories from both US and Dominican archives. In that sense, this book is concerned with how dictions—that which is written, said, or described—impact the way people, particularly those considered ethnic minority, colonial, or racialized subjects, are imagined and produced across national paradigms.

Chicana feminists Gloria Anzaldúa and Cherríe Moraga called for a theorization "from the flesh" in order to contrast the epistemic violence that perpetually excluded minoritized people's knowledge and histories from the archive.[15] Following this call, critics Walter Mignolo and Nelson Maldonado-Torres have urged us to think from the position of suppressed and marginalized in order to "decolonize knowledge."[16] Though skepticism surrounds intellectual projects that are not solely evidence based, I argue that finding a more complete version of "the truth" requires us to read in contra*diction*, paying attention to the footnotes and silences left in the dominant archives. To do so, I follow Elizabeth Grosz's groundbreaking proposition of the body as a central framework for the construction of subjectivity.[17]

If the body, as Grosz argues, can be a "thing" through which the dominant rhetoric of sex and gender can be contested, I argue it can also be a site where the violence and silencing of the borders contained in the nation's archive can be contra*dicted*. If the body of the racialized subject can carry the burden of coloniality ("good rum and cheap whores"), becoming a screen onto which colonial desires and fears can be projected, this book argues it can also become a site from where the histories and stories that perpetuate and sustain the oppressive borders of the nation can be interpellated.[18] I propose the body—the racialized body of dominicanidad living in El Nié—as a site for negotiating the narratives of race, gender, and cultural belonging that operate in bordering the nation.

Race and Borders

The study of the US-Mexican border has been central in establishing the growing fields of border studies and Latino/a studies in the United States. Though the importance of the US-Mexican border is undeniable, my book invites the reader to think about how other geographical and symbolic borders have been significant in imagining the national identity of the United States, particularly as related to race (blackness) and ethnicity (Latinidad). The United States' centrality in the formation of Dominican racial discourse is key to my analysis of the different ways in which dictions have shaped how Dominicans negotiate racial identities and national belonging across geographical and symbolic borders.

The noun "border" alludes to tangible objects (a sign, a site, or even wall) that can arbitrate people's access and belonging to a particular territory. A border, though often invisible, can be named, crossed, and sometimes even erased. "Bordering," on the other hand, evokes a continuum of actions that affect human beings. Bordering implies an actor (one who enacts the bordering) and a recipient (they who are bordered). As my experience with the professor shows, bordering can take place even when geographical markers are absent; bordering cannot be geographically contained.

This book suggests the border between Haiti and the Dominican Republic as a locus for understanding how race and nation intersect in the bordering of a people. As people and ideas travel back and forth, borders are reaffirmed, contested, and redefined through official and unofficial actions. Increased Haitian immigration to the Dominican Republic since the US intervention in Hispaniola (1914–34) and the massive Dominican emigration to the United States that began after the assassination of dictator Rafael

Leónidas Trujillo in 1961 largely shaped Dominican understanding of race and citizenship. *The Borders of Dominicanidad* insists on the centrality of the Haiti-DR border as a site that is both historically linked to and symbolically present in the United States through the body of the Dominican racialized immigrant/minority subject.

My repositioning of the Haiti-DR border within US history requires two disruptions of the current temporal and geographical notions guiding our understanding of race and ethnicity in the United States. The first disruption requires the reader to sustain the idea that "fear of Haiti"—the overwhelming concern that overtook slave economies like the United States and Spain following the slave revolt that began in 1791 and led to Haitian independence in 1804—is foundational to the production of US notions of race and citizenship. Fear of Haiti dominated the young and robust, slavery-driven US economy and determined the Empire's relationship to the two Hispaniola republics.[19]

During the early years of the foundation of the Dominican Republic (1844–65), the United States supported the idea of Dominican racial superiority over Haiti and disavowed Haiti as racially inferior and thus unfit for self-government. This dichotomist view of the two Hispaniola nations shaped the relationship between the Dominican Republic and Haiti. It also shaped how the two nations and the relationship between them were imagined, and continue to be imagined and produced, across the globe.[20] Fear of Haiti combined with Dominican *criollo* colonial desire and the threat of US expansionism impelled nineteenth-century Dominican writers and patriots such as Félix María del Monte and Manuel de Jesús Galván to produce dominicanidad as a hybrid race that was decidedly other than black, and therefore different from Haiti's blackness. They did so through literary and historical narratives of *mestizaje* that substituted notions of race (*mulato, prieto*) with nation (*dominicano*). The foundational myth of the Dominican hybrid nation has led to the continuous physical and epistemic violence against Dominican blacks, *rayanos* (border subjects), and Haitian-Dominicans. It has also contributed to military violence against rayano and Afro-Dominican religious groups at the hands of totalitarian and repressive regimes that dominated the twentieth-century Dominican Republic (US military: 1916–24; Trujillo dictatorship: 1930–61; US military: 1965; and Balaguer regime: 1966–78).

The history of US blackness is also largely intertwined with the history of Hispaniola's independence projects. With the emergence of two black and mulato-led republics (Haiti in 1804 and the Dominican Republic in 1821), Hispaniola became an international locus for black resistance and liberation as well as the object of fear in the antebellum United States.[21] At the beginning of the Haitian Revolution, thousands of French planters fled the island, taking refuge in the United States; many took slaves with them.[22] By 1792, more than two hundred white Saint Domingue families had moved to Philadelphia.[23] Following the fall of Cap-Français in 1793, the number of refugees increased daily, at one point reaching a rate of ten thousand per day for over a week. Most refugees went to the United States in the hopes of continuing to participate in a slave-driven economy.[24] The Saint Domingue events arguably influenced early abolitionist efforts and black insurgency in the nineteenth-century United States. Examples of this influence can be found in the Gabriel Conspiracy (1800), a plan by African American slaves to attack Richmond and destroy slavery in Virginia that "Frenchmen" allegedly orchestrated, as well as the famous Vesey Plot of Charleston (1822), in which the accused mentioned the Haitian Revolution as their inspiration for insurgency.[25]

During the second half of the nineteenth century, blackness was an important category in the definition of US destiny. A nation that was built at the expense of black people's freedom now had to figure out a way to redefine itself as multiracial, facing its great crime and finding ways to deal with the trauma of slavery. In this atmosphere—which coincides with the progression of Manifest Destiny, and the growth of the "White Man's Burden" ideology in Washington—US discourse of blackness that, as I argue, emerged in dialogue with Hispaniola, traveled back to Hispaniola through political and cultural imperialism. Nineteenth-century African American abolitionists such as Frederick Douglass and Martin Delany, as well as early twentieth-century thinkers such as W. E. B. Du Bois and Arturo Schomburg, located in Haitian slave rebellions the spirit of liberty and freedom needed to fight for the equality of races.[26] Some of these figures would eventually argue for emigration efforts of free American blacks to Hispaniola. Between 1823 and 1898, as many as twenty thousand black Americans emigrated to the southern part of Cap-Haïtien and to the Bay of Samaná, eventually forming communities and influencing the culture and history of both nations of Hispaniola.[27]

Frederick Douglass, who joined the Republican Party and participated amply in the imperial project, was appointed to the Commission of Inquiry for the Annexation of Santo Domingo, in 1871.[28] Douglass, an ex-slave and great defender of racial equality, actively participated in a project that would end the sovereignty of a nation ruled by African descendants. Reconciling his desire for equality and justice with his idea of a cohesive nation, Douglass got behind the Manifest Destiny of the United States. He believed that in order for the black race to move forward, it needed the support and strength of a strong nation and its leaders. Douglass believed "Santo Domingo could not survive on its own," but could be great as part of the US Empire.[29] Douglass, an expert on race, believed Santo Domingo would be a refuge for African American professionals and scholars seeking to escape the oppression of the post–Civil War United States to develop their full potential as humans: "This is a place where the man can simply be man regardless of his skin color. Where he can be free to think, and to lead."[30] But Douglass was not the first American to describe the Dominican Republic as a form of nonblack racial other. The US commission from 1845 in charge of assessing Dominicans' ability to self-govern found Dominicans to be "neither black nor white."[31] Assuaging public anxiety surrounding the potential emergence of another black nation, both commissions (the 1845 commission led by white American diplomat John Hogan and the 1871 commission in which Frederick Douglass served as secretary) insisted on the difference of Dominican *mulataje* as an advantage in the future progress of the young nation, in contrast with the disadvantageous blackness of neighboring Haiti.

Though Douglass found Dominican racial mixtures promising, particularly as compared to Haiti, he also found Dominicans to be generally uncivil and in need of much guidance and teaching. Consciously or not, Douglass, the voice of black thought in US politics of the late nineteenth century, established US blackness—which he embodied in the eyes of his nation—as an authority for determining the racial, political, and cultural implications of blackness in Hispaniola. His legacy of US black intellectual dominance continues to shape scholarly discussions about Dominican blackness to date.[32] If white Americans, like Hogan, were endowed with the power to govern and instruct young nations, black Americans—Douglass's actions seem to suggest—had the burden of teaching other blacks how to be black, civil, and free. In this framework, which would be expanded to the rest of the Hispanic Caribbean after the Spanish-American War, we can find that the roots of the "complicated" Dominican blackness are deeply intertwined with the economic and political ambitions of expansionist post–Civil War United States.

My proposed genealogy and geographical triangulation of the US-Haiti-Dominican borders can shed light on the contemporary prevalence of anti-

Haitianism in the Archive of Dominicanidad.[33] At the same time, it offers a way out of the discursive checkmate that persistently produces Dominicans and Haitians as racial opposites. Contemporary studies about Hispaniola tend to cast Dominicans and Haitians as enemies, the former being (more) successful, yet negrophobic and anti-Haitian, while the latter often being romanticized as poor, yet symbolic of black pride and black resistance. The common juxtaposition of Haiti and the Dominican Republic—which appears in the works of Henry Louis Gates Jr., Michelle Wucker, and Dawn F. Stinchcomb, among others—although important in beginning a conversation about the complexity of transnational race studies, can reproduce a decontextualized understanding of anti-Haitian discourse as a postmodern and local phenomenon resulting from twentieth-century Trujillo nationalism. Such an anachronistic approach obscures the fact that anti-Haitianism is a colonial ideology that traverses Hispaniola's historical struggle with European colonialism and US imperial expansionism. It also erases the fact that present-day Dominican anti-Haitianism is founded on nineteenth-century global anti-Haitianism. A more productive examination of the Dominican-Haitian relationship thus requires our awareness of the intricacies of Hispaniola's border history in dialogue with US history. Such analysis would also lead us to recognize the present Haiti-DR border as a product of the US Empire.

Disrupting Latinidad

The second disruption I propose as a way of expanding our understanding of race, nations, and borders as central in producing the US ethnoracial category of Latino/a. This epistemic interruption decenters the experiences of migration and border crossing—the movement of the body from one location to the other and/or the shifting of geographical frontiers that end up moving a community or locale from one nation to another. Rather, I argue that US political, economic, and military expansion over Latin America—which began circa 1790 with the slave revolts that led to the Haitian Revolution—are foundational to the production of Latino/a as a US racial category and consequently to the process of US cultural bordering that continues to render Latina/os as foreign. To explain this process, I examine dominicanidad neither through the dominant yet mutually exclusive temporal and geographical lenses dividing island and US Dominicans, nor through the polarization of migration-minority experiences. Instead I approach Dominican racialized subjectivity through a study of the palimpsestic coexistence of colonial impositions that are projected on the racialized body of subjects living on the island or the United States.

Borders are often imagined as a locus of migration or as a national landmark dividing citizen from immigrant subjects.[34] My analysis goes beyond this dichotomist view by insisting on the border as both a tangible location where subjects live as well as an embodied location—El Nié—where the multiple impositions of the nation-state and the imperial-colonial discourses coexist. The dictions that produce border subjectivity are thus always historical and translocal.

Foregrounding El Nié does not intend in any way to diminish the importance of the experience of migration in the construction of Latino/a ethnicity in the United States. Rather, I am bringing attention to an *other* way to expand our knowledge of Latinidad by looking at the significance of nineteenth-century US imperialism over Latin America for present processes of bordering, racialization, and exclusion of Latino/as from the United States and its archive. In this way, my proposed disruptions contribute to and expand the intellectual labor of US-Mexican border scholars Nicole Guidotti-Hernández, Laura Gutiérrez, and Raúl Coronado in their historical and geographical repositioning of relationships between US Latino/as and Latin Americans as shaped by the continuous presence of European and US American colonial impositions on the bodies of racialized subjects.

Coronado's "history of textuality," for instance, invites us to imagine Texas not as we do today, "as some behemoth of nationalist independent feeling," but rather as an "interstitial colony shaped by a long history of imperial jockeying among New Spain (now Mexico), French Louisiana, and the expanding United States."[35] Similarly, Guidotti-Hernández urges us to think beyond the dominant narratives of resistance associated with Chicana history to uncover the "interstices of multiple colonial regimes" that operate in the production of racialized subjects, "showing how language is what makes the subject and the body."[36] Coronado and Guidotti-Hernández's interpellations of US Mexicanidad pose urgent critiques of dominant epistemological approaches to Latino/a studies by insisting on the need to historicize the colonial contra*dictions* that operate to produce the racialized subject. My proposed genealogy of dominicanidad and the disruptions produced by the triangulation of US-DR-Haiti further demonstrate *how* racialized Latino/a voices, bodies, and dictions are silenced from multiple archives across time and geographies, but it also simultaneously creates an alternative archive that allows readers, if they so choose, to read in contra*diction*.

Contradicting the Archive

In order to understand my proposed geopolitical triangulation, *The Borders of Dominicanidad* examines the structural foundations of what I call the Archive of Dominicanidad—historical documents, literary texts, monuments, and cultural representations sustaining national ideology—through which I argue the criollo elite sought to define the racial borders of the nation following independence from Haiti (1844) and throughout the second half of the nineteenth century. I trace how these foundational ideologies have been interpolated, institutionalized, deployed, and embodied through repetition at five critical moments in the history of the nation: (1) the murders in 1822 of the Andújar sisters, better known as the Galindo Virgins, during the Haitian unification of the island of Hispaniola; (2) the killing of Afro-Dominican religious leader Olivorio Mateo in 1922 during the first US military occupation of the Dominican Republic; (3) the Massacre of 1937 of more than twenty thousand ethnic Haitians and Afro-Dominicans in the northern borderlands during the Trujillo dictatorship; (4) the 1965 military intervention of the United States in the Dominican Republic and the subsequent emigration of one million Dominicans to the United States; and (5) the earthquake that devastated Haiti and parts of the southwest region of the Dominican Republic in January 2010.

The time period encompassed in this study (1822–2010) is sizeable. However, I am not interested in producing a historical survey of dominicanidad. Rather, my work traces the genealogy of Dominican discourses of nation and race, and their appearances, reconstructions and interpellations across time and space through the literary representations of the five historical episodes at key moments in the nation's political history. Michel Foucault proposed the concept of "genealogy" as one that does not produce history as causal to the present or that pretends to "go back in time to restore an unbroken continuity." Instead, he argued: "Genealogy allows us to see how the complexity of the present is somehow linked to the errors, the false appraisals, and the faulty calculations that gave birth to those things that continue to exist."[37] My book creates a genealogy of dominicanidad through a careful reading of the conflicts and incongruities that appear in the dictions performed through the multiple repetitions of the five episodes *The Borders of Dominicanidad* proposes as key to the foundation of the nation and its archive.

The term "contra*diction*" frames my analysis of the ways in which narratives produce nations through the violence, exclusion, and the continuous control of racialized bodies. Contra*diction* explains, for instance, how dominicanidad became simultaneously a project of the criollo elite and the US Empire in their common goal of preserving white colonial privilege in the mid-nineteenth century. "Diction" refers to the distinctiveness of speech through which meaning is conveyed and understood. Thus, in its basic implication, "diction" signifies the performance of language and meaning. The larger way that "diction" works throughout the book is through the contrapuntal analysis of the historical (documents presumed to be evidence of fact such as military memos, newspaper articles, decrees, court transcripts) and the literary (which I broadly define so as to include different forms of cultural productions such as films, performances, and songs). My interrogations of the texts bring attention to the contra*dictions* that surge within and between history and literature, showing how literature works, at times, to sustain hegemony, while at others, it serves to contest it.

The epistemological break between history and literature is always expressed concretely through the historically situated evaluation of specific narratives. Yet the very disruption between history and literature offers a way to challenge what we have come to regard as truth, or as Michel Trouillot put it, "the ways in which what happened and that which is said to have happened are and are not the same may itself be historical."[38] My book thus examines how "truths" contribute to the violence, silencing, and erasure of racialized people and their truths.

The five historical episodes that frame my analysis of contra*dictions* demonstrate the lasting effects of dictions on the lives of human beings as narratives become "truth" and as "truth" becomes the basis for exclusionary laws that sustain the ideological and political borders of the nation. Insisting on the consequences that silences produced by history have on the sustenance of power and inequality, Trouillot argues that each historical narrative renews its own claim to truth through acts of epistemic repetition.[39] Repetition of historical events, whether through historical or fictional narration, can replace the actual trauma of violence with the symbolic effect of the particular act of violence on the hegemonic project of nation-bordering.

One of the ways silencing through repetition becomes visible in the dictions I analyze is through passive voice interference in literary and historical narration of violent events, which often materializes through allegorical and metaphorical language. The passive voice often interrupts and exculpates the pain and trauma caused on the bodies of the victims of violence (the Galindo Virgins, Olivorio Mateo, the twenty thousand rayanos and ethnic Haitians killed in 1937), delaying both the traumatic historical confrontation of the event and the possibility of healing. Allegorized rather than confronted, violence becomes a vehicle for the nation's bordering, which is reinforced through the constant, but indirect, repetition of the traumatic event in literature and history.

One well-documented example of the effects of silencing and repetition is the Massacre in 1937 of twenty thousand rayanos and ethnic Haitians that I study in chapter 3. The multiple, mostly foreign, studies about the Massacre of 1937 further exacerbate its erasure by casting it as an anti-immigrant state-sponsored crime against Haitians living on the Dominican side of border rather than as the genocide of the intraethnic border population of rayanos who lived and worked in the northwestern border towns of the Artibonito Valley. Thus, repetition contributes to erasing the fact that in 1937 Dominicans killed their own. Though the massacre is the most recurrent event in the historical and literary archives of twentieth-century Hispaniola, the actual violence on the bodies of victims has yet to be acknowledged. There are no memorial sites, official commemorations, or state-sponsored efforts for peace and reconciliation of the victims and survivors.[40]

In *Silencing the Past*, Trouillot insists on the relationship between power and the production of history, reminding us that silences enter every stage of constructing the historical archive: "at the moment of fact creation (the making of the sources); the moment of fact assembly (the making of the archives); the moment of fact retrieval (the making of narratives); and the moment of retrospective significance (the making of history in the final instance)."[41] A better way to find out "what happened" or what Trouillot calls "the final product of history" requires the reading of the creation of silences: a reading from the silences *left* by history. To do so, Trouillot urged us to be less concerned with what history is, but rather how it works.[42]

The methodology I follow throughout the book guides the reader to see *how* literature and history have silenced black lives, actors, and histories from the Archive of Dominicanidad, and *how* these silences have, in turn, produced violence and exclusion of actual human beings throughout the history of the nation. Diana Taylor, Pedro San Miguel, and Doris Sommer have insisted on the complicity between history and literature in the construction of the Latin American archive since the emergence of the modern nation in the nineteenth century. Taylor argues that this complicity also allows for "public acts of forgetting" that blur the obvious discontinuities, misalliances, and ruptures that founded and sustained the myths symbolically bordering the nation.[43] Following Taylor, Nicole Guidotti-Hernández warns us that these "public acts of forgetting" happen because of, rather than in spite of, the constant repetition of historical events. Repetition is another way of silencing.[44]

The Borders of Dominicanidad assumes the enormous challenge of reading in contra*diction* by analyzing the silences created by the repetitions and passive voice interferences that inhabit the Archive of Dominicanidad. To do so, I analyze a wide variety of texts including never-before-studied evidence-based documents found in historical archives in Santo Domingo, Port-au-Prince, and Washington, DC, as well as lesser-known literary texts, *salves*, photographs, performances, oral interviews, and films. The chronologically, formally, and linguistically diverse readings of materials both contra*dicts* the hegemonic Archive of Dominicanidad and produces a new archive of contra*diction* that I hope will invite further studies.

Archiving Contradictions

The majority of scholarship focusing on the Dominican Republic concentrates on the study of the Trujillo dictatorship (1930–61), the effects of sex tourism since the 1990s, and the present state of Dominican migration to the United States. Though many scholars are concerned with questions of racial identity and representation, these questions are typically examined through a contemporary lens. I argue, however, that to understand present-day dominicanidad and the borders that have produced it, we must look at the historical and rhetorical narratives of the early nineteenth century that sustain racism in the Dominican Republic. Such historical grounding would lead us, for instance, to understand that the present-day extreme xenophobia better known as anti-Haitianism that led the Dominican government to denationalize more than 200,000 citizens in October 2013 is the result of a colonial bequeath that was in turn upheld and sustained by the United States to preserve its own imperial ventures, rather than the recent legacy of the Trujillo dictatorship.

Part I, titled "Founding the Archive," examines the considerable role that Haiti played in the process of imagining and narrating dominicanidad along racial, cultural, and political lines during the critical years of the birth of the

Dominican Republic and through the first half of the twentieth century. Chapter 1, "The Galindo Virgins: Violence and Repetition in the Archive of Dominicanidad," shows how the racialized and sexualized body of the Dominican subject—exemplified in the case of the Andújar Murders of 1822—is objectified, violated, and sacrificed for the benefit of the nation-state. The chapter traces the transformation of the historical crime against the Andújar family into the symbolic rape and murder of the Galindo Virgins at the hands of the state-serving *criollo letrados*. The chapter examines the court transcripts of the proceedings against the murderers of the Andújar family in contra*diction* with the multiple literary repetitions of the crime that begin with Félix María del Monte's epic poem *Las vírgenes de Galindo* (1860). In their efforts to preserve their own white colonial privilege, del Monte and his successors produced Galindo as a crime of barbaric black Haitians against white civilized Dominicans. The production and repetition of the Galindo Virgins, I argue, is foundational to Dominican anti-Haitian rhetoric.

Chapter 2, "Of Bandits and Wenches: The US Occupation (1916–1924) and the Criminalization of Dominican Blackness," proposes Afro-religious rituals of possession (*montarse*) and storytelling through *salves* (sacred songs) as important contra*dictions* of the dominant exclusionary archives that underlines my analysis of the 1922 murdering of Afro-religious leader Olivorio Mateo at the hands of the US Marines during the military intervention of 1916–24. My historical analysis sheds light on how the US military intervention in the Dominican Republic shaped the Haitian-Dominican border, and contributed to further erasing and disenfranchising of black Dominicans. Through close readings of military records related to the persecution of Olivorio Mateo; traditional liborista salves; oral interviews; letters; and the novel *Song of the Water Saints* (2002), by Dominican American author Nelly Rosario, I analyze how the logic of the occupation contributed to imagining the Dominican body as a site that needed to be controlled and civilized. The chapter also recovers and preserves the multiple ways in which racialized subjects contra*dicted* the epistemic violence imposed on them by the Dominican and the US states through reading of letters, literary texts, and oral interviews. The variety of evidence this chapter engages creates a sensible account of the US military intervention that shows not only how the marines implemented US policies in the Dominican Republic, but also how these policies affected the everyday life of Dominican citizens at the time.

Chapter 3, "Speaking in Silences: Literary Interruptions and the Massacre of 1937," looks at the killings of ethnic Haitians and rayanos as remembered in four fictional accounts: the short story "Luis Pie," published in Havana in 1942 by exiled Dominican writer Juan Bosch; the Haitian novel *Compère Général Soleil* (General Sun, My Brother), by Jacques Stéphen Alexis (Port-au-Prince, 1955); a *testimonio El masacre se pasa a pie* by Freddy Prestol Castillo (Santo Domingo, 1973); and the celebrated novel by Haitian American writer Edwidge Danticat, *The Farming of Bones* (New York, 1998). My analysis links the Massacre of 1937 to the anti-Haitian dictions of the early republic examined in the first chapter, showing how diction became law and epistemic violence transformed into physical violence. Without diminishing the importance of the horrific nature of these events, my analysis of the massacre moves beyond the trauma of 1937, provoking a conversation among Haitian, Dominican, and US American texts to analyze the rhetorical significance of the massacre in shaping racial ideologies during the second half of the twentieth century. In addition, the chapter insists on the persistence of xenophobic nationalism in present-day Dominican Republic.

The second part of the book, "Diaspora Contra*dicts*," engages the impact of transnational interventions in contesting hegemonic notions of dominicanidad. This section shows how contra*dictions* take various forms throughout the twentieth and twenty-first centuries as other narrations of dominicanidad emerge, particularly in the diaspora. Historical novels dominate the bulk of Dominican American literary production, as evidenced in the works of Julia Álvarez, Junot Díaz, and Nelly Rosario. Diasporic contra*dictions* thus, on the one hand, place the Dominican experience within US history, insisting on the long and unequal relationship between the two nations that has resulted in the massive migration of 10 percent of the overall population to the United States in the last fifty years. On the other, they historicize the Dominican experience from the perspective of people who have been silenced in the nation's archive: women, migrants, peasants, blacks, LGBTQ, and the disabled.

Chapter 4, "*Rayano* Consciousness: Remapping the Haiti-DR Border after the Earthquake of 2010," was inspired by a photograph I saw one week after the Haitian Earthquake in 2010 of a rayana woman, Sonia Marmolejos, nursing a severely injured Haitian baby. The image provides an analytical framework for understanding the borders of dominicanidad in a global context. The English translation of the word *rayano*, "borderer," invites us to think about the Haiti-DR border within the framework of border studies, inevitably summoning a relational critique of the continued persistence of

US colonial domination on foreign territories, which shapes national identities, cultures, and bodies. My conceptualization of rayano consciousness creates a transnational, transtemporal interchange that I hope produces new ways to theorize Latino/a studies, inciting fruitful dialogues that can help us rethink how power and politics interact with the production of symbolic and geographic borders that shape our understanding of race, nation, and culture. Transcending the political and conceptual limits of the Haitian-Dominican border, rayano consciousness, as I define it, encompasses the multiplicity of borders—transnational, interethnic, and multilinguistic—that characterize the Dominican experience on and beyond the island. Rayano consciousness thus refers to the historical and present awareness of Dominican borders—symbolic, political, and geographical—a process that includes marginalized subjectivities in the imagining and narrations of dominicanidad. Following the structure of previous chapters, chapter 4, while focused on the present, puts into dialogue a variety of temporally, linguistically, and formally diverse texts: *Cantos de la frontera*, the poetry collection (published 1963) by Dominican nationalist writer Manuel Rueda; a series of performances and videos (2005–10) by David "Karmadavis" Pérez; and "Da pa lo do," a song and music video by writer and performer Rita Indiana Hernández (2011). The diversity of the texts studied in the chapter moves my analysis toward a decolonial turn, to borrow from Caribbean critic Nelson Maldonado-Torres, that helps us better understand dominicanidad within its context while proposing the possibility of a hopeful dialogue of solidarity that can contribute to dismantling anti-Haitian and xenophobic discourse on the island and beyond.

Chapter 5, the final chapter, "Writing from El Nié: Exile and the Poetics of Dominicanidad *Ausente*," proposes that rayano consciousness informs the creation of an alternative poetics of dominicanidad in the diaspora. Historically rooted in the 150 years of unequal relationship between the United States and the Dominican Republic, and particularly in the trauma of the US intervention of 1965, I argue that this poetics of dominicanidad ausente breaks away from the nostalgic trope of migration narratives in order to propose a critique of the relationship between power, the production of history, and the construction of transnational citizenship and identities. The chapter offers a reading of works by Dominican American artist and writer Josefina Báez in dialogue with twentieth-century Dominican narratives of exile, as exemplified in the seminal works of Juan Bosch and Pedro Vergés. In so doing, the chapter awards the opportunity to explore the ways in which a poetics of dominicanidad ausente has emerged as a dialectic process of transnational interpellation of the official national narration of dominicanidad solidified during the Trujillo regime. This final chapter demonstrates that marginality becomes a transnational experience for Dominican Americans who are the same poor, black, marginal subjects who have been historically oppressed and exiled from the nation-state.[45]

The borders of dominicanidad are many, encompassing the transnational and diasporic experiences of Dominicans in the United States and elsewhere; the existence of a community of Haitian-Dominican peoples on the borderlands; and the growing presence of Haitian immigrants living in Dominican cities. *The Borders of Dominicanidad* bridges the multiplicity of margins of dominicanidad while also bringing attention to the intangibility and elusiveness of the divisions that emerge on the individual as well as collective levels of the population. My book thus suggests a reimagining not only of the physical, militarized borders that separate the two nations that inhabit Hispaniola, but also of the series of loose articulations, discourses, traumas, myths, contradictions, and historical events that have informed the Dominican subject's understanding of him or herself in relation to Haiti and the United States. Borders are about regulating, controlling, and prohibiting the free crossings of bodies and objects from one locale to another. They are also about containing the undesirable outside of the nation's center. Thus the body of the (undesirable) border crosser is inscribed with the historical, social, and legal events that seek to contain/control it. These inscriptions can in turn become another way of understanding "truth." The body of the border subject—the prieto, the rayano, the Haitian immigrant, or the Dominicanyork—can also become an archive of contra*diction*.

I

FOUNDING THE ARCHIVE

CHAPTER I

The Galindo Virgins

Violence and Repetition in the Archive of Dominicanidad

Dominicans should never forget the inherent ferocity of those monsters that penetrated our homes . . . and even the innocence of our candid virgins destroyed.
—FÉLIX MARÍA DEL MONTE, "Canción dominicana," 1844

Let us not forget all that we suffered under Haitian oppressing rule. . . . Even our tender virgins were raped at the hands of those beasts.
—MANUEL ARTURO PEÑA BATLLE, *Discurso sobre la cuestión fronteriza*, 1944

All those enemies of our nation . . . who forget the incredible sufferings that under the forced occupation of 1822 our nation endured. . . . That even the fragile bodies of young virgins were raped and killed.
—VINCHO CASTILLO, "Discurso," 2014

On May 31, 1822, during the first year of the Haitian Unification of Hispaniola (1822–44), widespread panic overcame residents of Santo Domingo after a leaflet that read "Beware of Rapists and Killers" appeared around the main plaza in the city center.[1] The pamphlet described the events that had happened the day before: three men, armed with machetes and rifles, killed three girls and their father in the vicinity of Galindo.[2] The dismembered bodies of the children were found in a well.[3] On June 8, owing to the testimony of a woman identified as Ysabel, the house servant, members of the military government of Spanish Haiti (now the Dominican Republic) apprehended Pedro Cobial, Manuel de la Cruz, and Alejandro Gómez in connection with the crime.[4] The men were "wanted criminals from the Spanish Era who had escaped prison during the political transition from Spanish colonial rule to independence."[5] Cobial, de la Cruz, and Gómez self-identified as Spanish Dominicans from East Santo Domingo.[6]

Map 1.1 Map of Santo Domingo East, circa 1822. Created by Kilia Llano.

After a celebration that included drinking, dancing, and cockfighting, Cobial, de la Cruz, and Gómez broke into a stable near Los Minas (see map 1.1) belonging to a man identified as José de los Santos. They stole a horse, a rifle, and couple of machetes.[7] At dawn the bandits left en route to San Pedro, where Cobial was from. About nine kilometers east of old Santo Domingo (today Zona Colonial), they encountered a well-dressed lone rider, Don Andrés Andújar, who was headed to the city center for business. Andújar was a widower. He lived with his three daughters—Águeda, fifteen, Ana Francisca, ten, Marcela, six—and their nanny, Ysabel, in Galindo (see map 1.1), a six-hacienda community located west of La Caleta.[8] Still drunk from the night before, the three men attacked Andújar, who was also armed, with the intention of stealing his horse. Though Andújar resisted, he was outnumbered and eventually killed at the hands of Cobial.[9] The bandits then proceeded to the Andújar Hacienda, where the girls still slept. It was six in the morning.

No one knows if the criminals woke the children before they killed them.[10] Some said the men raped the girls.[11] The criminals then threw the lifeless bodies of the children in the well, raided the hacienda, lit it on fire, and left.[12] They spared Ysabel, presumably because they believed her to be mute. On June 11, 1822, a tribunal of Spanish Haitian judges convicted Cobial, de la Cruz, and Gómez for their crimes. They sentenced de la Cruz and Gómez to forced labor and five years in prison. Cobial was given the maximum sentence: fifteen years in prison. [13]

Through a narrative of repetition, silencing, and exculpation that resulted in what I call the Archive of Dominicanidad, nineteenth-century Hispanophile writers—who privileged Spanish language, Hispanic culture, the traditions of Spain, and whiteness—memorialized Águeda, Ana Francisca, and Marcela Andújar as white virgins and the first female martyrs of the nation, comparable only to the martyrdom of the revered Mirabal sisters.[14] Cobial, de la Cruz, and Gómez in turn became bloodthirsty black Haitians. The invention of the Galindo Virgins eventually replaced the memory of the violent act and the subjecthood of the victims. This discursive strategy helped to sustain elite desires for European cultural identity while appeasing global anxiety over the potential creation of another free black nation on the island of Hispaniola. Literature and History worked together in the production of Dominicanness in contrast to Haitianness; Galindo became one of the most important motifs for sustaining anti-Haitian ideology as the crime became a metaphor for the Haitian unification.

The nation-building project, as Franklin Franco argued, "aceleró por un lado el definitivo estrangulamiento de la deformada incipiente burguesía colonial esclavista española e impulsó por el otro la formación de una burguesía criolla profundamente integrada racialmente" (accelerated the definitive decline of the incipient, malformed proslavery colonial Spanish bourgeoisie, and sparked the creation of a criollo bourgeoisie that was profoundly racially integrated).[15] However, it also resulted in a contradictory national narrative that sought to produce a sovereign nation while simultaneously appeasing criollo colonial desire to retain whiteness and European cultural dominance.[16] During the second half of the nineteenth century, this contra*diction* manifested in a literary tradition that romanticized the Spanish colonial past and demonized the Haitian unification as "the darkest period in Santo Domingo history."[17]

The first reference to the Galindo murders appears more than three decades after the incident occurred, in Nicolás Ureña's poem "Mi patria"

(1853).[18] Writing from exile in the neighboring Spanish colony of Puerto Rico, Dominican romantic writer and Liberal Party leader Félix María del Monte revisited the story in his epic poem from 1860, *Las vírgenes de Galindo o la invasión de los haitianos sobre la parte española de Santo Domingo* (The Galindo Virgins or the Haitian Invasion on the Spanish Side of Santo Domingo). Del Monte's poem is the first account to explicitly change the identity of the convicted men from Dominican to Haitian.[19] Inspired by del Monte, criollo Alejandro Bonilla, one of the most successful Caribbean visual artists of the time, painted the scene (1883) as a gruesome crime perpetrated by black Haitian soldiers against visibly white women. The painting gained significant recognition nationally and abroad.[20] At the end of the nineteenth century, *costumbrista* writer and journalist César Nicolás Penson repeated this version of the crime in his celebrated historical legend (*tradición*) *Las vírgenes de Galindo* (1891).[21] Though there is evidence that Penson had access to the *Sentencias de los reos de Galindo* (1822), the official court transcripts, he based his historical legend on del Monte's poem from 1860, making it the first instance in which the fictionalized version of the event was presented as historical truth.[22] Penson sustained his claims to historical authenticity through the use of journalistic writing techniques and temporal exactitude, and by claiming access to eyewitnesses of the crime.[23] More than a century after the murders, and writing as part of the Trujillo intelligentsia, Max Henríquez Ureña, son of the celebrated poet Salomé Ureña, revisited the episode as imaged by Penson in his novel, *La conspiración de los Alcarrizos* (1940), linking it to the failed criollo independence plot of 1824.[24]

The contra*dictions* that exist between the historical court transcripts of 1822, on which I base my reconstruction of the violent crimes at the beginning of this chapter, and the subsequent abundant repetitions, illustrate the process by which the *diction*s of history and the *dictions* of literature have operated to produce an acceptable version of Dominican cultural and racial identity. This hegemonic dominicanidad is culturally Hispanic, therefore white, ethnically opposed to Haiti, which is rendered black, and ultimately defined on and through the body of the Dominican woman, who is also imagined as white.[25]

Between 1822, when the violent episode occurred, and 1860, when Félix María del Monte wrote his poem, there are only minor cursory mentions of the Galindo murders.[26] Similar temporal gaps exist between del Monte's poem and the publication of Penson's version in 1891, and between the latter and Henríquez Ureña's novel of 1940. These significant temporal gaps also suggest a conscious political attempt to recuperate the trope of the Haitian unification—displaced by the Galindo Virgins—as a collective traumatic experience at critical moments in the definition of the Haitian-Dominican border. Del Monte's epic poem, for instance, was written during the Spanish reannexation campaign (1860–61) and circulated shortly after the passage of President Gregorio Luperón's Treaty of Peace, Friendship, and Commerce with the Haitian state (1867), which resulted in a new diplomatic crisis with the neighboring nation over frontier demarcations in the Northwest.[27] Similarly, Henríquez Ureña's version from 1940 follows the Haitian-Dominican international crisis that emerged as a result of the massacre in 1937 of an inter-ethnic borderland community, which I study in chapter 3. The reappearance of the Galindo allegory reminded people of their national loyalty to Hispanism so that, as del Monte better explained in the prologue to the 1885 edition of his *Las vírgenes de Galindo*, "Dominicans would never forget Galindo as a symbol of the inherent ferocity of those monsters that occupied us . . . and avoid at all costs, a new intervention."[28] As if following del Monte's mandate, Dominican elite writers reiterated the Galindo case at various moments in the history of the nation. Violence served as a historical reminder of the threat Haiti represented against the sovereignty of the Dominican nation.[29]

Though studies about anti-Haitian ideology dominate the bulk of intellectual and historical inquiries about the Dominican Republic in the US academy, the case of the Galindo murders is rarely mentioned. The few cursory allusions to the violent event that do appear in contemporary historiography and literary criticism rarely consider the contra*dictions* and repetitions of the crime, acknowledging only its allegorical nature. This chapter calls attention to the multiple ways in which Dominican elite criollo writers fictionalized and produced the Galindo crimes to sustain hegemonic dominicanidad through a multilateral writing process that: (a) invented Dominican whiteness as a cultural category linked to Hispanism; (b) displaced black bodies and black experiences from the nation-narration through a manipulation of popular multicolor identification into mestizaje (Indian and European racial and cultural mixture); (c) co-opted, silenced, and whitened Dominican women's bodies as sites for contesting ideologies of race and nation; and (d) erased Dominican criollo culpability for ethnic, sexual, and physical violence. By studying the multiple repetitions of the Galindo murders within the historical context in which they were produced, we better understand the significance of History and Literature in the violent process of bordering and producing the modern nation-state.

Foundations of Contradiction

Étienne Balibar argues that in the modern nation there can only be one founding revolutionary event.[30] For the Dominican Republic this foundational event is the Trabucazo (the blunderbuss shot) that on February 27, 1844, ended twenty-two years of island unification under the Haitian flag.[31] But arriving at this Dominican Republic birth date has been a rather complicated question. The Spanish-speaking portion of Hispaniola declared its independence three times: twice from Spain (1821 and 1865) and once from Haiti (1844). The establishment of 1844 as the nation's foundational moment represents a trifold process of ideological contra*dictions*. First, the two dominant ideologies guiding the process of national independence were in opposition, one demanding racial erasure and the other proposing racial unity. Second, ensuring sovereignty depended on the global conviction that Dominicans were indeed (racial) antagonists to Haitians. Finally, nineteenth-century Hispanophile writers were caught between their own ideological desire to preserve an "essence" of dominicanidad and maintain Spanish cultural identities. These contra*dictions* materialized in political turmoil, despotism, and the inability to unify and integrate the majority of the population into a national project until the twentieth century. Further, they led to multiple independences that make establishing the birth of the Dominican nation a project of historical and rhetorical contra*diction*.

The Spanish Colony of Santo Domingo obtained its first independence from Spain on December 1, 1821. During the period known as España Boba (1809–21), Spain neglected its American colonies as it faced Napoleon's invasion (1807) and the aftermath of the Peninsular War (1807–14).[32] Taking advantage of the widespread discontent that overcame Santo Domingo's criollos amidst the growing economic decline of the colony and Spain's neglect, writer and politician José Núñez de Cáceres rallied them to seek separation from the European nation. Known as the Ephemeral Independence for its short duration (December 1, 1821, to February 9, 1822), the first República del Haití Español did not abolish slavery, and thus had scant popular support. Dominican mulato *hateros* (cattle ranchers) and farmers reacted by rallying behind Haitian president Jean-Pierre Boyer to unify the island and abolish slavery. Boyer's hatero supporters eventually formed the Radical Party, while Ephemeral Independence leaders organized under the Liberal Party.[33] The two political factions dominated the bulk of nineteenth-century Dominican politics.[34]

Three years after the unification of 1822, following increasing international pressures, Boyer signed the Reparations Act of 1825 in which he promised to pay France 150 million gold francs in compensation for the European nation's "lost colonial investment" and in exchange for recognition of Haiti's independence.[35] Haiti had won the war against France in 1804, but Europe and the United States refused to acknowledge the black nation's sovereignty, a fact that affected President Boyer's ability to participate in international trade. After the passing of the Reparations Act of 1825, Spain, the United States, and England also recognized Haiti's sovereignty, lifting a twenty-one year economic embargo. To meet French demands, however, Boyer was forced to increase taxation among landowners of East Hispaniola. Widespread discontent over crippling taxes soon resulted in a unified Liberal and Radical revolutionary front that, under the leadership of French-educated criollo Juan Pablo Duarte, eventually founded the independent Dominican Republic in 1844.

In 1861, fearing another unification under the Haitian flag, Pedro Santana (1801–64), a criollo, sought the support of Liberal elites to request that the Spanish queen, Isabel II, reannex Santo Domingo to Spain. Santana rationalized his treason by insisting on the patriotic need to protect the prosperity of Dominican "Hispanic essence."[36] During the Haitian unification of 1822, Spanish-language books and newspapers were censored and universities closed. Early republic intellectuals and politicians used the Spanish language, Hispanic traditions (music, dances, literature), and cultural attributes (holidays, religion, foods) to rebel against political opposition to Haitian censorship. Haitianness became equated with anti-intellectualism while Hispanism became a political strategy for creating a sense of national identification and culture.

Santana's reannexation was possible precisely because he utilized the same language of nationalism that had engendered the Dominican Nation in 1844. In the face of what appeared to be impending foreign invasions of French-speaking Haitians or English-speaking North Americans, Hispanic colonialism was equated with national belonging. Haiti and the United States defined the political, cultural, and ideological borders of the nation from its conception. After the violent two-year Restoration War (1863–65) led by mulato general Gregorio Luperón with support from Haitian allies, the Dominican Republic obtained its third and final independence on August 16, 1865. Over the next decade, Luperón worked with Haitian politicians to draft clear geographic frontiers between the two nations and to create international commerce and political treaties aimed at protecting the young republic from further invasions.

The question of how Dominicans came to settle on the independence of 1844 as the nation's foundational event is puzzling to many historians. Some believe the decision responds to Dominican "colonial yearning" and to the inherently "anti-Haitian nature of the Dominican independence project."[37] But such arguments rely on the same decontextualized and extemporal view of Hispaniola that has sustained the two dominant and pervasive views of dominicanidad in the US academy: that anti-Haitianism was the driving force of Dominican independence from Haiti in 1844, and that white elite Dominican criollos decided the destiny of the nation. This myopic vision of the 1844 foundation effectively erases Dominican blacks and mulatos as political actors.

Let us remember that Dominicans of color effectively terminated two governments: Cáceres's Ephemeral Republic in 1821 and Boyer's Unified Island in 1844, mainly because these governments did not serve their racial interests. The production of the independence of 1844 as anti-Haitian and negrophobic at its origins also perpetuates the myth that the complicated border crisis that affects Hispaniola in the twenty-first century is historically grounded in racism rather than stemming from both nations' historical colonial relationship with Europe and the United States. To avoid falling into a similar "colonizing trick," a contextualized interpretation of the contra*dictions* leading to the consecration of the 1844 nation foundation in the Archive of Dominicanidad becomes urgent.[38]

The foundation of the 1844 independence in the Archive of Dominicanidad does emerge out of the multiple racial and ideological contra*dictions* that characterized nineteenth-century Santo Domingo dominant elite criollos. However, the actual Trabucazo of 1844—the revolutionary event Balibar speaks of—was the result of a political consensus to establish a unique national identity for both the nation-self (the potential citizens) and the world (particularly the United States and Europe). Hispanism and *mulataje* became the diction of revolution and mobilization against the unified Haitian government. This revolutionary strategy was co-opted and manipulated by the elite writers of the late nineteenth century and early twentieth, such as César Nicolás Penson, who desired the establishment of clear and containable borders for the nation-state. Similarly, elite writers and ideologues from Puerto Rico and Cuba, fearing US expansion, also turned to Hispanism as a way to counteract Anglo-American expansion at the turn of the century, as can be seen in the works of Puerto Rican novelist Alejandro Tapia and Cuban poet Nicolás Heredia.[39] The colonial impositions that led to the division of the island of Hispaniola into two separate states, and its people into two ethnicities, also led to the existence of two ideological borders for the Spanish-speaking portion of Hispaniola. Such ideologies effectively forced Hispaniola's people to experience the epistemic violence of colonialism in the reaffirmation of their national identities. The independence movement of 1844, then, did not emerge out of antiblackness in its conception. Rather, it resulted from a profound political awareness on the part of both leading parties, Radicals and Liberals, of the impossibility of building a free nation on Hispaniola without the support of the great majority of the nation's population, which considered itself of color. Hispanism came to signify national unity among the diversity of colors that made up Dominican racialization.

In his seminal text *La ciudad letrada* (1984), Ángel Rama argues that elite criollo Latin American writers functioned as agents at the service of colonial power structures, facilitating "la jerarquización y concentración del poder, para cumplir su misión civilizadora" (the hierarchization and concentration of power, in order to fulfill their civilizing project).[40] *Letrados* also allied themselves to the nation-building project, facilitating the narration of a homogenous national discourse that sought to unite a racially diverse population that resisted their ideological paradigms. Nineteenth-century Latin American letrados often used literature as a vehicle to write their ideological models of the nation, using poetic license to reimagine historical events to benefit their own ideology. The fact that criollos letrados owned the majority of newspapers and printing presses served to solidify an ideological monopoly of the nation's political thought. The nineteenth-century Latin American letrado was thus a proxy of the nation-state, writing the borders of civilization and civility by privileging his own (European) cultural desires. The particular way Dominican lettered men wrote their version of the nation resulted in a production of dominicanidad as a race that was decidedly mixed, yet other-than-black. Hispanism (Christianity, Spanish language, and the elevated cultures of our "mother Spain"), and mestizaje (the mixture of European and Taíno blood) explained the colors of Dominican "race" while also affirming Dominican cultural and racial difference from Haiti in the eyes of the world.[41]

The letrado to first articulate the Dominican racial contra*dictions* into a cohesive political project was French-educated criollo Juan Pablo Duarte

(1813–76). Following the principles of the Illuminati and Freemasons that had been so successful in the early stages of organizing during the French revolution, Juan Pablo Duarte formed La Trinitaria Secret Society in 1838. La Trinitaria launched the political and military actions that led to the 1844 independence. Along with Duarte, the founding members of La Trinitaria—Santo Domingo philosopher Juan Isidro Pérez, and Azua hatero Félix María Ruiz—believed the "ideological differences between Haitians and Dominicans made it impossible to continue governing as a unit."[42] The Trinitario Manifesto of 1838 thus identified the need to break away from Haiti as political and ideological in nature. Difference, though irreconcilable, did not appear in ethnic or cultural terms. Rather, it was Haiti's crippling debt following France's imposition, paired with continued international disapproval of Haiti's sovereignty due to the nation's self-proclamation as a black republic that preoccupied hateros and criollos as the volatile economy made the future unstable and vulnerable to US expansion.[43]

Duarte understood that to remain free from colonial or US intervention, Dominicans needed to separate from Haiti and secure immediate international recognition from both Europe and the United States. To reach this goal, the founding father needed the support and trust of all Dominican races. Duarte's awareness of the need to ensure racial inclusivity in the nation is crystalized in his poem "Unidad de las razas" (published 1839):

los blancos, morenos, cobrizos, cruzados
marchando seremos, humildes y osados
la patria salvemos de viles tirano
y al mundo mostremos que somos hermanos.[44]

[White, brown, red, mixed-race people
will all calmly march together with determination and courage
to save the fatherland from the vile tyrants
and show the world that we are brothers.]

Duarte's *diction* "hermanos" calls for a symbolic embrace of the nation's emerging mixed-race patriarchy. A Mason, Duarte's notions of kinship and community were grounded in a homosocial space of solidarity and civility. Jossianna Arroyo argues that the Masonic Hall allowed for the inclusion of blacks and mulatos in politics and in the writing circle, particularly during the various Caribbean independence movements.[45] The lodge itself represented a place for intercultural and transnational intersections throughout the Americas. The Masonic lodge was a powerful global institution with its own rules and regulations that created an international brotherhood based on history, knowledge, and trust. The founding father's poem, which some believe the patriot envisioned as the first national anthem, engaged popular color identifications—"blancos, morenos, cobrizos, cruzados"—and called for symbolic inclusion of Dominican self-defined racial diversity, and in particular of the multiple ways for naming blackness that had characterized Dominicans since early colonial times.

As early as 1608, the Spanish colony of Santo Domingo began to see what some historians have called a "de facto emancipation."[46] Looking for fortune, many rich criollos sailed to new territories, leaving behind a few sugar plantations and scattered communities of cattle ranchers and farmers who survived through commerce and contraband with French and Dutch seamen, pirates, and explorers who were beginning to take interest in the region. To control contraband in the colony, Governor Antonio de Osorio demanded everyone to abandon the northwest lands and to relocate closer to the city of Santo Domingo, where illegal exports could be controlled.[47] Known as the Devastaciones (1605–6), these evictions resulted in the speedy economic decline of Santo Domingo and the eventual colonization of western Hispaniola by the French.[48]

Another unintended consequence was the freedom (either by release or rebellion) of nearly 60 percent of African slaves working in the cattle industry, and the increased mestizaje among blacks, Indians, and whites who took to the *montes* (wilderness) in armed resistance.[49] Pedro Francisco Bonó, writing in 1857, argued that free blacks and mulatos who escaped to the mountains during the Devastaciones of Santo Domingo gradually began to understand themselves as different from black slaves of neighboring Saint Domingue.[50] These free mixed-race communities eventually began to use other names and descriptions to assert their difference from both the European colonizers and the African slaves. Interesting terms such as *blancos de la tierra* (whites of the land) and *moreno oscuro* (dark brown) emerged as a result.[51]

Duarte believed Dominican multicolor racial understanding to be strength in the process of nation building: "Unity can arise from difference if we all march to the same goal."[52] Rather than substitute race with nation, as letrado José Martí would propose at the end of the nineteenth century in the case of Cuba, Duarte asked all "Dominican races" to work together and "save the nation from the tyrants."[53] These "tyrants," the patriot warned, could come not just from West Hispaniola, but from Europe, North America, or "even from within our own entrails."[54] In 1839, Ramón Matías Mella, a blanco, and Francisco del Rosario Sánchez, a moreno, joined the tripartite government of La Trinitaria, leading the military battles that ended the Unification. Along with Duarte, Sánchez and Mella came to be remembered as the founding fathers of the nation. The first decree of the new Dominican Republic on February 27, 1844, converted the symbolic (Duarte's poem) into action, declaring "slavery forever abolished and terminating the legal discrimination of human beings based on their color."[55] In one of the earliest modern attempts to create a multiethnic nation, Duarte's dominicanidad contradicted criollo colonial desire for white supremacy, ending three hundred years of colonial rule.

Although the majority of mulatos and farmers supported Duarte, not all criollos bought into his proposal for a racially integrated nation. Many, like the criollo letrado Félix María del Monte (1819–99), believed the mandate should be to "restore Santo Domingo to the Civilization and Progress we [criollos?] inherited from our Mother Land."[56] A self-identified *dominicano español*, del Monte was, in addition to an independence leader, one of the most influential literary figures in nineteenth-century Dominican letters.[57] His work was instrumental in the consolidation of a literary tradition based on a combination of *indigenismo* (mythical exaltation of Native Taíno heroes), European aesthetics, and colonial nostalgia that dominated the bulk of Dominican literature for over a century. To del Monte, Dominicans owe the use of the diction "Hispanic" as a signifier of ethnic dominicanidad contra *haitianidad* (Haitianism) during the early republic years (1845–61). He is also responsible for the establishment of the trope "Santo Domingo was the city Columbus loved the most," which has become a commercial motto for the tourism industry in the new millennium.[58]

Del Monte's "Canción dominicana," which the author envisioned as the first national anthem of the 1844 Dominican Republic, directly opposed Duarte's multicolor nation. Replacing Trinitaria's political process, which was accomplished with national war and ideological disagreement with a military adversary, del Monte writes:

¡Al arma españoles!
¡Volad a la lid!
Tomad por divisa
¡Vencer o morir!

[Take up arms, Spaniards!
Fly to the lines!
You must decide
Victory or death!]

¡Nobles hijos de Santo Domingo
erguid vuestra frente guerrera
y sañudos volad tras la *fiera*
que el *solar de Colón* devastó
¡No hay piedad, el haitiano insolente
penetrando hasta nuestros hogares,
profanó nuestros templos y altares,
nuestros fueros osó atropellar,
y el pudor de la *cándida virgen,*
y las canas del mísero anciano,
y cuanto hay de sagrado en lo humano
ultrajó con orgullo voraz.[59] (emphasis added)

[Noble children of Santo Domingo
Keep your warrior chin up
When confronting battle
And against the *wild beast*
That destroyed *Columbus's land*
No mercy for the insolent Haitian
who *penetrated* our homes
desecrated our temples and altars,
dared to destroy our dwellings
And the modesty of our *candid virgin,*
and the gray of our sad elderly,
and all that is sacred and human
destroyed with voracious hunger.]

Though del Monte's *Canción dominicana* (1844) did not become the national anthem of the Dominican Republic as the letrado had envisioned, it constitutes the first written model for Hispanophile ideology that Trujillo-serving intellectuals solidified in the twentieth century.[60] Joaquín Balaguer, Trujillo's right hand and most important intellectual ideologue, for instance, quotes del Monte to insist that "Santo Domingo es . . . el pueblo más español" (Santo Domingo is . . . the most Spanish nation) of the Americas.[61]

Urging Spaniards to defend their colonial legacy, del Monte's poetic diction *"solar de Colón"* (Columbus's plot) simultaneously reminds criollos of their (supposed) birthright to Santo Domingo—presuming or making *criollismo* and Hispanism essential to dominicanidad—and of the need to "take up arms" to defend their colonial inheritance from foreign (meaning Haitian) invasion. In contra*diction* with Duarte's uplifting and inclusive invitation to a unified and plural nation, "los blancos, morenos . . . marchemos serenos, humildes y osados" struggling for the common goal of progress, del Monte's *"¡Al arma españoles! ¡Vencer o morir!"* performs criollo anxiety over the simultaneous contradictory desire for sovereignty and for maintaining colonial privilege and whiteness.

Del Monte's *Canción* establishes Haiti as the nation's enemy, and vengeance, rather than political sovereignty, as the motive for rebellion. Converting the Haitian Unification (1822–44) into a "forced occupation," del Monte's call to arms in *Canción* also marks both the cultural and racial borders of dominicanidad through the same rhetoric of civilization versus progress that Argentina's letrado Domingo Sarmiento popularized a year later with the publication of his novel *Facundo* (1845).[62] Through the repetition of physical violence exemplified in the implicit raping of the "cándida virgen" and cultural violence embodied in violation of the sacred—"¡No hay piedad, el haitiano insolente penetrando . . . cuanto hay de sagrado"—del Monte renders Haitians as animalist and barbaric ("voracious beasts"), a trope he would later repeat in his better-known 1860 poetic rendition of the Galindo crimes, *Las Vírgenes de Galindo*. The epic poem juxtaposes Haitian savagery ("voracious beasts") with Dominican civilization ("Noble children of Santo Domingo!"), which del Monte's diction suggests rests on the country's Hispanic heritage and particularly on Dominican military superiority ("warrior chin"). The claims to Hispanic heritage, as well as military ability, became the nation's most important weapons in the struggle between civilization and barbarism.

Duarte and del Monte represent the two contradictory ideologies dominating the preindependence Archive of Dominicanidad. Duarte believed that naming diversity and promoting a sense of duty and patriotism through the respect and inclusiveness of ethnic groups would make the nation stronger internally and in front of the world. Del Monte's unity plan, on the other hand, actively replaced racial difference with his version of Hispanic culture (Spanish language, Catholic religion, and European literary traditions). Though their strategies for achieving national unity were in direct contra-

diction, both criollos knew they would not be able to achieve independence unless all races came together under one nation. Though seemingly irreconcilable, both ideologies came together as one party in 1844 to create the independent Dominican Republic. Del Monte and Duarte's seemingly oppositional ideologies became the basis for the Archive of Dominicanidad, as well as the blueprints from which letrados of the second half of the nineteenth century produced dominicanidad in literature and history. Gradually, Duarte's multicolor dominicanidad was transformed into a discourse of hybridity that allowed postindependent letrados "to manage racial politics either by promoting cultural over racial hybridity," as Shalini Puri argues often happened in postindependent Caribbean republics, or by producing racial mixes that they found acceptable.[63] Thus, during the second half of the nineteenth century, letrados, including Manuel de Jesús Galván and César Nicolás Penson, embraced del Monte's proposed Hispanism as a legitimate form of "Dominican culture" while transforming Duarte's multiracial unity into a rhetoric of mestizaje that allowed them to justify racial hybridity. The marriage between del Monte's and Duarte's ideologies in post-1844 literature allowed for the solidification of "Dominican" as a nonblack race. Dominican nonblack racial hybridity substituted the living African with a digestible fabrication of European and Taíno mestizaje.[64]

Reflecting on the way history and literature have operated in the production of cultural identities, Édouard Glissant suggests that the majority of people, most of all those at the margins of the nation, experience history through repetition.[65] The repetition and institutionalization of the Archive of Dominicanidad at the hands of elite Hispanophile writers under the Trujillo regime solidified mid-nineteenth-century literary Liberal elite narrations as historical truth, eventually completely erasing black and mulato histories from the national imaginary. Though the 1844 independence was a project of interracial cooperation and unity, the posthumous narration of the 1844 foundational date—even by contemporary critics—continues to erase Dominican blackness by privileging the critique of elite white supremacist and anti-Haitian discourse. I argue that the pervasiveness and persistence of anti-Haitian violence, as evidenced in the multiple versions of the Galindo crimes that inhabit the Archive of Dominicanidad, is to blame for the abundance of such myopic readings of Hispaniola's history. Focusing on the silences reproduced by the multiple repetitions of anti-Haitian violence is the only way to (re)focus our historical gaze and gain some perspective, even where evidence seems absent.

Doris Sommer argues that nineteenth-century Latin American literature produced "foundational fictions" based on allegories of romance and unity that ultimately helped consolidate the nation.[66] Almost inevitably, such romances display stories of lovers who represent particular regions, races, and economic interests and whose "passion for conjugal and sexual union spills over to a sentimental readership that would ideally desire the kind of state that allows such a union to occur."[67] The "foundational fiction" of the Dominican Republic is, according to many literary scholars including Sommer, Manuel de Jesús Galván's celebrated novel *Enriquillo* (1879).[68] Based on the journals of Bartolomé de Las Casas (1484–1556), the Dominican friar memorialized as the "protector of the Indians,"[69] Galván's novel recounts a love story between the Taíno cacique Guarocuya—who led the last and longest indigenous rebellion against the Spanish colonial government in Santo Domingo (1519–33)—and Princess Mencía, the mestiza granddaughter of the last Taíno queen, Anacaona.

Titled *Enriquillo* (little Enrique), after the cacique's imposed Castilian name, Galván's interpretation is a bildungsroman that privileges mestizaje, or rather, a form of mestizaje in drag, as the epitome of Dominican identity: "Enriquillo iba vestido . . . con un traje de terciopelo color castaño y ferreruelo de raso negro forrado de un seda carmesí, a la moda de Castilla" (Enriquillo went dressed . . . in a chestnut-colored velvet suit and a black satin cape lined with red silk, in the Castilian style).[70] "Dressed" with Spain, Galván's Guarocuya materializes as a dark-skinned criollo in a drag-mestizo performance of Hispanism—"vestido a la moda de Castilla"—that incarnates the criollo-preferred version of Dominican racial hybridity. Colonial Hispaniola historians agree that the Guarocuya Rebellion resulted precisely from indigenous rejection of forced Hispanic cultural impositions, which manifested in the form of forced conversion to Catholicism and European dress codes.[71] Yet Galván, a self-proclaimed "hispano dominicano," produced an indigenous mythical hero who was culturally Hispanic "a la moda de Castilla" but racially marked as nonwhite. This rhetorical ambiguity effectively inscribed on Galván's Guarocuya the prevalent contra*diction*s of nineteenth-century criollo political desire: to achieve unity among the multiracial citizens of the nation and to preserve the dominance of European cultural identity.

As we saw in del Monte's early writing, Hispanism was essential in sustaining Liberal criollo ideology. By the end of the nineteenth century, ideologues such as Galván interpolated Liberal criollo Hispanism into a malleable discourse of cultural inclusivity that ultimately erased racial diversity from nation-narration. If mulatos were economically and politically powerful, Galván's novel suggests, they could also become social equals, provided they were willing to dress white, "a la moda de Castilla." It was not the color of a person's skin (race) that made her *hispano*, Galván's *Enriquillo* posits, but rather his performance of Hispanism (culture) as the union holding together the multicolored bodies of the Dominican hybrid nation Duarte had created in 1844.

Galván's *Enriquillo* is part of the corpus of late nineteenth-century *indigenista* literature, which also include the seminal works of celebrated writers Salomé Ureña and José Joaquín Pérez, that "played Indian" as a way to explain and substitute the multiple ways of naming blackness dominating the nation's popular ideology since the seventeenth century and that Duarte believed should serve as the nation's foundation.[72] However, the process of founding the written archive of a nation is never solely derived from an affirmative *diction*—"Dominicans are Indians"—but also from a contra*diction*—"Dominicans are not black"; the affirmation depends on the perpetuation of the negation.

The founding story of Indian affirmation in the Archive of Dominicanidad is de Las Casas's legendary *Brevísima relación de la destrucción de las Indias* (1552), in which the Dominican friar denounces the mistreatment and destruction of Native Americans at the hands of Spanish colonizers. Yet de Las Casas's affirmation of indigenous humanity is simultaneously contra*dicted* by his negation of black humanity. De Las Casas suggests the importation of African slaves "who are more fit to endure the harshness" of forced labor as a solution to the colonial "labor problem."[73] De Las Casas's affirmation thus resulted in the beginning of a long history of black dehumanization (negation) in the Americas. Following the friar's lead, nineteenth-century Hispanophile letrados, such as Galván, equated the affirmative diction "We are Indians" to national belonging, while negating the diction "African" by displacing it in *haitianismo* and therefore rendering black bodies foreign. Affirming both dominicanidad and blackness became, at the hands of turn-of-the-century Hispanophile letrados, an ontological impossibility and a semantic contradiction.

While Galván's drag mestizaje, *Enriquillo* (1876), became the most celebrated affirmation of the mythical foundation of dominicanidad, César Nicolás Penson's *Vírgenes de Galindo* (1891) became, in turn, the negation that sustained it. The foundation of the Archive of Dominicanidad is therefore grounded on a dual rhetorical contra*diction* between indigenista "foundational fictions" and anti-Haitian myths. The multiple literary repetitions of the Galindo crime constitute a textbook model for analyzing the structures that produced the anti-Haitian ideology that has dominated Dominican politics since the late nineteenth century. Two factors contributed to the transformation of the Galindo crime into such a foundational trope in the Archive of Dominicanidad. First, the Galindo murders were a historically verifiable event that took place during the first year of the unification, 1822. This chronological concurrence added legitimacy to the retrospective fictional renditions of the historical crime that inundated late-nineteenth-century to mid-twentieth-century literatures. Second, the fact that the victims included three young girls made it possible for the authors to transform the crimes into what Sybille Fischer calls a "pornographic crime story" through which elite racial desire for an other-than-black Hispanic nation could be articulated.[74]

If a pornographic crime story is what the Galindo murders have become, the most renowned and influential version is undoubtedly César Nicolás Penson's tradición, *Las vírgenes de Galindo* (1891). A journalist, educator and poet, Penson (1855–1901) was one of the most influential intellectuals of all time. His first dictionary of *dominicanismos*, as well as a vast collection of Dominican oral poetry (*décimas*), contributed to the consolidation of a Dominican literary canon that prevails to date. In addition to his important contributions, Penson's classicism, which is reflected in the nostalgic reminiscences of the colonial Hispanic period (1492–1821), as well as his blatant racism against black Dominicans and ethnic Haitians, have influenced Dominican political and cultural discourse. This is evident in the writings of his admirers, Manuel Arturo Peña Batlle (1902–52), Max Henríquez Ureña (1886–1968), and Joaquín Balaguer (1906–2002).

Following the model popularized by Peruvian Ricardo Palma (1872–1910), Penson's tradición is divided into nine parts that contain long customary descriptions and multiple dialogues that legitimize the text as historical truth.[75] The first part of the story, titled "Preludios," takes on a nostalgic tone to describe what the author perceived as a better epoch, when luxury and tranquility reigned in Santo Domingo prior to the Haitian unification of 1822: "Entonces vivía uno a sus anchas en esta bendita tierra en que no se conocían pobres. . . . Todo el lujo de la época, que no era ostentador ni insolente, se echaba allí" (Back then one lived freely in this blessed land that did not know poverty.... All the luxury known to that era, which was neither ostentatious nor insolent, could be found there).[76] Depicting Santo Domingo as the cradle of Hispanic grandeur, Penson's sentimental and almost romantic lament of the long-lost Hispaniola in which "poverty was unknown" is anachronistic given the international climate of 1891: Cuba's and Puerto Rico's revolutionary movements were at their height and the US Good Neighbor Policy, which was in its early stages, particularly threatened the sovereignty of Hispaniola.[77] The journalist's extemporal colonial desire is better understood when read in tandem with del Monte's epic poem, also titled *Las Vírgenes de Galindo o La Invasión de la Parte Este de la Isla* (written in 1860, published in 1885), in which Penson interpolates his fin de siècle rendition of the crime.[78]

Del Monte's *Las vírgenes* begins with a similarly nostalgic tone:

Sobre el Indiano mar en la ancha espalda
Una ciudad modesta se reclina...
Es su nombre inmortal "Santo Domingo";
Otro tiempo lo fuera La "Española"
Cuando en sus sienes refulgente aureola
La magnánima Iberia colocó...[79]

[Over the expansive Indian sea
A modest city rests...
Its immortal name is Santo Domingo;
In a former time it was Hispaniola
When upon its brow brilliant praise
was bestowed by the magnanimous Iberia...]

But the tranquility is rudely interrupted by the Haitian Unification of 1822:

Acércase las huestes haraposas
De opresión y pillaje al par sedientas
Y ¡ay de los hijos que en tu seno alientas Misteriosa Ciudad
    monumental!!![80]

[The ragged masses approach
Oppressing and pillaging, all together avaricious
and Oh, pity be on the children you shelter at your breast, monumental
    Mysterious City!]

Identifying symbolically with Spain, while also alluding to Taíno heritage ("the Indian sea"), the introductory stanzas of del Monte's *Las vírgenes* disavow Haiti as a "foreign" force that threatens the essence and integrity of dominicanidad, which the poet locates in the colonial inheritance of Hispanism ("que la Iberia colocó"). Del Monte's Galindo responds to the author's colonial investment as well as his political aspirations to become a national leader. Let us remember that at the height of the *trinitario* revolutionary movement (1836–44), del Monte rallied criollos to oppose Duarte's vision for a racially united nation and proposed instead a reversion to colonial rule, which would guarantee the permanence of a criollo political leadership.

Writing in 1860, del Monte sought to memorialize "nuestros agravios, evocando el imperecedero recuerdo de los ultrajes inferidos bajo aquella vergonzosa dominación, y de los dramas sangrientos que aquí se representaron" (our grievances, evoking the everlasting memory of the injustices inflicted beneath that shameful domination, and of the bloody calamities which took place here) in order to justify his political support for Santana's reannexation plan (1861) and to obtain Liberal criollo backing for divesting mulato power.[81] Though Spanish colonization was far bloodier than the Haitian unification—causing the extermination of the indigenous population of the island and the death of thousands of African slaves—del Monte, who wrote for criollo whites, insists it was the Haitian unification they should never forget. Capitalizing on criollo fear that resulted from the political instability following the first three decades after the Trabucazo of 1844, del Monte gained political support for Santana's reannexation plan.

Between 1844 and 1861, there were multiple Haitian military attempts to occupy the lost territory of the east. Lacking the support that mulato ranchers and the general population of Dominicans of color lent Boyer in 1822, Haitian military efforts did not lead to any serious threats to Dominican sovereignty. Yet del Monte tried to instill fear of Haiti in his criollo compatriots by reminding them of the shared "shameful" experience of being dominated by what they considered to be an inferior race. Galindo came to symbolize this threat and del Monte's hope for restoring lost criollo political power.

By 1891, when Penson wrote his tradición, Haitian interventions did not pose a realistic threat to national sovereignty. But the prevalence of a large multiethnic rayano population who did not adhere to any national plan, as well as the constant revolts caused by *caudillismo*, made the unity of Eastern Hispaniola under a common flag a complete impossibility.[82] The

Galindo murders that had inspired the outrage of criollo patriot Félix María del Monte in 1860 provided Penson with the perfect symbol of the open wound of elite political failure at bordering the nation. The crime provoked what both authors describe as "unspeakable fear," leading the majority of the elite families to exile and, as Penson put it, "bankrupting the culture and spirit of our young nation."[83] Reminiscing on colonial splendor, and lamenting the loss of Hispanic "civilized" culture at the hands of the invading "barbaric" Haitians, Penson altered the rare and isolated crime into an example of the "shameful" injustices that the nation suffered at the hands of the invading force. Unlike del Monte, though, Penson did not only write for the Hispanophile elites.

Sociologist Francisco Bonó and Puerto Rican educator and thinker Eugenio María de Hostos insisted on the mulato identity of late-nineteenth-century Dominicans, who they believed existed somewhere between "US American Whiteness and Haitian blackness."[84] Penson was preoccupied precisely with the potential threat that Dominican mulataje could pose for the nation's progress. Anti-Haitianism became, as April Mayes argues, a "convenient strategy . . . to divide the laboring classes."[85] Through his depiction of Galindo, Penson sought to historicize the Haitian unification as the catalyst for Dominican patriotism and national essence, replacing the gray and dangerous border of Dominican mulataje with the more desirable and containable Hispanism that early-nineteenth-century letrados had preferred. In turn, this ideology also consecrates 1844 as the nation's true independence, and thus Haiti as the nation's eternal threat to sovereignty: "No hay episodio más conmovedor . . . y símbolo más caracterizado de la línea moral divisoria y del abismo que separa a este pueblo de Haití . . . ¡Primeros ímpetus patrióticos del pueblo recién independizado *de su mayores* y recién pisoteado por una sedienta nación bárbara!" (emphasis added) (There is no episode more moving . . . or symbol more characteristic of the moral dividing line and of the chasm that separates this nation from Haiti . . . The first patriotic impetus of the nation newly independent *of its elders* and recently trampled by an avaricious, barbarous nation!).[86] Penson's diction is loaded with the ambiguities of criollo colonial desire. He suggests that Haiti, not Spain, is the perpetrator who comes to interrupt Dominican life. Spain, on the other hand, is merely an "elder," a benevolent guiding parent from whom the criollo son parts to find his own way. By establishing Haiti as the perpetual enemy of the nation, Penson paves the way for criollo colonial desire, epitomized in Hispanophile ideology, to seamlessly emerge as essential to national identity for all races. Spanish colonization thus becomes a forgivable sin expiated through cultural and racial mestizaje à la Galván while Haiti takes the place of the nation's enemy in the struggle for sovereignty and democracy.

Penson's representation of the Galindo murders summons del Monte's anti-Haitian diction and then transforms it into a politicized racialization of Dominican citizenship as decidedly nonblack. Though del Monte is notable for being the first writer to change the identity of Cobial, de la Cruz, and Gómez to unnamed Haitians, Penson is responsible for transforming the killers from unnamed Haitians to nonhuman black Haitian soldiers, effectively changing an act of banditry into a state crime. The killers thus become actors of the Haitian state, and the victims, in turn, representatives of the Dominican Nation: "Horribles aparecieron las *negras y feas* estampas de los *soldados haitianos*. . . . Ved a los tigres, saciando su nauseabundo apetito y su sed de sangre, revolcándose en la inocencia de las pobres niñas frías ya por la muerte; vedlos consumando su obra inicua!" (emphasis added) (The horrible shadows, *black and ugly*, of the *Haitian soldiers* appeared. . . . See the tigers quenching their nauseous hunger and thirst for blood, rolling in the innocence of the poor girls who laid there dead, cold; see them completing their cruel plan!).[87] In this third section, Penson's *Vírgenes de Galindo* shifts from the descriptive romantic narration of colonial splendor that opened his tradición to a quasi-fantastic story of the struggle between good and evil. The killers take on supernatural, monstrous physiognomies, appearing at first as *estampas*, as nonbodies and phenomenological shadows that then morph into bloodthirsty cruel beasts. Penson's depiction of the killers not only dehumanizes blackness, but also portrays the Haitian state as an evil and superhuman "shadow" that spreads fear and devastation.

While the author's anti-Haitian rhetoric is foundational to Dominican literature, I argue it is also part of a larger corpus of anti-Haitian world literature that gained strength at the end of the nineteenth century and beginning of the twentieth. As the second independent republic in the Americas (1804) and the first nation led by descendants of black slaves, Haiti occupied a central place in the political and cultural imaginary of many diverse, and oftentimes oppositional, groups. Fear of and disdain for Haiti reflected in anti-Haitian and negrophobic literary and cultural productions throughout the world.[88] Novels, theatrical performances, and, later on, zombie films about Haiti produced in the United States and Europe represented Haitians as monsters, savages, childlike, and incapable of governing themselves.[89] Media depictions of Haitian women insisted on their hypersexuality, while

Afro-religious Haitian rituals were viewed as savage and uncivilized.[90] Penson's *Vírgenes* is part of an emergent world literary tradition of the late nineteenth and early twentieth centuries that was decidedly anti-Haitian. In the Dominican context, global anti-Haitianism reached a greater magnitude as it was met by the local elite Hispanophile, Indian-masked ideology of the likes of Galván, and by increased political preoccupation on the part of both Liberals and Radicals with the project of nation bordering.

Penson's strategy for narrating *Vírgenes* tries to fit a legal ruling into an anti-Haitian nationalist discourse that disavows blackness from the nation-building project by displacing black in Haitian, therefore rendering Dominican blackness a marker of potential treason. The author's characterization of Ysabel, the nanny, further epitomizes this formulation: "Hacíales compañía la esclava sordo-muda llamada Ysabel, quien, *aunque cuando podía gozar de entera libertad con el nuevo orden de las cosas reinantes*, había preferido permanecer con las tres doncellas" (emphasis added)[91] (Their mute and deaf slave named Ysabel, *who even when she was able to enjoy freedom due to the new order of things*, preferred to stay with the three girls). Depicting Ysabel as a grateful slave who owed her new freedom to the Haitian flag ("the new order of things"), Penson reminds his readers that the Haitian "Occupation" of 1822 was possible precisely because (Dominican) blacks aligned themselves with Haiti in exchange for emancipation. If, as Galván and del Monte insisted, the cultural essence of dominicanidad was found in the nation's "essential Hispanism," Penson clarifies that Dominican Hispanism is not *just* a cultural category. Ysabel, an ex-slave, though Dominican born and Spanish speaking, could not be "fully Dominican," because she was not mulata but black; her lack of whiteness became a source for suspicion and potential treason.

According to statistical documentation, Andrés Andújar manumitted Ysabel in 1803, before the girls were born and almost two decades prior to the Haitian unification.[92] Both Ysabel and her son Goyo lived with the Andújar family of their own will. Although the court documents state that Ysabel had "problems communicating," which I assume to mean some kind of speech impediment, they also insist that her testimony was clear and crucial in solving the case and prosecuting the three men:

Que la doméstica Ysabel único residuo de la familia Andújar a todos tres ha acusado y acusa de un modo claro y perceptible como autores de los asesinatos cuyas sospechas se agravan con las circunstancias mencionadas, y por la presunción que tienen contra si, especialmente el Cobial a quien ya se imputó en tiempo del Gobierno Español con bastante fundamento la muerte de un nombrado Gabriel . . . Firmado Antonio Madrigal Greffier.[93] (emphasis added)

[The domestic servant Ysabel, the only remainder of the Andújar family, has accused all three, and accuses them in a clear and perceptible fashion, as the perpetrators of the killings whose suspicions are worsened with the mentioned circumstances and for the presumptions held against them, especially Cobial who, during the time of the Spanish Government, was already charged with sufficient grounds with the death of one named Gabriel . . . Signed, Antonio Madrigal Greffier.]

Penson, a costumbrista writer and a journalist who prided himself on "not novelating but telling the truth," rewrites the Galindo proceedings in a way that discredits Ysabel's testimony and gives historical validity to criollo rumors that Haitian soldiers perpetrated the crime.[94] Legitimized by the resources of the tradición model—interviews, dates, customary descriptions—Penson contradicts the historical evidence by questioning the existing court transcripts as fraudulent because legal proceedings took place "under the watchful eyes of the Haitian beasts."[95]

Penson's repetition is grounded in del Monte's documented "gut feeling" that the convicted men were indeed innocent.[96] Del Monte's half-brother, Joaquín del Monte, was one of the judges in charge of the Galindo trials that culminated in the conviction of the three Dominican men.[97] The prologue titled "Advertencia" to the poet's 1885 edition points to a potential nonconformity with the verdict, suggesting disbelief that the crime had been indeed committed by Dominicans: "I, like many other patriots, have always known the truth."[98] Writing from Puerto Rico in 1860, del Monte makes a conscious decision to recover the case of the Galindo murders as a symbol of what he believed to be a "shameful domination."[99] Yet the poem went unpublished in the Dominican Republic for more than twenty years because, according to the author, "events made its publication unnecessary."[100] The unnecessary event the author refers to is the 1861 reannexation of the Dominican Republic to Spain, of which del Monte was a strong proponent. His insistence that his poem was written "out of necessity" points to the way in which literature sustained the criollo political project to cast Haitians as potential threats to the nation. Interpolating del Monte, Penson also insists that "the people knew the (real) killers were Haitian," and then proceeds to cite at least five witnesses: "Suministraron estos datos las señoras M.D.F. de C., C.T., A.Q. y señores Dn. F. Ma. D."[101] Though almost impossible to decipher most of his sources, the last one—Dn. F. Ma. D.—clearly corresponds to Don Félix María del Monte, whose poem, the author states, "informs" his descriptions of the girls and the details of the crime. Penson's narrative effectively substitutes history (in the form of the court transcript) with literature (del Monte's Poem), and testimony (Ysabel's words) with rumor (del Monte's gut feeling).

Whether the criminals who ended the lives of the Andújar family were ethnic Haitians or ethnic Dominicans is inconsequential given that the evidence surrounding the Galindo Murders proves it an isolated event. Yet for Penson and del Monte, declaring the ethnicity of the killers was essential to establishing the myth of the Galindo Virgins as allegorical to dominicanidad. Penson's narrative provided the initial preformulations of ethnic and racial prejudice in Dominican society. His discrediting of Ysabel—who was the main witness to the crime and key in identifying, capturing, and sentencing the criminals—is one of the most significant influences in the racial bordering of the Archive of Dominicanidad. If Ysabel, a Dominican descendant of slaves, could *turn* on her own nation, aligning instead with those who shared her skin color and history, Penson seems to warn his readers, other black Dominicans can also turn on their nation. The project of setting and guarding the borders of the nation—bordering—should thus belong to those who align with Hispanism: white and mulatos who enjoy economic and social mobility because of their light-skin privilege.

Though different in style and genre, the two versions of the Galindo Virgins, del Monte's and Penson's, function as complementary evidence in the foundation of the Archive of Dominicanidad, particularly as linked to the political process of bordering the nation that began after the Restoration War in 1865 and continued until the Massacre of 1937 during the Trujillo dictatorship. But if del Monte saw Galindo as a by-product of Haitian barbarism, Penson took the argument one long step further by locating the crime as part of the military actions of the Haitian state and as a "national wound" that needed to be remembered and possibly avenged by the Dominican patriarch in order to regain his honor.[102] The murders of the Andújar family thus became an almost anonymous example in a list of "ultrajes, vicisitudes, y desvergüenzas" (insults, vicissitudes, and shameless acts) suffered at the hands of the inferior occupier.[103] For del Monte, Galindo is a historical lesion that, though healed, must be remembered, while for Penson it remains an open wound that continues to bleed and has the potential to spill over and infect the rest of the nation. Blackness, for Penson, is figured as a disease.

Allegorizing political concerns of the multiethnic border community of rayanos, Penson's writing warns the reader to think about the need to contain blackness—Haitianness—or else run the risk of infecting dominicanidad. Penson's warning also alludes to the potential threat of rayanos who, like Ysabel, do not clearly fit into the Hispanic Dominican nation narrative. Defining the Haitian-Dominican border, Penson appears to insist, is incredibly urgent to protect the image of the nation from Haitian "infection":

> Y déjennos en paz los que confunden y barajan a cada paso, por pura ignorancia de la geografía y la historia, las dos porciones de la isla *esencialmente distintas en raza, idioma, costumbres, civilización, historia, orden social, constitución política, aspiraciones, carácter nacional y cuanto hay.*[104] (emphasis added)

> [And leave us in peace, those of you who confuse and hesitate at every step because of your sheer ignorance of the history and geography of each of the two parts of this island that are *essentially different in race, language, customs, civilization, history, social order, politics, aspirations, national character, and all that there is.*][105]

Setting the record straight by reminding foreigners that the two nations are indeed racially different, Penson's version of the Galindo Virgins thus not only establishes that the two peoples of Hispaniola are different, it also explains *how* they are different in a universal language of anti-Haitianism grounded in the perpetual struggle of civilization against barbarism.

But how could Penson completely eliminate the majority of the population, which consisted of mulatos and blacks, from the national imaginary? Indigenista narratives such as Galván's *Enriquillo* offered a solution for explaining color diversity: Dominicans were of color, but their color was different from Haiti's blackness. The Dominican Race was a product of benevolent, civilized mestizaje that resembled Hispanic culture and embodied civilization. Blackness or Africanness was a reminder of slavery, which could only be embodied by Haitians. Thus Dominicans, as imagined by Penson, were decisively nonblack, even if their skins were not white. At the hands of twentieth-century letrados who served the Trujillo dictatorship, Penson's narrative came to be historicized and legalized as truth. Writing in 1941, for instance, Joaquín Balaguer, Trujillo's right-hand man and puppet president, opined that Penson's "eloquent historical account of the death, misery and superstition of the unjust massacre of our own virgins" was the most vivid reminder of the "essential abyss that separates our Hispanic nation from Haiti."[106] If the late nineteenth-century Hispanophile letrados laid the literary foundation upon which the Archive of Dominicanidad would be erected, Trujillo materialized rhetoric into tangible objects and actions. The symbolic archive that emerged through the complementary narratives of Galván and Penson were transformed into physical monuments to Hispanism in the buildings, busts, and statues Trujillo built as a monument to Dominican high culture. The Plaza de la Cultura (Culture Square) located in the heart of Santo Domingo became a landmark of progress and civilization and publicly affirmed Hispanism as the historical and cultural roots of dominicanidad.[107] Through the construction of La Plaza de la Cultura and the institutionalization of the arts and education, the Archive of Dominicanidad became law. This transformation from myth to law required a series of rhetorical strategies and the complicit cooperation of history and literature in the production of monolithic cultural figures that silence and contain Dominican blackness.

White Virgins, Failing Patriots

Nineteenth-century literature is foundational because it sought to define a kind of universal identity for Dominicans within the political framework of the nation. Like many other "foundational fictions," Dominican literature formulated "the woman" as a monolithic cultural category.[108] She was represented more often than men and placed within a more constricted hegemonic patriarchal space that supposed her to be the mother of the patria and constricted her to the private home space. The Dominican patriarch, in turn, needed to be watchful and ready to defend the woman (nation) or else risk her demise at the hands of the perpetrator (Haitian). The criollo elite version of the nation, as literary critic Catherina Vallejo argued, thus co-opted gender so that "there was a stronger effort to define women than to define men."[109] To Vallejo's argument I would add that Liberal elite writers only defined women in two ways: as a Madre-Patria (Mother-Nation) or as a Virgen-Tierra (Virgin Land), universalizing dichotomies that are prevalent in the foundational texts of del Monte, Penson, and Galván.

The Galindo virgin-martyrs set the stage for founding the Dominican nation around three main figures: the woman, the patriarch, and the Haitian intruder. But unlike Patria, Minerva, and María Teresa Mirabal, the twentieth-century heroines of the Trujillo dictatorship, not much is known about the Andújar sisters except that they were killed during the Haitian unification.[110] Stripped of any identity or history, the girls became, at the hands of elite writers such as del Monte and Penson, "no tres mujeres / sino tres ángeles bellos" (not three women / but three beautiful angels), their suffering elevated to a form of martyrdom from which Hispanophile patriotism could be justified and articulated.[111]

Though undoubtedly seeking to establish a striking contrast between the criminal Haitian "black shadows" and the white virgin victims, Penson leaves his readers with, rather, an analogous superhuman rendering of the Andújar sisters; they are not girls but "Vírgenes de mármol," not human bodies but "immortal statues of beauty" (literally, marble). Penson then breaks their bodies into several pieces of an artistic puzzle—"ve los brazos de alabastro, y cuellos de animado mármol" (see the alabaster arms, and necks of living marble)—converting their mutilation into art that further solidifies the contrasting views of Haitians (barbaric) and Dominican (civilized) essences.[112] In his effort to immortalize the Galindo Virgins as eternal martyrs of the nation, Penson uproots the Andújar children from history while simultaneously grounding their symbol—las vírgenes—as the motive for Dominican independence from Haiti.

One of Penson's most unsettling rhetorical strategies in the repetition of the Galindo crimes is the transformation of the children into virgins—into deferred sexual beings—their immature bodies robbed of innocence to be converted into the virgin-land women onto which the nation's border could be drawn. Penson, like his predecessor del Monte, focuses his narrative gaze on the oldest of the three daughters, fifteen-year-old Águeda, whose body Penson unrobes even before the killers arrive at the scene: "Reclinada la cabellera descuidada en una mano fina y transparente . . . entreabierta la finísima camisa que dejaba desnudos su cuello y redondos brazos y el arqueado y terso pecho" (Her hair rested carelessly upon a refined and transparent hand . . . her half-opened exquisite shirt exposed her neck and her rounded arms and arched and smooth breast).[113] Self-conscious about his voyeurism, Penson is careful to explain his prurient diction in the context of the mundane and the natural: "It was indeed so hot . . . in the dark living room of the modest dusty home."[114] His narrative is not one of lust and desire, he reminds his readers, but a faithful collage of the multiple memories surrounding the evening that have been entrusted to him by the unnamed "witnesses" he interviewed.[115]

Intimately related to the family as the posthumous historical narrator-avenger, Penson suggests that the undressing of Águeda was not *his* decision, but that of the collective voices—the sources—that informed his customary narration of the "infamous day."[116] One of the ways Penson exculpates his role in the voyeuristic mutilation of Águeda is through the use of the passive voice ("I was told"), which interferes with the historical exactitude of his narration. The passive voice simultaneously creates distance from any blame ("Though I was not there") and complicity with the shared responsibility with the reader in the protection of the future ("we must never see our land invaded again").[117] The passive voice renders Águeda as a sexualized ornament in the dusty home of the Andújars. Ultimately the success of Penson's narrative depends on the presumed (male) readership participating in his narrative counterpoint of distance and desire; Dominican patriots must desire Águeda so that the pain of losing her to black "tyrant monsters" can be greater.

Resembling the sublime chronicle of colonial Santo Domingo that opens the first section of Penson's tradición, the peaceful life of the Andújars is also abruptly interrupted in the fourth section, "La Tragedia," by the "horrible shadows" that appear in the Andújar homestead with the sole purpose of causing destruction. The story then moves quickly from Penson's human-male gaze to the beastlike desire of the Haitian criminals, whose hairy hands cover the girls' mouths as machetes cut their throats and rip their dresses to ultimately rape the dead bodies of the girls. Through the use of necrophilia in his repetition of the crime, Penson defines the ultimate border between Dominican civilization and Haitian barbarism. Thus Haitian desire is not just foreign, but beastly and inhumane: "Ved a los tigres saciando su nauseabundo apetito y su sed de sangre . . . revolcándose en la inocencia de las pobres niñas, ya frías" (See the tigers quenching their nauseous hunger and thirst for blood . . . possessing the innocence of the poor girls who laid there cold, dead). In his famous lectures from 1917 on the theory of sexuality, Sigmund Freud qualified necrophilia as horror, and the ultimate limit of human desire.[118] Similarly, literary scholar Sybille Fischer, borrowing from psychoanalytic theory to approach Penson, asked what it meant for the desire of Haitians to be imagined as horrific: "It is a desire that is not only unnatural but posthuman in that is satisfied only after humanity is vanished."[119] Penson's depiction of Haitians in *Las vírgenes* is not only that they are barbaric, but monstrous, for Haitian desire cannot be satisfied with mere invasion (rape); it requires the annihilation of Dominican subjecthood (necrophilia). Unlike Spanish desire, which resulted in the "benevolent mestizaje" Galván suggested in *Enriquillo*, Haitian desire, Penson implies, can only result in sexual violence, desecration of the dead, and the complete destruction of Dominican civilization.

Literary critic Jean Franco has insisted on the significance of gender-related terms—castration, violation, prostitution, and impotence—in narrating Latin American struggles with colonization.[120] In the case of the Dominican Republic, the rhetorical labor of nineteenth-century writers such as Penson sought to replace the crimes of the Spanish conquest with the trauma of the Haitian unification.[121] Penson's Galindo Virgins are not only symbols of the (violated) nation, but they also serve as epitomes of whiteness and virginity, their mutilated bodies becoming testimonial evidence of the penetration by a race that is foreign and inferior. Penson's fictionalization of Galindo thus transforms a political conflict (Dominican struggle for independence from Haiti) into an international common trope of gendered racialized ideology (the raping of white women by black men).

Despite the fact that since the sixteenth century the majority of the Dominican population was mulato, elite writers such as Penson and Galván whitened the nation-woman through Europeanized descriptions of feminine beauty that portrayed Águeda as "a marble Venus" and a "fragile drop of snow."[122] Gender, like race, served as a fundamental category in the narration of the Dominican Nation in which "the (white) woman" became the guardian of the dominicanidad. Simultaneous to the production of white Dominican womanhood, elite writers disavowed black women as "tristes extranjeras" (sad foreigners) in the tragic hands "de miseria africana" (of African misery),[123] or as oversexualized "reina[s] de Saba / que domina[n] al hombre con una mirada" (Queen[s] of Sheba / who dominate men with one look).[124] The black woman—writes José Joaquín Pérez in his poem *Etnaí* (1883)—is "essentially different" from the criolla, as she is a "ferocious lion," unlike the "mansa oveja" (tame sheep) that is the white criolla. The black woman, as elite writers such as Pérez defined her, therefore did not need protection for the sake of nation-state.[125]

Nicole Guidotti-Hernández, writing about the US borderlands, argues that violence is an ongoing social process of differentiation for racialized, sexualized, and gendered subjects in the nineteenth and early twentieth centuries. Violence, she asserts, forms "the foundations of national histories and subjectivities" in the borderlands through repetition of the violent events that often erased or silenced the physical bodies onto which the violence is being committed—in this case the bodies of Águeda, Ana Francisca, Marcela and Andrés Andújar—while simultaneously celebrating the event as important and foundational to the nation. Thus repetition, as Guidotti-Hernández insists, may actually be a way of "instructing us to forget" precisely because the cursory references say nothing and say everything about the effects of violence.[126] The repetition of Galindo eventually replaced the bodies and identities of Águeda, Ana Francisca, and Marcela Andújar with the figurative and symbolic "Galindo Virgins"—their martyrdom serving as a reminder of the need to protect the virgin-land and virgin-bodies from black invasion.

Penson's beautified narration of the Andújar crime simultaneously reminds us of the "espanto indecible" (unspeakable horror) that the Haitians enacted upon the Dominican nation, while denying the reader the possibility of confronting the actual violent act on the physical bodies of the victims. The "unspeakability" of the crime negates the possibility of confronting the truth of the historical event—that three girls and their father were killed in a horrendous crime—and substitutes the tangible horror with the unspeakable symbol: that black Haitian monsters attacked (and therefore could attack again) white Dominican virgins. The institutionalization of the myth of the Galindo Virgins simultaneously requires, as Guidotti-Hernández would argue, that we remember the violence while forgetting the subjects onto whom the violent acts were committed. The lasting impact on the nation and its subjects is alarming, for the repetition of violence, instead of reproducing violence as the single act (the killing of the Andújar family), transforms it to a paradigm of "the series of unspeakable acts" suffered at the hand of the invading Haitian forces. Violence thus becomes the only way to avenge national honor and protect the fragile borders of the nation-virgin-land from future destruction.

Rendering the Andújar girls as the virgin-land, which is violated by the foreign invader, Penson encapsulates his tradición within a paternalistic discourse of the nation. However, this narration also points to Penson's preoccupation with the Dominican patriarch's inability to produce a cohesive nation, a fact that manifested in the continued disenfranchisement of the borderland population. Penson allegorizes his patriarchal anxiety through the characterization of Andrés Andújar:

[Andrés Andújar] en sus diligencias se iba a la ciudad continuamente, y pues tenía que dejar solas a las pobres niñas en aquel desierto; pues la estancia quedaba enclavada en el corazón del bosque. . . . *Y acaso más que sus diligencias, el fatal vicio que le dominaba.* Así que días y aún noches lóbregas pasaba la familia de Don Andrés aislada en medio de la selva mientras él tiraba de la oreja al burro en indignos garitos de la ciudad o echaba una fortuna a las patas de un gallo en las galleras. De aquí que la desazón y el disgusto de las personas que tenían afecto a las niñas fuese grande y en aumento.[127] (emphasis added)

[(Andrés Andújar) would always go to the city to run errands, and so he would have to leave the poor children alone in that desolate place because the Hacienda was buried in the heart of the forest. . . . *And more than going to run errands, he would go because of that horrible vice that dominated him.* Therefore the family would spend days and even nights isolated in that forest while he would get drunk in the bars of the city or spend a fortune betting in the cockpits. This is why those who loved the girls were increasingly upset and angry.]

Andújar, a criollo, appears in Penson's narrative as a failed patriarch who is careless, selfish, and childlike. It is Andújar's cavalier lifestyle and "vices," Penson suggests, that ultimately caused the demise of his own daughters. *The Galindo Virgins* is not only a story about the perverted Haitian desire that resulted in the obliteration of Dominican virgins, but also about the impotence of the Dominican patriarch who failed to protect them. Penson writes for men, appealing to their sense of duty and patriotism by reminding the Dominican patriarch of his past failure to protect the white virgins (nation) from black Haitian rape (invasion).

Penson's disappointment at Don Andrés is symbolic of criollo trauma of Cáceres's Ephemeral Independence (1821), when the last hopes of creating a white-led nation were crushed by the unification of black and mulato leadership. Penson therefore speaks to three generations of patriarchs: the Liberal elite of the early nineteenth century who failed to protect the nation; the turn-of-the century generation of elites to which Penson belonged and which he believed responsible for the task of bordering the nation; and, most important, the future generation of patriarchs who the author thinks should "never forget the horrible crimes suffered under Haitian rule."[128] Penson's timeless message is thus: We Hispanic Dominican men must never fail to protect our nation from black Haitian invasion again or we risk losing our Hispanic culture, that is, our white privilege.

Directly responding to Penson's critique of the Dominican patriarch, twentieth-century Hispanophile elite and Trujillo-serving intellectual Max Henríquez Ureña published the historical novel *La conspiración de los Alcarrizos* in 1940.[129] The novel reconstructs the events surrounding the Liberal criollo plot of 1823 to overturn the Haitian government, directly linking it to the Galindo murders through the main character in the novel, Lico Andújar. Lico is imagined as the surviving cousin of the murdered girls and Águeda's fiancé.[130] Organized in Los Alcarrizos, a community located fifteen miles north of Santo Domingo (see map 1.1), under the leadership of Baltazar de Nova, Antonio González, and Vicente Moscoso, *La conspiración de los Alcarrizos* sought to restore colonial ties with Spain.[131] Henríquez Ureña describes the Galindo crimes as a decisive moment in the consolidation of "Dominican Race" as different from Haitianness and as a catalyst to the 1844 independence movement: "Ese crimen espantoso, obra de bestias y no de hombres, es el fruto de la ignominia en que vivimos. . . . Ya no podemos figurar más en la lista de países civilizados. Hemos retrogradado a la barbarie" (This horrifying crime, the works of beasts rather than men, is the fruit of the ghastly times we live in. . . . We can no longer appear in the list of the civilized nations. We have devolved to barbarism).[132] Henríquez Ureña's novel ventriloquizes Penson and del Monte, reminding his (Dominican) readers of the "essential difference" that existed between the two peoples that inhabited the island of Hispaniola, and of the perpetual threat to sovereignty Haiti represents.

Writing only three years after the Massacre of 1937, Henríquez Ureña, like other Trujillo-serving intellectuals of the period, justifies the violence that ended the lives of more than twenty thousand people, through a repetition of the historical wound of the Haitian unification of 1822, allegorized in the Galindo Virgins. Violence became, at the hands of the dictatorship, the logic for bordering the nation. The repetition of the Galindo Crimes, as an example of the horrific violence that sent Dominicans to "barbarism" in the nineteenth century, served as both the motive (vengeance) and the justification (reciprocity) of the brutal state massacre on the multiethnic community of the northern borderlands. If nineteenth-century literature provided the foundation for the symbolic erasure of blackness from the Archive of Dominicanidad, twentieth-century literature became the historical diction that justified the multiple acts of violence that target and destroy black bodies. The epistemic violence of Penson and del Monte materialized into tangible acts of violence and destruction.

Through the transformation of the Galindo murderers into barbaric black Haitians and the victims into white young virgins, Dominican Hispanophile writers facilitated the erasure of plural histories of solidarity surrounding the Haitian unification of the island (1822–44) while imposing a history of violence that would further the project of border making and civilizing of the newly birthed Republic as desired by the dominant criollo elite. As we will see in chapters 2 and 3, in the twentieth century this criollo-based ideology served as historical justification for the passing of xenophobic legislation and racist crimes against the Afro-Dominican religious, the rayano, and the ethnic Haitian by the US military government (1916–24), the Trujillo dictatorship (1930–61), and the Balaguer regime (1966–78).

School curricula throughout the twentieth century indoctrinated children into the process of national disidentification with blackness and upholding Hispanism. As minister of education (1949–55) during the Trujillo dictatorship, Joaquín Balaguer required that all schools teach Penson's 1891 tradición in the middle and high school curricula.[133] Balaguer's logic responded to increased anxiety among the small but powerful white elite class over what they perceived as the rapid "ennegrecimiento del país y la pérdida de nuestra cultura hispánica" (blackening of the country and the loss of our Hispanic culture), embodied in the growth of the borderland intraethnic and multilingual communities of Dajabón, Elías Piña, Monte Cristi, and Jimaní (see map 3.1). To this day, Penson's *Vírgenes de Galindo* and Galván's *Enriquillo* are mandatory readings in all public middle and high schools throughout the country.

Along with indigenista literature such as Galván's *Enriquillo*, Penson's *Las vírgenes de Galindo* became complementary narrations of an elite-preferred version of dominicanidad that reinforced prejudice against Africanness and blackness while delineating the cultural and racial borders of the nation. Though the narration of the Galindo Virgins arguably did not translate into tangible actions during the nineteenth century, the posthumous consecration of Galván's affirmation ("we are Indians") and Penson's negation ("we are not black") would found the cultural, political, and historical origins of the nation-state during the Trujillo dictatorship (1930–61). Sadly, contemporary Dominican arts and literature continue to repeat the violence of Galindo as the catalyst for the 1844 independence, following a Pensonian lens. The most recent example is a theatrical representation entitled, once again, *The Galindo Virgins*, which debuted in the Dominican National Theater December 10, 2013, following the international crisis that emerged after the Dominican Constitutional Court approved a law that effectively denationalized more than 200,000 Dominican-born ethnic Haitians. Like Henríquez Ureña's novel, this state-sponsored production by Hamlet Bodden reminded Dominicans of the violence of Galindo in order to justify the dehumanization of ethnic Haitians at the hands of the state.[134]

The following chapters establish that the contradictory ideology that grounds the Archive of Dominicanidad continues to color notions of citizenship and belonging in twentieth- and twenty-first-century Dominican Republic as ideologues and politicians such as Vincho Castillo, whose remarks from 2014 open this chapter, continue to manipulate historical events and myths in their effort to disunite and divest the poor. Yet their rhetoric does not go uncontested. Dominican blacks have continued to shatter the silences, questioning and challenging the racist norms that sustain the borders of dominicanidad at home and abroad. Producing an archive of contra*dictions* that has begun to dismantle xenophobia and marginality within political, literary, and historical discourse as well as in the public sphere, *dominicanos*—particularly, I argue, those in the diaspora—place their racialized bodies at the center of history, contra*dicting* Hispanophile ideologies that insist on erasing them.

CHAPTER 2

Of Bandits and Wenches

The US Occupation (1916–1924) and the Criminalization
of Dominican Blackness

Cuando yo me muera que me toquen palos
que no llore nadie y que me canten salves
Pañuelo rojo, traje blanco
y que los quijongos no se callen
Ya verás cómo vuelvo hecho todo aire
a contarle al mundo dos o tres verdades.

[When I die, play me some *palos*,
no one crying, all singing salves.
Red bandana, white dress
and let the drums do the crying.
You shall see how I come back through the air,
to tell the world one or two things about the truth.]
—Popular Dominican *salve*

On Pentecost, 1922, Dominga Alcántara prepared for the most important celebration of the year. As the queen of the *Cofradía del Espíritu Santo*
(Brotherhood/Sisterhood of the Holy Spirit) of San Juan de la Maguana, she
was entrusted with the great task of organizing the annual festivity to honor
the incarnation of the Holy Spirit in the living *fieles* (the faithful).[1] Though
Alcántara always took great care in leading the cofradía's sacred celebrations,
she was particularly excited about this year's Day of Holy Spirit, for rumor
had it that Olivorio Mateo, the San Juan Valley prophet, would come by to
give her a special blessing.[2]

Days prior to the June 4 celebration, Alcántara had begun to make palm

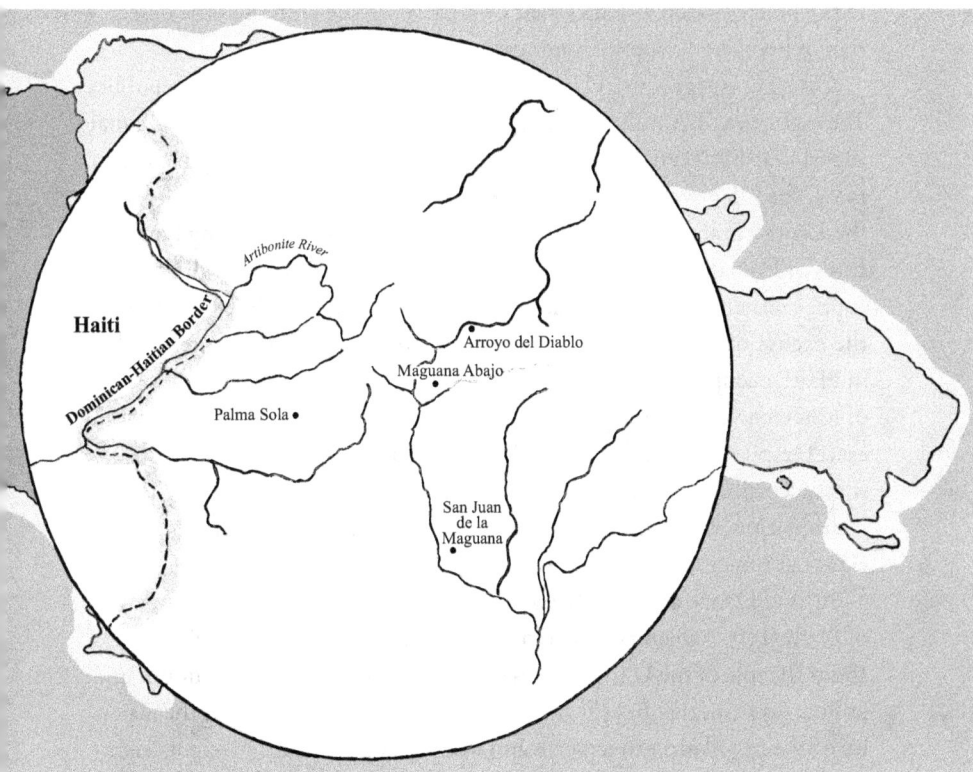

Map 2.1 Map of San Juan Valley and the liborista territory. Created by Kilia Llano.

crucifixes, which she carefully dressed in yellow and red to place on the altar along with *velones* (large candles used for religious rituals) and marigolds, as is customary in the *batey* celebration.[3] Early that Pentecost Sunday, when the women of the cofradía arrived at Dominga's house to prepare the stew of *chivo con chenchén* (goat with corn meal) that would be served for the occasion, Dominga was ready to receive her blessing.

At two in the afternoon, shortly after the three sacred drums had been blessed with rum and prayer, the feast began.[4] But just as the *palo mayor* (main drum) redoubled to signal the beginning of the first danceable *atabal*, a group of armed *guardias* commanded by US Marine Captain G. H. Morse Jr. stormed into Alcántara's home, declaring that "the party was over."[5] The marines ordered people to disperse and go home "if they did not want to spend the night in jail."[6] They then took the rum, tobacco, and sacred drums to the police station and had their own party. As she witnessed the desecration of her sacred drums, Dominga wept with rage.[7]

On May 15, 1916, the United States invaded the Dominican Republic. The eight-year US military occupation followed two decades of unequal tug-of-war between the Empire and the two nations of Hispaniola. In 1904, the US government had seized Dominican customhouses. In 1905, the United States issued sanctions and ultimatums, threatening both nations of Hispaniola with the possibility of intervention if they did not get "upheavals and banditry" under control.[8] Finally on July 28, 1915, with the excuse of protecting US interests in the region, US Marines landed in Haiti, occupying the second-oldest nation of the Americas for a period of nineteen years. A few months later, in May 1916, the occupation spread east. Despite the local armed and intellectual resistance, the US military was successful in controlling Hispaniola's population through censorship, intimidation, fear, and military force, breaching the two nations' sovereignty at imperial will.

A brief glance at the early twentieth-century United States occupation of Haiti (1915–34) and of the Dominican Republic (1916–24) tells us a lot about the role of the United States in the creation of unequal economic and political systems that benefit rich corporations while condemning the majority of the population to poverty and disenfranchisement. During its eight-year occupation of the Dominican Republic, the US government handed Dominican finances over to the National City Bank of New York, which would later be controlled by the Rockefeller Group. This move facilitated corporation ownership of Dominican land for sugar production.[9] Another bequeath of the US occupation was the creation of the Guardia Nacional Dominicana (Dominican National Guard, or GND), which served as a vehicle for the ruthless dictatorship of Rafael Leonidas Trujillo (1930–61), the US occupation's right-hand man and appointed general.[10]

An equally violent, though not yet studied effect of the occupation is the criminalization of Afro-religious practices and practitioners through official and unofficial channels. These measures included, as evidenced in the story of Dominga Alcántara, the public desecration of Afro-religious articles, particularly sacred drums; raids of religious celebrations, including birth blessings and funerals in the borderland towns; the imprisonment of *santeros* under vagrancy laws; and the branding of the Afro-religious as savage or bandit.[11] Much like the actions of US military personnel in Abu Ghraib during the Iraq War (2003–4), the confiscation and desecration of Alcán-tara's sacred drums epitomized the marines' racism and intolerance toward local cultural and religious practices.[12] Letters from marines stationed in the border region spoke of drumming as "haunting and scary" practices of "criminals and savages."[13] Some marines even complained the drumming was driving them mad.[14] The confiscation of drums and the punishing of drummers became a common practice of the occupying marines in their efforts to "civilize" Hispaniola, and as a response to their fear of blackness.[15]

Disconcerted by the sacrilege of the Cofradía she had been charged with guarding, Alcántara wrote a letter to the military governor of Santo Domingo, General Harry Lee.[16] In it, she denounced the confiscation of the sacred drums of the Holy Spirit and demanded their immediate return:

> Ciudadano Almirante: Después de saludarlo tomé de mi vil pluma para reclamar me devuelvan los quijongos del espíritu santo que le dicen los palos camitos del espíritu santo que en San Cristóbal lo tocan como devoción, en Las Matas también y a ninguno los han aprehendido solo los de San Juan que los hizo preso al capitán Morcia [Morse] y hasta la fecha están presos. Pues yo quiero que Ud. me diga si los palos del espíritu santo son del gobierno o son de las gentes del batey. Ud[.] puede informarse con el General Wenceslao Ramírez si esa hermandad no es muy vieja y el gobierno nunca nos había *probado* hasta hoy. Pues me despido con to respeto y esta *única ama* de dicho quijongo y del espíritu santo queda en espera de su contesta. Dominga Alcántara. P.D. Ahora lo tienen en la gobernación como distracción y como ud. comprenderá esos son palos benditos y se usan solo cuando se necesitan.[17] (emphasis added)

> [Citizen Admiral: After greeting you, I took up my mundane pen to demand the return of the drums of the Holy Spirit, which are also known as the sticks of camitos of the Holy Spirit, and which are played in ceremonies in San Cristobal and also in Las Matas.[18] And none have been confiscated except for those from San Juan that were stolen by Captain Morse. So I would like it if you told me to whom those drums belong. Do they belong to the government or to the people of the batey? You can ask General Wenceslao Ramírez about this brotherhood, about how old it is and how the government had never *tested* us, until today.[19] This servant of the Holy Spirit and *only master* of those drums respectfully salutes you and waits for your response. P.S. Now they have them (the drums) at the

Police Station, and they play them for fun, and as you may well understand those drums are sacred and are only to be used as needed.]

On June 27, 1922, following a memo by General Harry Lee, Captain Morse
returned the drums to Alcántara.[20] I am inclined to believe that Alcántara
was never again tested.

Alcántara's story is more than a case study of the ways in which the Afro-
religious, particularly those who resided in the borderland communities of
the southwest Captain Morse commanded (see map 2.1), experienced the
violence of the intervention. Alcántara's letter to General Harry Lee, the
highest commander of the military government, constituted an important
documented contra*diction* that not only illuminates the seemingly incon-
spicuous ways in which the violence of the US occupation of the Dominican
Republic (1916–24) marginalized Afro-Dominicans from the nation and its
archive, but also of how this community contested oppression. Her diction,
"the government had not tested us," more than a plea, was a challenge that
embodied both her faith-based conviction and her political power. Though
the Cofradía del Espíritu Santo was a peaceful religious community organization, Alcántara's diction reminds Governor Lee that peace can always be
interrupted, whether by divine or worldly forces, for when the sacred is desecrated, gods and people get angry.

At the heart of the organizational structure of cofradías like Alcántara's
Espíritu Santo rests an important history of black Dominican colonial contestation. When blacks and mulatos were excluded from colonial societies
such as Masonic temples and *cabildos*, they formed their own organization,
the cofradías.[21] These spiritually based societies also performed a political
purpose: they were charged with representing free blacks in front of colonial
law. The leadership of the cofradía was often granted to the most learned,
usually a person who could read and write, and often a woman because it was
believed women held the ability to guard history for posterity.[22] Cofradías
thus hold an important historical archive of black dominicanidad, as well as
the institutional power to confront colonial oppression.

As the queen of the Cofradía del Espíritu Santo, Alcántara was entrusted
with the responsibility of defending it in front of the law, which in this case
meant the military government. Her position also meant that Alcántara had
some education and was literate. The queen of the Holy Spirit began her
salutation by asserting her literacy and authorship: "Tomé de mi vil pluma."
"Tomé" (I took) uses the first-person preterit conjugation of the verb *tomar*

(to take) in an active assertion that assumes the responsibility for the composition of the letter and the tone of its content. "Tomé de mi vil pluma" (I took my mundane pen) is a performative diction that reminds the reader of her action (writing) and the body that acts (taking of the pen with my fingers), in stark contra*diction* with the impersonal and passive tone that characterized official memoranda. The diction "I took my pen to demand my drums" thus reminds the military governor that weapons can come in many forms and shapes, and that war can be waged with guns, prayers, or pens.

The assertion of her literacy in the very first line of the letter places Alcántara in direct confrontation with the military government, a road seldom traveled by women of any race or class in early twentieth-century Hispaniola, "para reclamar los quijongos del espíritu santo" (to demand the Holy Spirit's drums). Though many letters addressed by women can be found in the occupation records, they mostly concern the release of a son, brother, or husband imprisoned by the marines, or a request for child compensation for the offspring of a marine. In such cases it was often men—lawyers, priests, or "officially" respectable members of the community—on behalf of the pleading women who wrote such letters, for in the 1920s Dominican Republic the majority of the poor, particularly women from farming communities, were illiterate.[23] But Dominga Alcántara knew how to read and write. More important, she recognized the power that her literacy conveyed. The queen did not plead to General Lee as did other female letter-writers; rather, she demanded ("reclamar") her property rights as sole and only owner of the drums ("única ama de estos quijongos"). In so doing, she also allegorized the US occupation of Dominican land in Morse's usurpation of the drums, reminding Lee of the impending possibility of rebellion.

Despite the fact that Alcántara wrote without intermediaries, she did not interpellate the military government alone. Her somewhat vague mention of General Wenceslao Ramírez, the most important caudillo of the region and with whom the military government had negotiated in order to establish a post in San Juan, contextualizes her political power as a respected community leader. Alcántara was careful to let General Lee know that she could, but chose not to, ask Ramírez to intercede on her behalf the way the caudillo often did for other *sanjuaneros* (people from San Juan) who had grievances with the marines. Instead Alcántara mentions Ramírez as a reminder that neither force—imperial nor national—had tested her, suggesting, perhaps, that they both should also fear the spiritual power she could summon.

Captain Morse's response to Harry Lee's inquiry about the confiscation of Alcántara's drums is a telling indicator of whom the military government feared: "The sticks in question were seized by the undersigned," Morse wrote, "due to the fact that the dance was next to the *cuartel* and the undersigned received information that a group of Mateo's people would be in town for the purpose of attacking the Police Barracks."[24] Olivorio Mateo was an Afro-religious messiah from the rayano farming community of Maguana Abajo, near the city of San Juan de la Maguana (see map 2.1) whom the military government had been chasing but unable to apprehend for nearly four years.[25] Though there is no historical evidence that Mateo ever attacked the police, Morse saw him as a potential catalyst for armed resistance throughout the San Juan Valley. Aware of the military government's fear of her prophet, Alcántara openly challenged the military regime, regaining her drums and reasserting her authority as a community leader.

Death of a God, Birth of a Movement

On July 27, 1922, exactly one month after Alcántara's drums were returned to her, a detachment of twelve men under the command of US Marine Captain George H. Morse Jr. and Lieutenant G. A. Williams killed Olivorio Mateo.[26] Papá Liborio, as he is still referred to by his followers, was shot fifteen times, until his fingers and limbs fell on the ground.[27] Unlike other executions enacted by the US military government during the eight years it occupied the Dominican Republic, Mateo's was a public event. The body of the spiritual leader was tied up in front of the San Juan City Hall for all to watch it rot (see figure 2.1). After three days of this macabre spectacle, Mateo was buried in the San Juan City Cemetery. The local paper, *El Cable*, published an obituary that read: "With the death of Olivorio, we consider his coarse religion to be finished forever. It constituted a disgrace for this municipality, particularly since the majority of its followers were *foreign elements*" (emphasis added).[28]

In the eyes of the marines, Papá Liborio was just "another gavillero bandit," a threat to US "appeasement of the Dominican population."[29] Guerrilla resistance had posed a significant challenge for the marines since their arrival.[30] Bands of Dominican guerrilla peasants from the eastern part of the country, known as *gavilleros*, waged a guerrilla war against the occupiers. The guerrillas significantly hindered the actions of the US military, creating public embarrassment and eventually forcing the United States to withdraw in 1924.[31] The final destruction of the Afro-religious prophet as-

2.1 Olivorio Mateo *en parihuela*, as exposed in front of the San Juan City Hall. Reprinted with permission from the Archivo General de la República, Santo Domingo.

suaged marine anxiety over the potential uprising of new dissidents. The *El Cable* obituary thus served in part as a precautionary note to other "bandits" who—whether through prayer, pen, or combat—might want to lead people against the imposed order.

But Olivorio Mateo was not only a problem for the US military regime. The otherwise vocal anti-US intervention intelligentsia celebrated Mateo's execution because, in the words of Max Henríquez Ureña, "it [Liborismo] constituted a disgrace to the civilization and unity of our Christian nation."[32] Elite disavowal of Liborismo as barbaric and foreign is a performative repetition of the diction of civilization versus barbarism that nineteenth-century letrados such as Félix María del Monte and César Nicolás Penson popularized in their efforts to mark the racial borders of Hispaniola. Let us remember that at the end of the nineteenth century, Hispanophile writers such as Penson and Manuel de Jesús Galván, through a rhetorical process of silencing and repetition, succeeded in solidifying a national myth that equated blackness to Haitianness, and thus rendered Dominican blacks exiles in their own nation. [33] The white intellectual response to Mateo's destruction at the hands of the marines, exemplified in *El Cable*, though paradoxical as it comes amidst wide opposition to US presence on the island, is congruent with the dominant narration of dominicanidad that emerged during the second half of the nineteenth century. The diction "foreign" that appears in *El Cable* validates the right of the United States to civilize black Hispaniola. Equally disavowed by the US military regime and the (white) Dominican opposition, Liborio's body became textual evidence of the cooperation between the US Empire and the Dominican white elite in bordering Hispaniola to exclude blackness from the nation.

It is said that Mateo's body was dismembered to such a fragile state that the marines had to wrap it in twine and rope to keep it from falling into pieces (figure 2.1). Others say the extra restraint was due to fear that his people might try to steal him in order to give the prophet a proper ceremonial burial. One could also speculate that Mateo's body was (overly) restrained because the US occupiers and the local elite feared that Liborio could indeed rise from the dead, escape, and avenge his murder. Mateo's murder epitomized Afro-religiosity as a potential locus for political contestation: Mateo's body could be re-membered, coming back to contra*dict* governments' oppression of him as a criminal. Yet, the impact of Olivorio Mateo's tale lies not in his lynching by the US military and Dominican allies, but in the legacy of contestation he bestowed upon the people of San Juan, as personified in Dominga Alcántara's letter to Governor Lee and in the many salves (Afro-religious songs), that, contra*dicting* the archive, continue to narrate an *other* history of the prophet's life.

The capture and assassination of Olivorio Mateo in 1922 marked a considerable advancement toward the goals of both hegemonic forces—the US government and the Dominican Hispanophile elite—because they believed, as stated in the obituary, that Liborismo indeed finished with Mateo. But the peasant religious community of San Juan Valley, led by priestesses and priests like Alcántara, differed in its viewpoint: Mateo's death did not cause distress or sadness because the Afro-religious had known, as predicted years earlier by their own leader, that Papá Liborio would indeed die at the hands of US soldiers. [34] They also believed his death to be a necessary yet temporary sacrifice, for Papá Liborio, like Jesus, would rise up in three days to inhabit the mountains of San Juan and reincarnate in the bodies of his followers for generations to come. [35]

A God with Balls

Despite being illiterate, Olivorio Mateo was a skillful reader. He read the sky for time, the grass for impending misfortunes, people's eyes for illnesses and secrets, and the river's movements for bad weather. In 1908, his ability to read led him to the mystical experience that transformed him from a farmer to a god.[36] The Great Storm of 1908 caused ferocious rain for more than a week, triggering floods that destroyed crops and dwellings throughout the Caribbean and the southeast United States.[37] Mateo walked into the storm and, as he would later tell his followers, in the clouds he read the wisdom of the Holy Spirit ("el gran poder de Dios"). He then walked in the valley, following the storm, and there he came "face to face with God."[38]

Assuming him dead, Mateo's family held a funeral in his honor. On the ninth day of the funeral, the last day of the customary mourning and burial rituals, Mateo returned to his community of La Maguana, surprising all.[39] His return on such a symbolic day contributed to his beatification. A popular salve remembers Papá Liborio's mystical disappearance and return during the 1908 storm as the source of his spiritual wisdom:

Liborio se perdió bajo un tiempo de agua
y volvió con un palo e piñón en la mano y la cara de Dios de su lado.
Liborio era un santo y nos vino a salvá
de la opresión, del hambre y la soledá.
Alabado sea Papá Liborio.

[Liborio disappeared amidst a storm
and came back with a blessed cane in his hand and the shadow of God
    on his side.
Liborio was a saint who came to save us
from oppression, hunger, and desolation.
Blessed be Papá Liborio.]

Garrido Puello also situated Papá Liborio's emergence as a religious leader in 1908, following his return from the storm.[40] Yet people who knew Mateo insist that he was always "special," possessing the kind of clairvoyant wisdom that drew people to seek his company and advice in times of trouble.[41] The link between Liborismo and a hurricane is noteworthy in two ways. First, it ties the religious movement closely to the island's environment, making it relevant to the everyday lives of farmers. Additionally, the storm chronologically locates the emergence of Liborismo, fitting with the popular practice of remembering through natural events that has allowed Dominicans to preserve important histories despite a lack of archives or access to writing.[42] A little over two decades later, in 1931, another hurricane would aid Trujillo in gaining the trust of a distressed people, perhaps appealing to memories of Papá Liborio the peasantry held.[43]

The salve historicizes Mateo's disappearance into the storm, as well as the maladies affecting San Juan Valley peasants at the turn of the twentieth century: "la opresión, [el] hambre y la soledá" (oppression, hunger, and desolation). At the emergence of Liborismo in 1908, the Dominican Republic was undergoing a series of political and economic changes due to the country's insertion in the global market, mostly through the sugar industry. A new and powerful middle class began to emerge, and the cities—particularly Santo Domingo, Puerto Plata, and Santiago—experienced a revival in the cultural and political scenes. This imminent "progress" affected farmers who, according to labor historian Roberto Cassá, became targets for those elite who sought to eradicate anything that opposed their idea of modernization and progress.[44] In addition to losing their crops to the storm, sanjuaneros also confronted increasing pressures from the central state seeking to insert them into the nation-modernizing process through land redistribution and taxation. The communal ways of Liborismo offered a solution to anxious farmers of San Juan who faced "oppression, hunger, and desolation."

Though hunger and oppression are well-defined socioeconomic conditions, the diction *soledá* (loneliness or desolation) summons both affective and effective connotations. In its spiritual and psychic inferences, *soledá* refers to the loss of guidance and accompaniment of leadership. *Soledá* could thus denote the spiritual condition of the Afro-religious community of San Juan Valley, who felt their faith shaken after the storm as people lost their crops, homes, and even lives.[45] In this sense, Mateo's return from the storm came to assuage the spiritual loneliness the community faced and community members' urgent desire to regain peace and faith after the storm. But desolation is also a diction often associated with the geographical area of the Haiti-Dominican borderlands.[46] Desolate, lonely, unaccounted for by the state, in the early twentieth century, the Línea Fronteriza, where liboristas resided, was still a disenfranchised location, imagined and produced as existing outside the nation.[47]

Rayanos such as Mateo and his followers lacked political leadership and representation at a moment in which the country was modernizing and the peasants were suffering the pressures of an imposing state-serving economy.[48] Like Moses in the burning bush narrative, Mateo's mystical experience as remembered in the salve allowed him to come back with the tools—*palo de piñón* (juniper walking stick) and the face of God—to lead a distressed people during arduous times, thereby becoming an important symbol of both spiritual and political hope.

News about Mateo's healing powers and abilities to predict the future spread throughout the country via rumors, newspaper articles, and salves. Marine memoranda list "letters coming from remote places as far as Higüey and Santiago in which people requested miracles and prayers to heal their ailments."[49] Mateo's biographer, Garrido Puello, wrote that as early as 1909 a community of over one hundred followers "from different parts of the Frontier" congregated as an independent brotherhood under the liborista principles of peace, community, and love.[50] Rapidly, Mateo's fame spread across the island, attracting the attention of both friends and foes.[51]

Jan Lundius and Mats Lundahl, in their extensive analysis of Liborismo, define it as a messianic phenomenon, the product of "a charismatic leader like many found throughout the history of humanity."[52] Mateo's success, the authors argue, is the result of people's perception that the leader possessed "thaumaturgic powers."[53] Though I recognize that Liborismo can be compared to a larger trend of socioreligious and messianic movements that took place in Latin America at the turn of the twentieth century, I must insist on its specificity as an organic and spontaneous socioreligious movement that emerged in peaceful contra*diction* with the church and the state. Liboristas imagined themselves as Catholic and Dominican, and did not believe their devotion to Liborismo opposed their religious or national affirmations. Additionally, unlike other Latin American messianic movements, Liborismo was not short lived; on the contrary, it has endured until the present, influencing other expressions of Afro-Dominican religiosity and quickly spreading into the US and European diaspora.[54]

It is possible, however, to find connections between the sociohistorical causes that allowed for the establishment of Liborismo and other Latin America social movements, such as the *canudos*, that emerged in Brazil beginning in 1893. Canudos, like *liboristas*, were farmers who faced similar socioeconomic challenges as Brazil grappled with the pressures to modernize following the Industrial Revolution, and particularly at the turn of the twentieth century.[55] Canudos operated as a communal group, practicing common ownership, and abolishing the official currency, as well as participating collectively in the management of the town under the spiritual leadership of Antônio Conselheiro. And like liboristas, canudos were eventually persecuted and their leader massacred. Like Mateo, Conselheiro became not only a spiritual symbol, but also an emblem of social justice who threatened the interests of the elite and the state.[56]

In popular literature and music, Papá Liborio is remembered not as a prophet but as a living god, an embodiment of the Holy Spirit who came to guide farmers in spiritual and human unity:

Viva Cristo, el rey mesías
viva la madre piadosa, viva Liborio,
esto es todo lo que anhelo
de aquí saldrá un presidente
que domine el mundo entero.[57]

[Long live Christ, the king messiah
long live the merciful mother, long live Liborio,
this is all I long for
from this place will go forth a president
who will prevail over the whole earth.]

The previous salve avows Mateo as both a worldly and a spiritual leader: the completion to the Holy Trinity and the "president who will prevail over the world."[58] Mateo's legacy, the salve suggests, resides in the marriage of his divine spiritual force with revolutionary authority. Papá Liborio was not only a god but "a god with balls," as Felipe Umberto Acosta, a present-day liborista explained to me; "Liborio had the balls to stand up to the gringos and to anyone who wanted to take advantage of him and his people. I don't go to church—churches are full of it [*pendejá*]—but Liborio, he is the real deal, like the famous song says: he isn't full of it [*no come pendejá*]."[59] Acosta's faith in Papá Liborio is not guided solely by the spiritual powers attributed to the prophet but also by the leadership he exercised in the fight against oppression, hunger, and desolation.

A picture of Olivorio Mateo from 1909 (figure 2.2) encapsulates the rugged masculinity of Acosta's (vulgar) description as a "god with balls," while simultaneously defying the US military and Dominican elite's complicit hegemony that sought to contain and criminalize Afro-religious expressions. Though a crucifix rests on his forehead, Mateo's image differs from the traditional benevolent depictions of Christian iconography. Mateo's eyes are

2.2 Portrait of Olivorio Mateo (left), circa 1909. Colección de fotos, Gobierno Militar (1916–24), Archivo General de la República, Santo Domingo.

strong, staring fiercely and intensely. His shirt is unbuttoned, revealing his chest, while his posture denotes alertness and physical readiness. We can see the muscle tension in his arms. Rather than offering the other cheek as suggested by Christianity, Mateo's picture seems to warn the viewer of the potential fist he would not hesitate to use in order to defend his honor and that of his community. The picture does indeed suggest that Mateo was "a god with balls," as Acosta reminded me, a (masculine) leader capable of contra*dicting* Dominican (failed) white elite patriarchy.

Mateo's performance of masculinity in the open-shirt photo (figure 2.2) summons action rather than the passivity that characterizes Hispanophile narratives of the turn of the century. Let us remember, as discussed in chapter 1, that in their writings Penson (1891), Galván (1871), and del Monte (1861) cast the Dominican patriarch as lazy, passive, and weak—a weakness, the authors suggested, led to the loss of dignity (Haitian unification 1822–44) and honor (raped virgins) at the hands of a foreign (Haitian) invader. Hispanophile letrados grappled with their colonial desire, fears of US expansionism, and racial anxieties by excluding blackness from the nation's narration. At the beginning of the twentieth century, and particularly during the US military regime, Hispanophile ideology fused with US paternalistic discourse—which was also a discourse of racial anxiety—contributing to the further erasure of black bodies from the nation and its archive.[60] Elite celebration of Olivorio Mateo's lynching, exemplified in the *El Cable* article only twenty-five years after the initial publication of Penson's *Las vírgenes de Galindo* (1891), confirms that the project of founding the Archive of Dominicanidad had been co-opted by Hispanophile letrados whose main concern continued to be—even at the loss of sovereignty at the hands of US Empire—the protection of their colonial investment in Hispanism and whiteness, rather than the liberty and freedom of Dominican citizens they often professed.

Mateo's naked torso contra*dicts* the elite version of dominicanidad, for rather than a passive voice that interferes, delays, and laments a lost colonial privilege, it promises protection against the concrete military and government forces that oppress dominicanos. Mateo's body language—his fierce eyes and open shirt, the alertness of his body—all seem to suggest he is ready to lead and ready to fight. His message thus reminded criollos of their own fear of black and mulato political power while sending US military forces a cautionary message of the potential expansion of peasant rebellion. Olivorio's performative diction of black masculinity placed him in direct confrontation with the powerful allegiance of the Hispanophile elite and the US empire.

Big Brother, Little Nation

Like other US occupations of the twentieth and twenty-first centuries, the Dominican intervention in 1916 was a complicated enterprise that engaged a heteronormative understanding of the world in which the United States, embodied in each of the marines, was entrusted with the duty to "protect" public order and safety. The rhetoric of the occupation painted the marines as "invaluable vessels of the mighty United States Government," a privilege that came with the duty to eliminate opposition and to dominate the local—and often resistant—population.[61] A memo by Commanding General Harry Lee in 1921 offers a helpful illustration of the rhetoric through which marines were invested in the imperial domination of the Dominican peoples in order to protect their notion of civility and democracy:

It is thought well at this time to remind all that we, a force of the United States, are in Military Occupation of the Republic of Santo Domingo, and that the territory has been placed under Military Government, and is in a modified way in a status of territory of a hostile state, over which military authority has been exercised. The authority of the legitimate power having passed into the hands of the United States, we as representatives of the occupant shall take all the measure in our power to insure public order and safety. . . . No cruel, harsh or unusual measures are permitted against the inhabitants. Measures to locate and apprehend or capture lawbreakers and *evildoers* such as *bandits* and other criminals must be taken in order to insure order and public safety.[62] (emphasis added)

The diction of the military memo is as fervent and strong as it is vague. Much is left to interpretation: Were "evildoers" robbers? killers? common criminals? Could a censorship violator such as a journalist or writer who criticized the military government be considered an "evildoer"? Could a sex worker be an "evildoer"? Could a santero (Afro-religious priest) performing a non-Christian ceremony in a public space? Could an American officer ever be an "evildoer," or could only a native do "evil"? The ambiguous language of the memo allowed for officers to interpret it using their own cultural logic to decide who was an "evildoer" and how this person should be punished. The result of this "flexibility" was what General Knapp described as a series of "undesirable" events, which often included the killing of innocent civilians, raids, rapes, and persecution, with an "unnecessary harshness, even brutality that was exhibited by the officers against local civilians as if Dominicans were in fact enemies of war."[63] The "unnecessary harshness" of the military during the US occupation of the Dominican Republic reflected the eugenicist-fueled racial ideology of the early twentieth-century United States in which whiteness was perceived as a sign of civility and in turn barbarity was a racialized characteristic of those who were perceived as other than white. This binary opposition, as historian Roxann Wheeler has argued, justified US imperial interactions throughout the twentieth century, as marines successfully embodied the rhetoric of the white heterosexual nation they represented.[64]

In his inauguration speech of 1904, President Roosevelt added a corollary to the Monroe Doctrine, which stated that European countries should stay out of Latin America. The Roosevelt Corollary took the Monroe Doctrine a step further by affirming that the United States had the right to exercise military force in Latin American countries in order to keep Europe out.[65] The Roosevelt Corollary justified US interventions in Cuba (1906–9), Nicaragua (1909–10, 1912–25, and 1926–33), Haiti (1915–34), and the Dominican Republic (1916–24) in the public eye as part of the nation's role as a leader and "big brother" to "less civilized" countries.[66]

Following Roosevelt's expansionist corollary, President Woodrow Wilson (1913–21) invigorated the US military to become a guiding force helping other nations become civilized: "If we have been obliged by circumstances . . . in the past, to take territory which we otherwise would not have thought of taking, I believe I am right in saying that we have considered it our duty to administer that territory, not for ourselves, but for the people living in it."[67] In Wilson's words, the interventions of Hispaniola were not criminal acts but, rather, acts of charity for those people who were "incapable of governing themselves."[68] The United States, like a foster parent, had to step up and govern Hispaniola for its own good.

The paternalistic rhetoric of US domination inundated the press and popular culture. Between 1904 and 1919, for instance, articles referred to Haitians and Dominicans as childlike, lazy, ignorant, and savage. The United States thus had to step in and rescue them from savagery. A political cartoon from 1906 (figure 2.3), for instance, depicts President Roosevelt as a robust man with superior virility exercising masculine dominance over the elderly (impotent) Spain. Between both men, the hypermasculine United States and the defeated Spain, lay infantilized Santo Domingo, hiding underneath the United States' phallic military protection. Writing about the Haitian occupation that began in 1915, historian Mary A. Renda argues that paternalist discourse was one of the primary cultural mechanisms by which the occupation conscripted men into the project of carrying out US imperial rule.[69] This imperialist logic was further complicated by the US racial system that had traditionally viewed blacks as inferior and childlike. Whiteness represented an "essential element of American manhood," and American men were poised to assert their manhood around the globe.[70] To be an American marine under President Wilson's government meant to be a "fatherly" (white) man to a less capable nation.

United States disavowal of Dominican and Haitian manhood was rooted in a domestic rejection of African American manhood. At the time of the occupation the US South was still segregated under Jim Crow. Wilson's diction "we must" was then an invitation not to American men but to white American men who, already carrying the "white man's burden" of

2.3 Political cartoon published in 1906 depicting Theodore Roosevelt using the Monroe Doctrine to keep European powers out of the Dominican Republic.

leading America, were now asked to undertake their younger sibling/children nations for the well-being of the Empire. Wilson believed, as one reporter stated, that "the Negro as a race, when left alone, is incapable of self-advancement."[71] Carrying this racialized idea of manhood and citizenship with them, the soldiers who landed in the Dominican Republic in 1916 believed it was their duty, as verbalized by President Wilson's agenda, to "help" Dominicans become politically sound and to "teach them how to govern themselves."[72] The majority of marines sent to the Dominican Republic and Haiti between 1914 and 1930 were white.[73] Whiteness legitimized the marines' ability to assert masculine authority while justifying criminal actions through the rhetoric of white civility and progress that Wilson institutionalized. As white, civilized men, marines were charged with endowing people with civilization—whether that meant confiscating drums or killing prophets—even if the process required the use of uncivilized "harshness."

But upon their arrival to the civilizing mission, marines stationed in the Dominican Republic faced terrible opposition—a fact that often took them by surprise and caused confusion and anger.[74] In the eastern towns of El Seibo and Higüey, farmers waged a guerrilla insurgency from early 1917 to the end of 1922, which prevented the marines from occupying the eastern provinces. The military government's training and weaponry were bested by the guerrillas' resilience and mobility, and widespread local support.[75] In addition to military action, the nationalist intellectuals launched an international campaign through the publication of essays, articles, and open letters that denounced the occupation as illegal.[76] These often resulted, as they did for Blanco Famboa and Fabio Fiallo, in exile or imprisonment.[77]

The challenges marines faced in "civilizing" Dominican people were intrinsically linked to the racist paternalistic ideologies they had brought with them, as evident in a report from the second commissioner dated June 11, 1918: "(a) Every Dominican is conscious of the instinctive racial antagonism between white and colored races; (b) No white nationality has less sympathy with colored races than American; i.e. the American goes farther than any other people in its race prejudice."[78] The US military government's awareness of the racial ideology affecting their ability to dominate further fueled their aspiration to control and "civilize" Dominicans—who were perceived as nonwhite, childlike and, therefore, inferior—in order to fulfill the "Manifest Destiny" of the United States.[79] The eventual persecution and killing of Papá Liborio and his followers was thus in great part an attempt to silence black Dominican self-governance and anti-US resistance in order to preserve the white American alpha male civilizing dominance depicted in the 1906 cartoon. Amidst such racial antagonism, it is not surprising that the marines and the military government found Mateo's open-shirt photo, and its masculine performance, threatening. If Dominican men were as brave as Mateo's photo suggested, they did not need US military protection. Mateo's performance of masculinity therefore epitomized two major concerns about the US military presence in the Dominican Republic: that the intervention was unnecessary and criminal; and that black men were indeed capable of governing and defending their nation.

Though little is known about the origins of the 1909 photo of Olivorio Mateo, we do know that it forms part of the military government's archive. One can thus maintain that the marines charged with apprehending and executing Mateo had to rely on that photo, the only one available to them at the time, to identify him.[80] Arguably, Mateo's rugged masculinity, encapsulated in Acosta's diction "god with balls" and performed in the photo, threatened the occupation's narrative of racial superiority and the marines' masculine authority. Mateo, the marines must have believed, had enough masculine courage (balls) to rally an army of rebels, spreading guerrilla resistance throughout the southwest. Mateo's performance of black masculinity, in turn, also led to his increased persecution and to the transformation of Liborismo from a peaceful religious community into a radicalized nomadic rebellious cofradía.[81]

Bordering Hispaniola

The occupations of the Dominican Republic (1916–24) and Haiti (1915–40) have traditionally been studied as two separate events.[82] Nonetheless, the fact that they took place at the same time and within an island shared by the two nations is extremely significant. Although, as previously discussed, there were many implications for the Empire, as the Hispaniola nations provided land, resources, and cheap labor for commercial exploitation, the intervention was more significant to the two nations sharing Hispaniola.[83] In 1918, for instance, US secretary of state William Jennings Bryan spearheaded a plan to write a new Constitution for Haiti. The new Constitution removed the original 1805 law that barred foreigners from owning Haitian land. The assistant secretary of the navy at the time, a young Franklin D. Roosevelt, took credit for writing Haiti's Constitution, which gave preference to American corporations for buying and owning Haiti's land.[84] The loss of communal land contributed to the strengthening of a new plantation system that condemned the Haitian peasantry to poverty.[85] Disenfranchised peasants would eventually look to the Dominican Republic for work in the US-owned sugar industry and through the US-established Hispaniola temporary labor program that imported Haitian laborers for cane cutting and West Indian specialized workers for management and office administration. This structure became the basis of the exploitative labor system dependent on undocumented Haitian workers that continues to foster race-based economic inequality of ethnic Haitians in the Dominican Republic.[86]

One of the missions of the US military regime was to create a clear national frontier to separate Haiti and the Dominican Republic. As early as November 1916, US preoccupation with the "Haiti-DR border problem" overtook the military officials, who grappled with concerns about "the lack of a clear borderline, the nonexistence of a border police and the prevalence of a mixed border population."[87] In 1917, a commission was established to assess the border situation and provide guidelines for a solution. The report stated that "until the frontier is definitely settled and permanently marked, it is believed that questions of border conflicts will constantly arise. . . . The recent violations of boundary by both Haitians and Dominicans show that such a tentative boundary will only hold good for military purposes, such as preventing patrols from crossing the boundary."[88] Following the 1917 assessment, the US military government created the first Hispaniola border patrol, a branch of the GND, which was charged with checking documentation and stopping illegal border crossing.[89]

United States Marines stationed in Hispaniola imagined Dominicans and Haitians as two racially and culturally distinct peoples, often referring to the latter as more primitive and blacker than the former. Many arbitrary military practices contributed to the marines' opposition of Haiti and the Dominican Republic, including one in which soldiers who misbehaved were transferred from their post in the Dominican Republic to the neighboring country as a form of punishment.[90] This dichotomist view—which, as demonstrated in the previous chapter, helped sustain anti-Haitianism—has influenced the relationship between the United States and both Hispaniola nations since Dominican independence from Haiti in 1844.[91]

As the first black nation in the Americas, Haiti has occupied a central place in the political and cultural imaginary of the modern world. Haiti's revolutionary success was inspirational to other American independence movements. Powerful leaders such as Simón Bolívar and José Martí relied on complicit support from Haiti in their countries' struggles for independence from Spain. During the Civil War, United States Union forces sought Haitian military aid to defeat the Confederate Army.[92] In addition, African American and Caribbean intellectuals, artists, and writers also found in Haiti a model from which to imagine a Pan-African identity and a source of African pride in the Americas.[93] But Haiti was also a threat to many. The slave-dependent modern world greatly feared Haiti precisely because of its symbolic status as a locus for racial equality and political contestation. "Fear of Haiti" also informed nineteenth-century narratives, particularly in the young, slave-dependent United States Empire and the last Spanish colony of Cuba.[94]

At the end of the nineteenth and beginning of the twentieth century, the growing literature of the Empire often portrayed Haiti as a land of savages without history.[95] Eugene O'Neill's play *The Emperor Jones* (1921) is an example of the kind of anti-Haitian literature of the Empire that circulated in

the public sphere in the United States during the occupation. The play recounts Brutus's life story in flashbacks as he makes his way through the forest in an attempt to escape former subjects who have rebelled against him.
O'Neill's play criminalizes black liberation through an allegory of the Haitian Revolution that depicts Christophe as a convict rather than a maroon.
The metaphoric maroonage of Brutus renders black freedom criminal while
simultaneously suggesting the impossibility of black leadership.

Much like the paternalist logic guiding the US intervention of Hispaniola, O'Neill's subtext is the place of US blackness in the post–Civil War
United States. The date of publication for *The Emperor Jones*, 1921, at the beginning of the Harlem Renaissance and during the height of a black political
and cultural movement, also suggests that O'Neill, like other antiblack writers of the time, was asserting his white masculine superiority amidst what
seemed like a potential change in the white-dominated US political scene.
The fact that black political writers and scholars such as W. E. B. Du Bois, Arthur Schomburg, and Langston Hughes publicly opposed the Haitian occupation further fueled anti-Haitian public discourse in the mainstream media,
literature, and the emerging film industry. This growing climate of "fear of
Haiti" and antiblackness traveled along with the soldiers who went to the
island during the nineteen years of the Haitian occupation and eight years of
Dominican occupation, its influence underpinning soldiers' military actions.

US anti-Haitian discourse also fueled marine persecution of Olivorio
Mateo, whom Dominican elites considered a "black man of Haitian ancestry."[96] Through a Pensonian trope, Dominican intelligentsia persistently
disavowed Liborismo as a "degrading and low class superstition of Haitian
influence."[97] Their disavowals focused on his race—"he was dark, short and
ugly"—and his thaumaturgic powers as markers of foreignness (Haitianness).[98] Between 1910 and 1916 the regional San Juan newspaper, *El Cable*,
continuously portrayed Mateo as foreign and barbaric: "The pestilent fake
leader who fools the poor . . . The uneducated Haitian voodoer."[99] However,
after the arrival of the US military troops in 1916, the disdain that existed
among the elites of San Juan was transformed into a military persecution:
the US regime viewed Mateo and his people not only as a "savage" but, like
O'Neill's Brutus, as a savage who had the potential to rally guerrilla resistance, further embarrassing the military regime amidst its struggle to contain
gavilleros in the east.

In 1922, in an effort to put an end to the fruitless and embarrassing four-
year persecution, Governor Harry Lee assigned the mission to capture and

kill Mateo to Captain George H. Morse Jr., an experienced officer with good knowledge of Latin America. Over the previous four years, Mateo and the liboristas had become a nomadic radicalized secret community. Fearing attacks, Mateo and many of the men were now armed. Yet there is no evidence the liboristas ever launched an attack or sought in any way to join the gavilleros.[100] Still, Morse pledged to find the last of the Dominican "bandits," and through local connections, torture, and bribes, he was able to find Mateo's temporary camp in Arroyo del Diablo, near Bánica in the southwest borderlands (see map 2.1).

On May 19, 1922, with four marines and a small detachment of the Guardia Nacional Dominicana, Captain Morse attacked the village of Arroyo del Diablo, brutally killing twenty-two civilians, including children:

> Accompanied by twenty enlisted men of the 19th company, GND, all of whom except two came from *the frontier posts*, the undersigned made an assault on the camp of *Dios Olivorio* Mateo at 5.20 a.m. May 19, 1922, which resulted in the death of twenty-two members of this band, including twelve men, eight women and two small children. The women and children were killed in their beds due to the concentrated fire into the shacks of the camp. . . . Four prisoners, two men, Pedro del Carmen and Enerio Romero, and two women, Ramona Bautista and Petronila Jerronemo, were captured. The number of men and women wounded is not known, however the sides of the mountains were covered in bloody trails, indicating that a large number of the band was wounded. The camp consisted of fourteen shacks, laying in a zigzag fashion on the side of the mountain. . . . Needless to say, the camp of Olivorio cannot be compared even with a *pigpen*. In searching the shacks, large quantities of foodstuffs were found, many empty bottles showing that a large amount of *Haitian rum* smuggled *across the border* reached Olivorio's camp. All kinds of letters and papers were found, the contents of which would disgust anyone. They show that Olivorio and his band are of the lowest order of human beings and that debauchery and prostitution were the only modes of living. People from all over the republic either visited his camp or received instructions on how to cure ailments, which was paid for by rum, tobacco, foodstuffs, and money.[101] (emphasis added)

One is led to wonder how Morse imagined himself in front of the liborista community. Did Morse see himself as a white Christian man? Was he conscious of the fact that his actions and words represented the United

States? Was the killing of Mateo's followers simply a part of Morse's duty as a marine, or was it a personal vendetta, a form of revenge for the embarrassment liborista power had posed for the US military post of San Juan over the years? Did he feel fear or hatred in addition to his clearly articulated disgust? Or was Morse so frustrated at the impossibility of capturing the dissident leader that he took out his rage on whoever was suspected of sympathizing with him? We will never know the exact answers to these questions; however, we can speculate that the imperial discourse of civilization and progress, as well as a history of US curiosity and exoticism of Afro-Caribbean religious practices, evidenced in the representation of Haitian vodou, for instance, could have informed the attitudes of Morse and his men.

Captain Morse, like many other marines who came to the Dominican Republic during those eight years, recognized himself as an authority over Dominican people, a symbol of the white civility he represented. As M. Jacqui Alexander argues, this type of understanding functions as an important way to maintain "the hegemony of imperial, capitalist power across geographical and psychological borders."[102] Morse's report describes every person as a bandit, as a morally corrupt subject, and less than human, reducing Afro-religious practices to debauchery and prostitution. Morse's report on the destruction of Mateo's camp not only reveals much about US military operations that targeted those perceived as rebellious against (or different from) the military regime, but it also offers glimpses of the cultural processes that shaped the violence of US imperialism in the Dominican Republic, and that contributed to the racial bordering of Hispaniola: the rum, the letters, and even some of the liboristas came from Haiti. Morse's report supports Dominican elite ideology that barbarism, in the form of Afro-religiosity, came from Haiti; containing the borders was thus an urgent matter in the process of civilizing Dominicans.

Imperialism requires money and weapons, but it also needs diction: stories and narratives to justify it. The stories of flesh-eating Haitian zombies and criminal black emperors the US Marines brought with them to the island probably grew as they met the local rumors of Haitian monsters who killed virgins and raped their dead bodies in broad daylight. Fear of Haiti and a lack of understanding of cultures and religion, mixed with rumors and stories propagated by the local anti-Haitian Hispanophiles meant that when encountering liboristas, soldiers would probably have seen them as Haitian-influenced "evildoers" who needed to be eradicated in order to insure the "safety" and civility of Dominican population they were charged with civilizing. This logic, complemented by the freedom to act and a vague notion of who the "evildoers" were, resulted in the persecution of religious communities on both sides of the island.[103] Further, one can speculate reading the *El Cable* article that the US military government appropriated anti-Haitian rhetoric in order to freely persecute and kill black "evildoers" without much opposition from the Dominican elite.[104] US literature of the Empire, as epitomized in O'Neill's play, worked together with Dominican anti-Haitian literature, exemplified in Penson, producing the diction that supported the military actions and resulted in the killing, marginalization, and silencing of blacks and rayanos from the Dominican nation.

The Possessed Text, Diaspora's Contra*diction*

Dicen que Liborio ha muerto
Liborio no ha muerto ná
Lo que pasa e que Liborio
no come pendejá . . .

[They say Liborio [Olivorio] is dead
Liborio ain't dead.
What's up is that Liborio
does not take any bull . . .]
—Popular salve from San Juan

At the heart of Afro-Caribbean religiosity is the practice of *montarse* (possession) through which the spirit of the dead enters the body of the devotee, reminding them of their worldly and spiritual history.[105] Through possession, Afro-Caribbean religiosity can offer the opportunity for making the invisible visible and for embodying resistance at moments of censorship and control because the dead, as M. Jacqui Alexander reminds us, "Do not like to be forgotten."[106] Liborismo, like other Afro-Caribbean religions (*santería, palo,* vodou), is a complex manifestation of geographical, epistemic, and historical contra*dictions,* which cannot be understood solely through traditional archival records.[107] Those documentations dismiss the very logic that guides and sustains Afro-religious narratives, stories, and epistemes.

In her deeply personal study of African divinity, Alexander proposes the concept of "embodied memory"—the memory that is passed on to the devout through the spiritual act of possession—as an antidote to "the alienation, separation, and amnesia that domination produces."[108] The author engages memory not as a secular, but rather as a "sacred dimension of the self," insisting that "Knowledge comes to be embodied through flesh, an embodiment of Spirit."[109] Following Alexander, I argue that the death of Olivorio Mateo has allowed for the collective embodiment of an *other* memory of the occupation among Afro-Dominican communities through songs, salves, and literary texts that contra*dict* the hegemonic Archive of Dominicanidad.

The salve that appears at the beginning of this section, "Dicen que Liborio ha muerto, Liborio no ha muerto ná" (They say Liborio is dead, Liborio ain't dead), is the best-known story of Liborismo in the present-day Dominican Republic. Popularized by the Left in the wake of the second US military intervention (1965), "Dicen que Liborio ha muerto . . ." is a performative diction that denounces the crimes of the military occupation against liboristas while simultaneously questioning the veracity of Mateo's death. "Dicen" (they say) interpellates the passive and indirect voice that dominates the Archive of Dominicanidad and that persistently exculpates criminals and erases the bodies of the victims of crimes. Disavowing the anonymous "they," the salve rejects what "they" said, contra*dicting* it with an *other* truth: "Liborio no ha muerto ná" (Liborio ain't dead). The fact that this salve became a common slogan for both the religious and the militant Left affirms the Afro-Dominican religious episteme as a source of historical contestation that summons the divine nature of Liborio: "he is not dead," and his masculine power: "Liborio no come pendejá" (Liborio does not take any bull), to remind the living of the possible union between the sacred and the earthly power through the act of montarse.

Afro-religious practices such as spiritual possession contest hegemonic understandings of dominicanidad at home and abroad by making visible the too-often silenced bodies of Dominican racialized subjects.[110] Through Afro-religiosity, artists, particularly diasporic writers, are finding a diction that allows them to interpellate the Hispanophile version of Dominican history, reimagining an *other* truth that can finally confront the passivity and silencing of hegemonic Hispanophile texts. In his acclaimed novel, *The Brief Wondrous Life of Oscar Wao* (2007), for instance, Junot Díaz writes *fukú*, an Afro-Dominican curse, as the cause of disasters and maladies such as the Trujillo dictatorship and the assassination of JFK. Much like salves, Díaz's fukú contra*dicts* the Archive of Dominicanidad by offering an *other* genealogy for understanding what happened and how it happened. Similarly, Angie Cruz, in her novel *Soledad* (2001), also invokes Afro-Dominican religiosity through the character Olivia, who is in a state of trance between a coma and a spiritual possession. Olivia's ailment allows the reader to see the truth of Dominican American experiences as the character remembers and memorializes the traumas of dominicanidad she carries in her own body.

As exemplified in the seminal works of Julia Álvarez, Angie Cruz, Junot Díaz, and Nelly Rosario, historical novels dominate the bulk of Dominican American literary production. [111] Dominican American contra*diction* on the one hand places the Dominican experience within US history by insisting on the long and unequal relationship between the two nations. On the other, these contra*dictions* historicize dominicanidad from the margins, letting other voices speak. Dominican diasporic texts are thus, I argue, *textos montados* (possessed texts) that, much like the salve that opens this section, allow for the possibility of finding a more complete version of the truth through the embodied memory of silenced histories.

Nelly Rosario's novel *Song of the Water Saints* (2002) is a texto montado that imagines how the occupation of 1916–24 affected the lives of black and poor women. By means of the life of Graciela, Mercedes, Amalfi, and Leila — four generations of women from the same family — Rosario creates a genealogy of Dominican trauma that begins with Graciela in Santo Domingo during the US occupation (1916–24) and ends with her great-granddaughter Leila in New York in the 1990s, who represents the massive migration of Dominicans to the United States (1965–2000). Rosario's genealogy of dominicanidad contra*dicts* the dominant chronology that locates the recent migration of more than one million Dominicans to the United States as a result of the Trujillo dictatorship (1930–61). As if answering the question, "What are you (Dominicans) doing here (in the United States)?" Rosario's contra*diction* tells us a story of the suppressed history of the US Empire, reminding readers of the multiple and lasting consequences of imperial violence on people and land.

Song of the Water Saints opens with a description of an archival document, a postcard dated circa 1900 in which two dark-skinned naked teenagers are shown in an erotic pastoral scene. The young couple sits on a Victorian couch; a backdrop of an American prairie frames the picture. They are mostly naked. Coconut trees and tropical flowers frame their young bodies, reminding the viewer of the couple's exotic location. The first chapter, "Invasions 1916," offers an immediate contra*diction* of the visual scene that imagines the various ways in which the United States occupied Dominican bodies in 1916:

With the promise of pesos, Graciela and Silvio found themselves in the Galician vendor's warehouse, where Peter West had staged many ribald acts among its sacks of rice. . . . The pink hand tugged at her skirt and pointed briskly to Silvio's hand. They turned to each other as the same hand dangled pesos before them. . . . In the dampness they shivered as West kneaded their bodies as if molding stubborn clay. . . . Then Graciela and Silvio watched in complicit silence as West approached the couch and knelt in front of them. . . . One by one, West's fingers wrapped around Silvio's growing penis. He wedged the thumb of his other hand into the humid mound between Graciela's thighs. Neither moved while they watched his forehead glitter. . . . As promised, the yanqui-man tossed Silvio a flurry of pesos.[112]

Postcards, as Krista Thompson argues, were important metropolitan texts that created a visual narrative of the Caribbean as a fantasy of colonial desire.[113] At the turn of the twentieth century, as photography and reproduction became more accessible, postcards became an important medium for disseminating travel stories across the world, becoming "readable" texts even for the illiterate. Rosario's historical contra*diction* of West's photo offers an *other* postcard of the occupation that shows how white American and European civilians also invaded Dominican bodies with the support of the US military. When a land is occupied, so are its inhabitants. Providing a backstory to the usually anonymous models that appear on commercial photographs, Rosario's text gives the "models" names and a history, contradicting the West(ern) archive that rendered them objects. More than characters, Silvio and Graciela appear as spirits, or rather as water saints that mount the novel and, like Afro-religious salves, sing truth. Both Silvio and Graciela die because of the impact of the occupation. Silvio is eventually "gutted by the Marines" after joining the gavillero rebellion. Graciela contracts syphilis after a sexual encounter with Eli, a European tourist drawn to the island after seeing West's postcard.

Rosario's story of the photographic scene imagines a genealogy of the prevalent present reality of the Caribbean sex industry in which women, young girls, men, and young boys become part of an exploitative system that sinks people deeper into the circle of poverty.[114] The postcard can be read as a premonition of the Internet sites and multiple cable television specials that sell the Dominican Republic as a "sexscape," to borrow Denise Brennan's term,[115] as a location for commercialized sexual exchange between white tourists and racialized locals, and Dominican bodies as sexually available for consumption. In sexscapes, Brennan argues, "there are many differences in power between the buyers (sex tourists) and the sellers (sex workers). . . . These differences become eroticized and commodified inequalities. The exotic is manufactured into the erotic—both privately in consumers' imaginations and quite publicly by entire industries that make money off this desire for difference."[116] Rosario locates the United States as a producer and consumer of the exploitative Dominican sexscape through the body of Graciela. She historicizes the Dominican sexscape as resulting from and sustained by the US Empire, contradicting the fantasy that renders it timeless. Through the genealogy it creates, *Song of the Water Saints* also reminds us that the Dominican immigrant woman, as exemplified in my own uncomfortable encounter with the professor that opens the introduction of this book, can also embody the complex dynamic of the sexscape, being perceived as both a fantasy and a threat by the receiving nation.

Rosario's historicization of the violence of the US occupation on Dominican female bodies contra*dicts* the Western production of the Dominican sexscape. The photographic scene sanctions the trauma of US-Dominican unequal interactions through the occupied bodies of the Dominican subject positioning (the) West as a penetrating force that, by means of the US military, objectifies, infantilizes, and violates the Dominican subject while justifying its action through financial assistance: "a flurry of pesos." For the US occupying forces, this assistance manifested in the various education, road, and sanitation programs it implemented. Rosario's contra*diction* of West's postcard seems to demand that the reader decide *how* to read Graciela and Silvio's black bodies: as an exploiter, a consumer, a voyeur, or a critic, contemporizing the postcard through the symbolic Caribbean fantasy it implies. In any given role, the reader must enter the text through the bodies that mount it. The postcard, rather than an objective story that circulates across the globe, appears in Rosario an expression of imperial will. The photographic scene is a transnational interpellation of the occupation that obligates the reader to confront the effects of US imperialism on the Dominican body.

According to the eugenics-influenced occupation logic, all (black) Dominican women were corrupt, available for consumption, and unworthy of protection.[117] The military sought to control the marines' sexual interactions with local women to protect the future of the American (race) embodied in the marines. Documents and memos warned stationed marines of the potential danger of sleeping with Dominican women, and often punished men who married them: "It is generally known that some enlisted men in various posts of the country are or have been living with native women as 'matrimonias.' Some of these women, undoubtedly without either the knowledge or consent of the men in question, have prostituted themselves."[118] The women in the report are imagined "prostitutes" and therefore corrupt, treacherous, and needing no protection.[119] On the contrary, the marines are exculpated; their transgressions are seen as worthy of forgiveness. This logic, much like the myth of the mulata that had circulated within colonial thought since the beginning of the seventeenth century, located in the racialized female body the potential for corruption and transgression. Carrying a form of "savage sexual magnetism," these women were capable of seducing even the most righteous men. It was them, therefore, and not the men, who needed to be controlled.

The official documents of the intervention tell us little about the extent of individual relationships between US Marines and the local population. However, we do know that efforts were made to keep marines from creating long-term ties with locals, particularly women.[120] Despite the official position of the government, we can speculate that many Americans, and especially many of the stationed men, ventured into the towns and befriended locals, especially women, who must have served as a bridge between both groups. As a result, the occupying regime exhibited a lot of concern for the role of women and their potential ability to distract and corrupt the marines.[121] However, often women who engaged in sexual relationships with the marines were labeled "wenches" or "prostitutes," becoming targets of the military government and local communities alike. This rhetoric contributed to a number of reported imprisonments and many other crimes against women.[122]

Dominican "prostitutes" were often accused of carrying venereal diseases and were quarantined. These practices became a common way to repress and contain female "troublemakers," or those women perceived as potentially dangerous to stationed men. At least 953 women were imprisoned during the intervention, accused of carrying venereal disease or prostitution.[123] Many others were routinely forced to attend local clinics to be checked for venereal diseases. The roundups of Dominican "prostitutes" were indiscriminate and often included young girls who were not sexually active.[124] That was the case for Luisa Salcedo, a seamstress from Santiago de los Caballeros. Captain B. F. Weakland, who was in charge of the Sanitation Office in La Vega, accused Salcedo of carrying gonorrhea and syphilis and consequently imprisoned her.[125] Salcedo appealed, with support from a local doctor who attested to her good health, at which point she was arrested a second time: "Luisa Salcedo, 21 years of age, single, a dress-maker by profession with her domicile in this city, accused of violating Sanitary Law #3338 . . . was found innocent, and immediately the Procurador Fiscal ordered that she be released, and to this effect, the prison warden of La Vega complied with the order. . . . The following day, as the government was not satisfied with this sentence, they arrested Miss Salcedo and imprisoned her for the second time, alleging, in order to justify the arrest, that Luisa Salcedo was a prostitute."[126] Many questions remain after reading Salcedo's file: Why did Weakland apprehend her? Was she really a prostitute? Was she or one of her family members a dissident who openly opposed the regime? Was she a victim of sexual assault who spoke up and was therefore punished as had happened to other women in the region?[127] Documentation of the eight-year occupation shows a number of complaints by women or on behalf of women who were raped, assaulted, or otherwise dishonored by a marine.[128] Some were pregnant or had birthed marines' offspring and demanded child support. Many, not knowing where to turn, resigned themselves to their fate and did not seek justice. But this was not the case for Salcedo. For many months, her family and friends wrote letters, pressuring the local government to review her case and release her. Many local leaders, including a priest, wrote letters to the admiral, attesting to the young woman's impeccable morals and work ethic.[129] One letter insisted on the young woman's virginity. But all efforts seemed in vain, as months later Salcedo was still imprisoned with no access to a lawyer or release date.[130] There are no documents recording her release.

Aimed at controlling the population, eugenicist theory allowed for the implementation of laws that targeted immigration, sanitation, and the reproduction of women and people of color.[131] In 1907, the US state of Indiana passed the first eugenics-based compulsory sterilization law in the world and was soon followed by thirty other US states. Although the Indiana Supreme Court eventually overturned the law, in 1921, the US Supreme Court upheld the constitutionality of laws that allowed for the compulsory sterilization of the mentally ill. In the context of eugenics, a concern with the female body as the potential carrier of future life emerged, which, in turn, caused prostitution to become an important topic of national anxiety—particularly as concerned with race and miscegenation in Jim Crow United States.[132] In the United States in 1910, the Mann Act prohibited "prostitution or debauchery."[133] Eight years later, the US Chamberlain-Kahn Act declared that the government could quarantine any woman suspected of having venereal disease "for the protection of the military and naval forces of the United States" and that the discovery of venereal infection upon examination could constitute proof of prostitution.[134] Under the Chamberlain-Kahn Act, any woman under the jurisdiction of the United States could be detained and medically examined if the officer was of the opinion that her "lifestyle observed or rumored sexual behavior indicated she might be infected."[135] Salcedo's case is a documented example of how eugenicist-fueled logic affected everyday citizens, particularly women, at the hands of the marines. Sadly, there are few documented cases that provide the backstory of women like Salcedo.

Rosario's *texto montado* provides us with the possibility of imagining how the policies implemented by the occupation affected the body as much as they affected the land. If the body of the black Dominican man, as exemplified in Mateo's lynching, could be mutilated and destroyed, the body of the Dominican woman, as seen in Salcedo's case, was imagined as a site for consumption and control. Where evidence is lacking, Rosario imagines, voicing the silenced histories of violence against black women during the occupation through the occupied female body:

> A woman with the carriage of a swan and a bundle balanced on her head walked from the nearby stream. Her even teeth flashed a warning as she stepped onto the road. . . . Graciela shaded her eyes. Tall uniformed men in hats shaped like gumdrops sat on the roadside. They drank from canteens and spat as far onto the road as they could. . . . The yanqui-men's rifles and giant bodies confirmed stories that had already filtered into the city from the eastern mountains: suspected *gavillero* rebels gutted like Christmas piglets; women left spread-eagled right before their fathers and husbands; children with eardrums drilled by bullets. Graciela had folded these stories into the back of her memory when she snuck about the city outskirts with Silvio. The yanqui-man in the warehouse seemed frail now, his black box and clammy hands no match for the long rifles aimed at the woman. "Run you Negro wench!" The soldier's shout was high pitched and was followed by a chorus of whistles. A pop resounded. Through the blades of grass, Graciela could see the white bundle continue down the road on a steady path. The woman held her head high as if the bundle could stretch her above the hats. Another pop and Graciela saw the woman drop to the ground. The soldiers milled around screaming and thrashing in the grass. Some already had their shirts pulled out of their pants.[136]

Literary critic Lucía Suárez argues that it is through diasporic literature that violence can be remembered in order to "refuse to let the violence of the past be buried."[137] Through the imagined episode of the Swan Woman described in the previous quote, *Song of the Water Saints* brings attention to the violence of the intervention and to the silences of Dominican history which, being traditionally held in the hands of elite white Dominican men, ignored marine violence because the woman in question was poor and black.[138] Much like the elite disavowal of Mateo, the rapes and murder of poor black Dominican women remain silenced; their lives deemed too disposable and redundant to be recorded in the Archive. The national racialized Dominican Madonna/whore rhetoric allowed US marines to rape, kill, and dishonor black Dominican women during the eight years of the occupation, while Dominican men were busy condemning Haitians for similar (imagined) crimes against young white virgins, as exemplified in the Galindo story.[139] But the fact that Rosario writes in English and publishes in the United States also relocates the crime of the Swan Woman within US history. In so doing, Rosario imagines the Dominican diaspora as a colonial, rather than postmodern, effect—a project of contradictory negotiation with the Empire's gaze. As evidenced in Captain Morse's report on the persecution of Olivorio Mateo or the imagined shooting and rape of the Swan Woman, the Empire's (racist) gaze could easily translate into violent actions against black bodies in the name of civilization and freedom.[140]

Through their actions, the interventionist forces sought to "civilize" the Dominican body for foreign consumption (labor, sex). Men were expected to join the GND, becoming obedient tools for the regime, while women were commodified for marine entertainment. Dissidence was equated to banditry and difference to savagery. In the name of progress and civilization, "bandits" and "savages" were persecuted, captured, punished, and, often, even killed. The ideology of the occupation, therefore, insisted on controlling not just the economy and the systems of government, but also the minds and bodies of the people who lived in the occupied land. Intellectuals and thinkers were often imprisoned, newspapers closed, literature censored, and gatherings controlled. Cultural practices, especially those of people of Afro-Caribbean descent, were ridiculed and often banned. Black women and Afro-Dominican religious practitioners were particular targets of the occupation, their bodies read as carriers of both pleasure and corruption.

In US history, the intervention of the Dominican Republic is but a minuscule footnote in the narrative of imperial expansion over the Caribbean territory, which became evident to the world with the Spanish-American War in 1898. But for Dominicans, the time the US military forces spent on the island radically changed the country's political, social, and cultural life. The agricultural laws promulgated in 1919, for instance, contributed to the strengthening of an economic system that condemned Dominican peasantry to poverty.[141] The establishment of the Guardia Nacional Dominicana in 1918 by the US Marines served as a vehicle for the founding of the thirty-one-year dictatorship of Rafael Leónidas Trujillo and many other ruthless and violent episodes in Dominican history. Mateo's obituary in *El Cable* was emblematic of the imperial rationality that qualified the US occupation. While elite writers portrayed Afro-religious believers such as the liboristas as "foreign," and potentially threatening Dominican cultural "essence," US foreign impositions altered every aspect of society. Baseball, for example, eventually replaced cockfighting as the national pastime; foxtrot and jazz were played in local bars while Afro-Dominican music was banned from public places; and US evangelical missionaries erected churches in many villages, whereas Afro-religious practices were declared illegal on the island.[142] Through US-centric ideas about race, gender, sexuality, religion, and exoticism, the US military intervention contributed to the disenfranchisement of black Dominican women and the persecution of people who practiced Afro-cultural and Afro-religious traditions. This legacy was continued under Trujillo during his thirty-one-year dictatorship, and persisted throughout the twentieth century.[143]

After the assassination of Trujillo in December 1962, following intense pressure from the US to eradicate all peasant and grassroots groups that could harbor communist sentiments, liboristas were once again attacked. President John F. Kennedy's anti-Communist plan meant that the United States kept a close eye on all aspects of Dominican life, making sure that it would become a democracy and not "another Cuba."[144] Thus, following Kennedy's plan for democracy, the US-formed GND, under US military observation, air-struck the liborista camp in Palma Sola, killing nearly two hundred unarmed civilians, including children, and taking more than six hundred people into custody.[145] The act, known as the Masacre de Palma Sola, was the climax of many decades of antiblackness.[146]

The beginning of the twenty-first century has brought more US involvement into the internal politics of underprivileged nations, as evidenced by the military occupations of Afghanistan (2002), Iraq (2003), and Haiti (2004). The Dominican intervention of 1916–24 is an important example for understanding the long history of US imperial interactions, which, veiled under the narrative of freedom and civilization, have dominated and influenced the world for over a century. In a struggle for "democracy," "civilization," and "freedom" (which sadly resonates with the contemporary rhetoric used to justify the wars in the Middle East), the intervention in the Dominican Republic systematically oppressed a large portion of the Dominican population that had already been pushed to the margins of the nation by the dominant elite and the white nationalists of the nineteenth century. Ultimately, the structures of power sustained by the military government served as the basis for Trujillo's thirty-one-year dictatorship, which continued to threaten Afro-Dominican cultural practices and promoted a vision of women as either mothers of the nation or sex objects. Fortunately, Afroreligious salves and embodied texts, such Rosario's, continue to emerge at home and in the diaspora, contra*dicting* of the hegemonic narratives that have engendered violence and oppression against black Dominican across geographies and time.

CHAPTER 3

Speaking in Silences

Literary Interruptions and the Massacre of 1937

Dèyè mon gén mon.
[Beyond the mountains, there are more mountains.]
—Haitian proverb

Driving around the Artibonito Valley in the northwest of the island of Hispaniola (see map 3.1), a person can suddenly feel overwhelmed. The large, curved mountains block all other views, forcing passersby to take in their majesty. Local santeros call the valley "the endless mountains," for it is difficult to see or imagine anything beyond them. The Afro-religious respect the valley and honor it because, to them, Artibonito holds "powerful, unmentionable secrets that concern us all."[1]

That which the local Afro-religious dare not mention is what foreign historians have termed the Haitian Massacre: the genocide of *rayanos* and ethnic Haitians that took place from October 2 to October 8, 1937, near the fatefully named Masacre River in the northern borderland (see map 3.1).[2] No one knows the exact number of victims.[3] Using machetes and knives to simulate a fight among peasants, Dominican military and civilian allies murdered an estimated fifteen thousand to twenty thousand people, converting a once peaceful, multiethnic border community into a site of horror.[4] Today, tourists hiking the mountains or travelers on the International Highway would never suspect the horrible secrets that dwell in them. That is because officially, according to the Dominican state, the Massacre of 1937 never happened.[5]

Contrary to Dominican state silence, US-produced historiography about Hispaniola has largely focused on the "Haitian Massacre." Some categorize it as the worst in the long list of the atrocities committed during the Trujillo

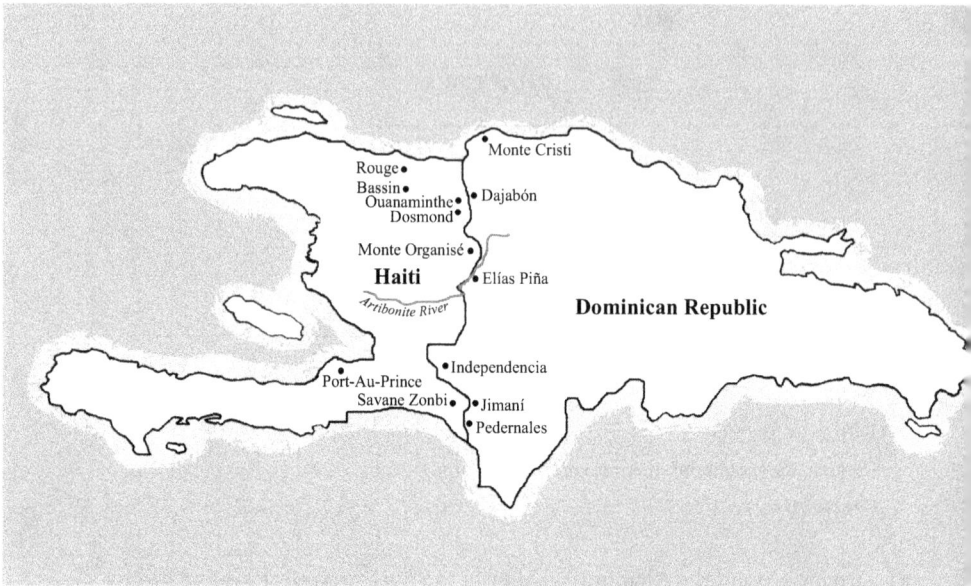

Map 3.1 Map of the Línea Fronteriza (Haitian-Dominican borderland). Created by Kilia Llano.

dictatorship (1930–61).[6] Others opine that it is the most important event in the history of Haitian-Dominican relationship.[7] Haitian and Dominican literature has also focused largely on the violence, often as a vehicle for denouncing present-day anti-Haitianism in the Dominican Republic. In her heart-wrenching interpellation of the violence of 1937, Edwidge Danticat locates the slaughter within the sugarcane *bateyes*, a strategic fictionalization that Dominican writers also employed in their literary renditions of the violence the decade following the massacre.[8] Together, history and literature have produced a vast archive of the Massacre of 1937. These works have greatly contributed to an engaged transnational dialogue about the genocide in the context of Haitian labor exploitation by the sugar corporations.[9]

But categorizing the 1937 violence as the "Haitian Massacre" has also had the unintended effect of perpetuating several myths about the people of Hispaniola: that Dominicans and Haitians are timeless racial enemies; that anti-Haitianism is a Dominican product rather than the result of colonial and imperial economic exploitation of blacks and rayanos; and that the Massacre of 1937 was a criminal act against unlawful Haitian immigrants rather than an ethnic cleansing of an ethnically mixed, highly transnational border population. Ultimately, the production of the 1937 violence as a "Haitian Massacre" erases the bodies of the multiethnic Afro-Hispaniola rayano population that was attacked and destroyed at the hands of the Trujillo forces. The label "Haitian Massacre" also delays Dominican confrontation with the traumatic historical truth that in 1937, Dominican military and civilian allies killed their own people.

In the Dominican Republic, the 1937 violence is remembered by the euphemism "El Corte" ("Kout kouto a" in Creole). The diction El Corte situates the genocide within the genealogy of Caribbean coloniality. Evoking *la zafra* (also known as *el corte*), the period in early fall when sugarcane is harvested, El Corte is reminiscent of the European sugar plantation economy that resulted in the largest slave population of the Americas. But "the cutting" also summons the contemporary global sugar plantation economy that exploits, once again, Hispaniola's black bodies for foreign benefit. Latin American decolonial studies have brought attention to the dynamics of global coloniality that operate whether or not a colonial administration is present. In the Dominican Republic, as we saw in chapters 1 and 2, colonial desire, structures, and thought continued to guide elite state-serving intellectuals and state administrators, shaping the nation's politics and the nation's archive. At the end of the nineteenth century and beginning of the twentieth century, US economic and political interventions on the island further complicated these colonial structures through racially based modes of labor exploitation.

Unlike other euphemistic dictions of dictatorial violence in Latin America—the *desaparecidos* of Chile and Argentina and the *olvidados* of Brazil—El Corte historicizes the gruesome violence as the diction describes *how* Trujillo's men killed the victims. The palimpsestic violence that inhabits the diction El Corte brings attention to the present and past structures that operate together in the process of silencing, erasing, and destroying the black body. Despite multiple historical and literary repetitions, it is silence that dominates the archive of the Massacre of 1937. Michel Trouillot taught us that truth is a construct of absences and presences substantiated by historical proofs. But those truths are neither neutral nor natural. Rather, Trouillot reminds us they are creations: "Truths derive from mentions or silences of various kinds of degrees. And by silences I mean an active and transitive process: One silences."[10] The silences surrounding the Massacre of 1937, and the transitive process that engendered them—the silencing—are not always equal; they do not emerge from the same source, and they do not seek the same objectives. There are unspeakable silences that erase the victims' bodies through the very repetition of the historical event; guilt-driven silences that exculpate the criminals through passive voice, allegory, or euphemism; and solemn silences held by those for whom speaking is simply too painful. This chapter is about the silences, absences, and suppression that inhabit the archive of the Massacre of 1937. But it is also about re-membering the mutilated, violated, silenced bodies destroyed at the hands of the 1937 murderers, and honoring the living, who everyday continue to embody the memory of violence so that the rest of us do not forget.

Unspeakable Silences

Rumor has it that Trujillo ordered the killings while drunk. When a captain interrupted a party to complain about unrest in Dajabón, annoyed, the Jefe responded: "Kill them fucking Haitians; kill them all."[11] To this day, however, no one knows with certainty how the massacre was put in motion. Did Trujillo plan it? Did the intellectuals suggest it? How exactly did the violence escalate to such a high number of victims? Whatever the motives and reasoning behind Trujillo's orders to "kill all Haitians" living in the borderlands, the results were "effective": the Haitian-Dominican frontier was forever redefined and, as historian Richard Turits argues, what was once a fluid, mixed population became divided.[12]

From the beginning of his populist regime, Trujillo promised a "permanent solution to the border problem" that had preoccupied the Dominican state since the second half of the nineteenth century.[13] Following in the footsteps of the United States military, the dictator attempted to control the flow of people and capital between the Dominican Republic and Haiti through legislation and militarization of the frontier.[14] As seen in chapter 2, during the US military occupation of 1916–24, Hispaniola's borders began to transform due to economic and political control.[15] Despite the occupation and nationalist efforts to modernize the frontier, rayano communities continued to develop somewhat independently of the two states. In chapter 1, I examined how early intellectuals of the republic César Nicolás Penson, Félix María del Monte, and Manuel de Jesús Galván produced dominicanidad as a hybrid, nonblack race. But while influential in shaping Dominican politics and public opinion, intellectual works did not contribute to a tangible redefinition of ethnic identities among the peasantry and the borderland's population. This complexity was in part because borders, both geographical and imaginary, continued to be fluid for the two nations sharing the island of Hispaniola. The people, particularly those who lived in the borderlands, often found common interests that united them.[16]

Prior to the violence of 1937, the Haitian-Dominican parallel borderlands constituted a bicultural area where generations of ethnic Haitians and ethnic Dominicans resided and interacted through commercial, religious, and, at times, political cooperation. Pedro Campo, a native of the southwestern border town of Jimaní (see map 3.1) recalls:

> Aunque yo era un muchachito en eso primero año de Trujillo, yo me acuerdo que eso tiempo eran diferente. Uno podía decí que sutano o mengano era haitiano o dominicano, pero aquí en Jimaní al meno, eso no era ná; nadie era mejor que nadie. Decile haitiano a uno no era un insurto en eso tiempo porque enante to er mundo tenía haitiano en su familia. En la mía había do, la mamá de mi mamá y el papá de mi papá.[17]

> [Though I was only a little boy during the early years of Trujillo, I remember that in those times things were different. You could say so-and-so was Haitian, or so-and-so was Dominican, but here in Jimaní that really did not mean much; it did not mean one person was better than the other. Saying a person was Haitian was not an insult back then because all families had [Haitians] in them. In my case I had two, my mother's mother and my father's father.]

Historical documentation of the turn of the twentieth century corroborates Campo's memories of La Línea Fronteriza as a fluid, transnational, and multicultural territory. Ethnic Haitians and ethnic Dominicans often crossed into Haiti to perform religious rituals such as baptisms, weddings, and cleansings.[18] Some crossed the border daily to work or visit their families because, as Campo recalled, "crossing the border just meant walking over to another neighborhood. It was not a big deal."[19]

My historicization of the fluidity of the Línea Fronteriza does not seek to romanticize the pre-1937 Haitian-Dominican border. Rather, I want to highlight that amidst the multiple understandings of ethnicity, culture, and race, and in addition to the colonial and early republican territorial conflicts, the Línea Fronteriza was as Campo remembers: a residential space where people lived normal and productive lives. The people who inhabited the area shared more than just land or the conflicts of two colonies and two fragile states seeking, unsuccessfully, to control them. The transnational nature of the rayano population of the Línea contributed to the construction and imagining of racial understandings of Afro-cultural and Afro-religious practices as "Haitian." Yet, as Derby argues, the cultural categorization "Haitian" did not preclude rayanos and ethnic Dominicans from participating in, preserving, and enjoying those cultural practices regardless of their citizenship or ethnic affiliation.[20] Further, the equation of Haitian with Afro-cultural practices did, in turn, facilitate political impositions under the Trujillo regime that came to divide people into two distinct races and cultures. But prior to 1937, regardless of how people chose to name themselves or their cultural practices, in the Línea Fronteriza "Haitianness" did not signify barbarism the way it did for elite state-serving intellectuals living in the cities.

It was precisely the fluidity and cultural hybridity of the Línea Fronteriza that preoccupied Trujillo and the Hispanophile intelligentsia. Manuel Arturo Peña Batlle, for instance, saw Haitian—meaning Afro-derived and rayano—cultural presence in the borderlands as a form of "invasion" of Dominican values, equal to the Haitian Unification of 1822.[21] The ethnic Haitian culture of the borderland, Joaquin Balaguer insisted, threatened national sovereignty and the Hispanic essence of dominicanidad:

> *Nuestro origen racial y nuestra tradición de pueblo hispánico* no nos deben impedir reconocer que la nacionalidad se halla en peligro de desintegrarse si no se emplean *remedios drásticos* contra la amenaza que se deriva para ella de la vecindad del pueblo haitiano. . . . Para corregirlo tendrá que recurrirse a providencias llamadas forzosamente a lastimar la sensibilidad haitiana. Lo que Santo Domingo desea es conservar su cultura y sus costumbres como *pueblo español* e impedir la desintegración de su alma y la pérdida de sus rasgos distintivos.[22] (emphasis added)

> [*Our racial origins and traditions as a Hispanic people* should not keep us from recognizing that our nationality is in danger of disintegrating if we do not employ *drastic measures* against the threat represented by the neighboring Haitian people. . . . In order to correct this, we might have to employ tactics that will, without a doubt, hurt the sensibility of the Haitian people. What Santo Domingo desires is to preserve its culture and customs as the *Hispanic people* we are, and to stop the disintegration of our soul and the loss of our distinctive characteristics.]

Ventriloquizing del Monte and Penson, Balaguer summons the "Hispanic origins" of dominicanidad as essential to the national identity. But unlike the nineteenth-century letrados, Balaguer does not use the euphemistic language of culture; instead, he speaks of race, inserting himself within the civilizing political project of twentieth-century eugenicists. Balaguer warns about the "dangers" of cultural and racial miscegenation. His concerns are therefore not about the Haitian immigrant, but rather about the rayano, whom he saw as a potential threat to his national project of ethnic cleansing. Referring to the border area as a site of risk, Balaguer claimed Haitian mixing posed a threat to the Hispanophile project of nation bordering. If the rhetorical project of nineteenth-century intellectuals such as Penson was to produce Haitians and Dominicans as two essentially different races, the project embodied by Trujillo's intelligentsia, as seen in Balaguer and Peña Batlle, was to extend the definition of Haitian (foreign blackness) to the mixed-race rayanos. I argue that when referring to "Haitians," Balaguer and Peña Batlle are also speaking of Dominican citizens who practiced Afro-religiosity, lived on the borderlands, or had an ethnic Haitian background.

Intellectuals such as Balaguer played an important role in drafting the ideology of the dictatorship, especially in relation to race, culture, and national borders, by drawing on nineteenth-century Hispanophile ideology à la Penson, and on early twentieth-century eugenicist theories.[23] Although during the first seven years of the regime (1930–37), there was little visibly state-sponsored anti-Haitian propaganda, the education, sanitation, and immigration policies reflected an increase in institutionalized racism and xenophobia.[24] Like Balaguer, many other important twentieth-century intellectuals worked to sustain the nationalist rhetoric of "the preservation of Dominican essence," allegedly threatened by Haitian immigration.[25] In this racist climate, the massacre then came to be a "solution" to the national threat the elite saw in the rayano population.

Appealing to the Hispanophile version of Haitian-Dominican history, Balaguer naturalizes the Massacre of 1937 as part of the Dominican struggle for sovereignty. As Nelson Maldonado-Torres reminds us, such a process emanates from the Eurocentric episteme of control that can create "radical suspension or displacement of ethical and political relationships in favor of the propagation of a peculiar death ethic that renders massacre and different forms of genocide as natural."[26] The naturalization of the Massacre of 1937 responded to the prevalence of colonial structures of the Dominican state that continue to "dehumanize subjects perceived as a menace to the nation" and relegate them to the margins, to displacement, or to death, whether physical or symbolic.[27] In the climate of a bellicose world, between

World War I and World War II, it was fairly easy for Balaguer to validate war against rayanos in 1937.

The Massacre of 1937 became the final solution to the bordering that had begun in 1907 when the United States took control of the customhouses and restricted border trade between the two peoples of Hispaniola. Under Trujillo's populist regime, however, ethnic separation from Haiti became a matter of life or death for the poor, and in particular, for rayanos. During his regime, Trujillo affirmed the working people as his "friends." Yet he also required the working people's devotion to his national project. Trujillo's performative embrace of the working class carried the simultaneous disavowal of the presumed national enemy: the political dissident, the tax evader, and the rayano.[28] The friend was thus obliged to participate in the destruction, ostracizing, and silencing of the foe. The Massacre of 1937 elucidated Trujillo's relationship with the population: he was "El Jefe," and all needed to follow him to escape peril.[29] The fact that Trujillo did not pay reparations to Haiti after the Massacre of 1937 also confirmed that the dictator operated with impunity—or, even worse, with US support.

In the decade following El Corte, Trujillo-serving intellectuals were charged with justifying the killings in front of the international community. Intellectuals such as Héctor Incháustegui Cabral and Ramón Marrero Aristy joined Trujillo's cabinet in the early 1930s, hoping to influence the dictator in pushing for a land reform that would end with the massive US expansion over the national territory that began at the dawn of the nineteenth century and spread during the military occupation of 1916. Trujillo's Partido Nacional promoted a nationalization agenda that capitalized on elite desire to eradicate the "larger-scale foreign land ownership" that was threatening "national sovereignty."[30] After the massacre, however, they had to confront international media and diplomatic pressures from the United States and Mexico (which had been selected as arbiter of the conflict) to explain and contextualize the killings.[31] As a response, Peña Batlle and Balaguer published multiple articles and volumes of books historicizing Haitian attempts to occupy Dominican territory since the 1844 independence. Along with Max Henríquez Ureña, Incháustegui Cabral and others, they built an archive of exculpation that presented the genocide as a conflict between Dominican peasants and Haitian (undocumented) immigrants, accusing the latter of trying to take over land and stealing cattle from Dominican borderland ranches. Summoning the history of the 1822–44 Haitian Unification of the island, Trujillo's writers presented the Massacre of 1937 as a necessary action taken by civilians in order to protect the borders of their nation from the tyrannical, neighboring enemy that was allegedly slowly taking over dominicanidad. In a letter to the editor-in-chief of Colombia's *El Tiempo*, one of the most important Spanish-language daily papers in the hemisphere at the time, Balaguer explained the allegiance of the intellectual class to the Trujillato: "Si los hombres de pensamiento, con tres o cuatro excepciones, respaldan el régimen del Presidente Trujillo, es porque el estadista dominicano está resolviendo, con iluminada devoción patriótica, los problemas fundamentales de cuya solución depende el futuro de la República Dominicana" (If thoughtful men, with three or four exceptions, support the Trujillo regime, it is because the Dominican statesman, with enlightened patriotic devotion, is taking on the solutions to fundamental problems upon which the future of the Dominican Republic depends).[32] Balaguer's diction, though adulatory of Trujillo's response to the feared "blackening" (*ennegrecimiento*) or "hybridization" of the Dominican race, is quite vague. He clearly states that Haitians are a problem for the "Hispanic culture" of Dominicans. However, he does not address *how* exactly Trujillo is "solving" this grave problem. The displacement of Trujillo's violence onto the euphemism of "problem solving" is exemplary of the passive diction that interferes in most narratives—whether anti- or pro-Haitian—about the Massacre of 1937.

The desire to maintain the illusion of Dominican whiteness moved intellectuals to actively support Trujillo's campaign and to defend state-endorsed racist ideologies. Balaguer, Max Henríquez Ureña, and Manuel Arturo Peña Batlle, among other important Hispanophile intellectuals supporting the regime, served as ambassadors to various European and Latin American countries, promoting *their* idea of Dominican national and racial identities and enthusiastically defending Trujillo's actions. This strategy continued and grew even after the dictator's decisions resulted in one of the most shameful crimes against humanity ever committed in the Dominican Republic. After the fall of Trujillo, anti-Haitianism continued to grow under Joaquín Balaguer, whose dictatorial regimes (1966–78, 1986–96) heavily influenced the nation for the greater part of the twentieth century.

Silencing Guilt: Sugar Allegories of 1937

Despite the number of anti-Haitian texts that inundated the Archive of Dominicanidad during the Trujillo Era (1930–61), and particularly surrounding the violence of 1937, critics have also categorized the decade that followed

El Corte as a period of human compassion and solidarity.[33] In an effort to respond to the political and economic realities of their nation, Dominican artists and writers began to produce works that denounced US economic exploitation in the region, as well as state violence against the poor and the dissidents, through what posthumously became known as the Literature of Compassion.

Dominican Literature of Compassion, like early twentieth-century social-realist texts in Latin America, such as Mariano Azuela's famous novel *Los de abajo* (1914), heavily focused on the underdogs—the people forcefully moved to the nation's margins in the name of modernity and civility. But the Dominican version of social realism was also heavily influenced by Négritude and *poesía negrista*, which, as David Howard and others have argued, had a late start in the Dominican Republic, making its debut in 1940 with Manuel del Cabral's publication of the epic poem *Compadre Mon*. It is in this sociopolitical and aesthetic context that Compassionate writers began to construct Haitian characters after 1937.

Ramón Marrero Aristy's novel *Over* (1939) and Juan Bosch's *Cuentos escritos en el exilio* (short stories written during his first exile; 1939–61) are among the most important examples of pro-Haitian Literature of Compassion. Marrero Aristy was one of the intellectuals who served Trujillo during the first decade of his regime (1930–40). Perhaps because of this fact, he has not been studied as a Compassionate writer. Yet, as André L. Mateo reminds us, no intellectual practice was possible outside of the Trujillo regime.[34] Therefore, all writers who did not manage to go into exile had to write *within* Trujillismo. Finding Compassion in texts published within the Trujillo dictatorship requires that we read in contra*diction*.

Over takes place in a sugarcane batey in the east, where the narrator and main character, Daniel, manages the company store, a bodega. Daniel's tone is often racist: "I see their dirty faces, deformed noses . . . their faces like bottoms of old *calderos* (rice pots)."[35] Yet underneath the narrator's diction lies a critique of the Haitian migrant's exploitation by the sugar corporations and of the race-based hierarchies they impose. Puerto Ricans, Daniel notes, are administrators and managers "because their skin is lighter"; Dominicans are watchmen and *bodegueros* because "they are strong and brute"; and Haitians are cane cutters, "for they are the darkest and most desperate."[36] Marrero Aristy's racialized labor stratification of the exploitative sugar corporation economy exemplifies the prevalence of US-imposed racial logic after the occupation of 1916. In 1917, a survey of potential locations for US military bases recommended building a naval base in Vieques, Puerto Rico, rather than in Samaná, Dominican Republic, because the native labor in Puerto Rico was perceived as "largely white." On the contrary, the survey shows that the available labor in Hispaniola was largely "Negro" and therefore less desirable.[37] During the intervention, Puerto Ricans often occupied clerical and managerial positions, while Dominicans were relegated to remedial jobs and Haitians only cut cane. Marrero Aristy interpellates the prevalence of US race-based economic inequality in Trujillo's Dominican Republic, allegorizing its corrupt and unethical basis through another euphemistic diction: the *over*.

The English term "over" references the value that cane weighers keep when they underrepresent the weight of cut stalks in order to make a profit. "Over" also refers to the amount the bodegueros must keep if they want to turn a profit. "Over" is the money payroll clerks steal from the workers' wages. "Over" ultimately symbolizes the effects of US capitalism in postoccupation Hispaniola. Seduced by the possibility of a profit, or forced by the need for survival, all employees of the sugar corporation participate in theft through the "over"—that is, all but the cane cutter who, though aware of the crime, can do nothing to contest it. Undoubtedly battling with the guilt and responsibility of the Massacre of 1937, Marrero Aristy's *Over* explains how in an economy of inequality, everyone participates in economic exploitation and social oppression. Survival, Daniel suggests, depends on one's investment in the racially based system of economic inequality. For the narrator, that requires buying into Trujillo's anti-Haitian narrative by reducing Haitian bodies to the collective anonymity of *haitianaje*. Marrero Aristy's utilization of the "over" functions as an allegorical critique of Trujillo's corrupt institutionalization of US imperial exploitation. During his regime, Trujillo appropriated state resources for personal use, leaving the country bankrupt upon his death. The novel warns the reader, in an almost premonitory tone, of the prevalence of corrupt capitalism in the Dominican Republic that, resembling a prison, will trap "everything, everywhere" without the possibility of hope or escape.[38]

Also critiquing the unequal race-based economy of the sugarcane company, Juan Bosch approaches the Massacre of 1937 through the allegorical figure of the cane cutter. Unlike Marrero Aristy, who writes under the gaze of Trujillo and is eventually murdered by the regime, Bosch writes from exile with the support of left-wing politicians and intellectuals from all over the Americas and Europe. Geographic distance allowed Bosch to clearly articulate his compassion for the Haitian subject, whom he depicts as the ultimate victim of the oppressive system that affected Dominican society during the Trujillo regime.[39] Born in the Cibao Valley, the most agriculturally productive area of the Dominican Republic, Bosch grew up interacting regularly with peasants and Haitian workers. His writing was heavily influenced by Marxism and is characterized by a desire to denounce socioeconomic injustices and by a romanticist vision of Dominican peasantry. Bosch's narrative project illustrates the feeling of impotence often provoked by dictatorships as the author confronts—from his own position of exile—the political reality affecting his nation. As a writer and a political figure, Bosch takes on the ambitious task of changing the island's social reality through his work (and later through political involvement), a common trend among Latin American intellectuals of the period.[40] The short story "Luis Pie" (1943) is Bosch's condemnation of the atrocities committed against Haitians and rayanos during the Trujillo regime. This seminal, pro-Haitian text, however, makes no direct reference to the actual crimes of 1937. Instead, it presents us with an allegory that employs the recurring trope of the oppressed Haitian sugarcane worker.

"Luis Pie" brings the reader inside the infernal world of a Haitian immigrant working and living in the bateyes. A widower and father of three, Pie leaves Haiti to work in the neighboring country's bustling sugarcane plantations. One day, Pie suffers a horrible machete accident—*un corte*—which makes it difficult for him to walk the several kilometers from the sugarcane field to his shack in the batey. Bosch's narrative takes place during the excruciating hours when Pie crawls through the ravines while begging God for strength so he can make it home to feed his little children: "Ah . . . Pití mishé tá esperan a mué—dijo con amargura Luis Pie. Temía no llegar en toda la noche y en ese caso, los tres hijitos le esperarían junto a la hoguera . . . sin comer" ("*Pití mishe* ['little kids' in Haitian Creole] are waiting for me, said Luis Pie sorrowfully. He was afraid he would not make it home tonight, in which case his three little children would wait by the hearth . . . hungry").[41] Within the first few paragraphs the reader becomes aware of Pie's fate, as the omniscient narrator's tone prophesies the Haitian man's future death.

While Pie crawls home to his children, the rich plantation manager, Pie's boss, accidentally starts a fire by throwing his lit cigarette out the window of his fancy car. Dominican overseers and military immediately go looking for the person responsible for this fire. They find Luis Pie, who had coincidentally lit a match to look at his wound, and accuse him of starting the fire:

Luis, con su herida y su fiebre delirante, había quedado atrapado dentro de un incendio que por descuido causó su patrón en el cañaveral, hecho por el que luego sería culpado. En momento de desesperación, Luis clama a Bonyé, al dios de los cristianos que según sus cavilaciones debe ser tan bueno como los "dominiquen bom" que le han dado la oportunidad de trabajar en su tierra.[42]

[Suffering from a delirious fever due to his infected wound, Luis was trapped in a fire caused recklessly by his boss, for which he would later be blamed. In the midst of his desperation, Luis prays to Bonye, the god of Christians, a god that, he imagined, must be as good as the "good Dominicans" that allowed him the opportunity to work in their land.]

Soon, the overseers tie Pie up and drag him across the batey while his children watch his execution: "Inmediatamente aparecieron diez o doce hombres, muchos de ellos a pie y la mayoría armados de mochas. Todos gritaban insultos y se lanzaban sobre Luis Pie" (Ten or twelve men showed up immediately; many of them on foot and almost all with machetes. They yelled out insults and lunged themselves on Luis Pie).[43] Confused by the sudden aggression, and not knowing what the accusations against him were, Pie prays, asking God to save him from what seems like his imminent death. But the Christian God does not listen to this Haitian man, and the story ends with the image of Pie's little children watching as their father is slowly murdered by an angry mob of Dominicans who seem completely blind to this poor man's suffering.

Bosch's depiction of Pie renders him a martyr—abandoned by the state, the community, and even God. Perhaps in an effort to recast a narrative tradition that has doggedly portrayed Haitians as inhuman, violent, and dangerous, the omniscient narrator who takes us inside Pie's torturous world shows us a man of spiritual strength and innate goodness, capable of being peaceful even at the time of his death. Taking various rhetorical steps, Bosch deconstructs the dominant literary characterization of the Haitian savage. First, the author shows us a Dominicanized Pie through the insertion of recognizable popular Dominican values, such as the relationship to the land, to family, and to a Christian God, even if this God is referred to in Créole as "Bonyé" (Bon Dieu). Then Pie appears as the victim of two systems of oppression: the sugarcane plantation economy and institutionalized racism. Finally, at the end of the story, Pie is rendered as a hero and a martyr; his suffering becoming the allegorical embodiment of the Haitian Massacre as the legacy of violence.

Bosch's rendering of Pie succeeds in evoking a critique of the US-imposed socioeconomic systems that reproduced poverty and oppression in many Latin American countries throughout the twentieth century. Pie is the victim of the powerful union between the Dominican state (allegorized in the soldier) and the sugar industry (the plantation owner who starts the fire). But such union, Bosch suggests, can only continue to destroy if the Dominican public remains passive. At the end of Bosch's story the reader is also left with the image of the orphaned Haitian children and the implicit question, "What will happen to these children?" Responsibility for the future of Haitian children on Dominican soil is placed upon the presumed reader, who must in some way continue Bosch's narrative. A contemporary reading of this ending calls to mind the persistent problem of ethnic Haitian children born to undocumented parents in the Dominican Republic who are not recognized as legal citizens by the Dominican state or by Haiti, and so are stateless.[44]

"Luis Pie" is an allegory of the Massacre of 1937. Pie's lynching summons El Corte, admonishing Dominican complicity in the horrific crime. Bosch's condemnation of the Massacre of 1937 and of the overall growth of anti-Haitianism in Dominican thought are evident in his speeches and interviews, and in his multiple letters to contemporary writers and scholars. In 1943, for instance, he admonished Dominican literary critic Emilio Rodríguez Demorizi for his lack of compassion and blatant racism against Haitians:

> Creo que Uds. no han meditado sobre el derecho de un ser humano, sea haitiano o chino, a vivir con aquel mínimo de bienestar indispensable para que la vida no sea una carga insoportable; que Uds. consideran a los haitianos punto menos que animales, porque a los cerdos, a las vacas, a los perros no les negarían Uds. el derecho de vivir.[45]

> [I think you have not meditated on the question of human rights; whether that human is Haitian or Chinese, he has the right to basic wellness so that life does not become unbearable. You consider Haitians to be less than animals because you would not deny pigs, cows, or dogs the right to live.]

More important, his conviction that anti-Haitianism was morally wrong, and that the island should exist in peaceful cooperation, guided Bosch's influential political thought, and led to his antihegemonic ideology that, as we will see in chapter 5, influenced national politics and diasporic writing during the second half of the twentieth century.

Though the story does not directly historicize the massacre, Bosch's narrative does not exculpate Dominicans from their participation in the horrific violence. Everyone is guilty: the soldiers who hit Pie, the overseers who ordered the lynching, and the people who watched silently and did not defend him. But while the narrative of Pie's tragic incident attempts to confront the guilt and responsibility of Dominicans in perpetuating anti-Haitianism, it also contributes to further solidifying the 1937 violence as "The Haitian Massacre" for Pie is a Haitian immigrant working in the bateyes, rather than a rayano from the borderland. Although the allegorical displacement of the Massacre of 1937 in the body of the immigrant cane worker allows for a critique of economic oppression of the sugar industry, it perpetuates the image of Haitians as foreign cane workers rather than as citizens of the Dominican nation. Bosch's allegory appeases the unstated anxiety produced by the knowledge of the potential killing of Dominican blacks and during the Massacre of 1937.

Bosch's narration of solidarity equates the Haitian worker with the Dominican peasant through a reinforcement of common cultural and religious values. Pie's submission to his Dominican aggressors and his eventual death are presented as examples of a superior spirituality that, the narrator suggests, can be obtained only through suffering and poverty. This alleged innate goodness is proffered as a lesson to the Dominican subject embodied in the figure of the soldier:

> El soldado se contuvo. Tenía la mano demasiado adolorida por el uso que le había dado esa noche, y, además, comprendió que por duro que le pegara Luis Pie no se daría cuenta de ello. No podía darse cuenta porque iba caminando como un borracho, mirando el cielo hasta ligeramente sonreído.[46]

> [The soldier restrained himself from hitting Luis. His hand was already hurting, and he also understood that no matter how hard he hit him, Luis would not feel the blows. He would not even notice because he was walking like a drunk, looking at the sky and smiling.]

Since the early nineteenth century, narratives about Haiti's magical powers have appeared in literature throughout the Americas, and especially in the United States and the Caribbean. Some authors, as seen in chapters

1 and 2, represented Haitians as savages, incapable of governing themselves, and as morally corrupt. Others—such as Bosch, Langston Hughes, and Alejo Carpentier—found in Haitians an inherent spirituality and goodness that was inspirational and mysterious.[47] As a response to the late nineteenth-century rhetoric of exploitation, and in the context of the Négritude movement, many African American and Caribbean intellectuals portrayed Haiti as a source of black inspiration.[48] These Haitian fantasy narratives inadvertently fall into what David Kazanjian calls a *colonizing trick*.[49] This trick perpetuates the exoticism of Haiti and ultimately renders it incapable of defining and governing itself. Jacques Derrida posits an analysis of the paternalistic construction of the other as a superior savage, arguing that "the critique of ethnocentrism ... has most often the sole function of constituting the other as a model of original and natural goodness, of accusing and humiliating oneself, of exhibiting its being-unacceptable-in an anti-ethnocentric mirror."[50] Bosch's critique of anti-Haitianism falls into this very trap, as the author offers us a subject that is ostensibly and inherently superior to Dominicans, owing to his innate benevolence and passivity. Pie's silence and ultimate demise can be read as the symbolic death of the Haitian subject as an agent within Dominican society, and his rebirth as a mythical figure from which a Dominican, in this case the author himself, can articulate a narrative of solidarity with the marginalized subject.

Contemporary analyses of Literature of Compassion tend to focus on the idea of solidarity with the marginal Haitian subject while positing a critique of anti-Haitian rhetoric. The idea of hybridization or even assimilation is often ignored, privileging notions of difference. Literary critic and author Fernando Valerio-Holguín examines the development of anti-Haitian discourse in literature, history, and journalism. He argues that through a barbarization of Haitians, Literature of Compassion asserts Dominican identity in opposition to its neighboring state.[51] Valerio-Holguín's argument insists on difference as the main narrative strategy for promoting anti-Haitian sentiment and reinforcing the national frontiers between the two nations. Following Valerio-Holguín's thesis, we can read Bosch's story as a contra*diction* of anti-Haitianism as the text posits an alternative vision of the Haitian subject through Pie's assimilation, and therefore as an early demonstration of what I call rayano consciousness, a revisionist articulation of the multiplicity of experiences, histories, borders, and ethnicities that make up dominicanidad. The story creates empathy by insisting that though Pie is not Dominican in the legal sense, he belongs to dominicanidad for he occupies an integral part of the nation through his role as a worker and as a father of possibly Dominican-born children. As we will see in chapters 4 and 5, this formulation of Haitian-Dominican subjectivity, exemplified in Bosch and other Literature of Compassion writers, served as the basis for important contestations of Dominican dominant ideology throughout the twentieth century on the island as well as in the diaspora.

But the insertion of Luis Pie into the nation reaches a certain discursive limit in the story that is resolved only through the embodiment of a mythic Haitian heroism that transcends the tangible reality of Haitian-Dominican relations. The recourse to mysticism within an otherwise social-realist text points to a common limitation Compassionate writers encountered in their struggles to articulate a new vision of the various Haitian-Dominican borders. They were haunted by the collective guilt and trauma of the Massacre of 1937. Despite these limitations, "Luis Pie" is the earliest example of a literary tradition seeking to contra*dict* Trujillo-based anti-Haitianism by pointing to the possibility of solidarity and reconciliation.

Silencing Guilt: The Two Borderlands of Prestol Castillo

We have studied thus far the complicated rhetorical process through which the archive of the Massacre of 1937 has silenced, even in texts that otherwise deconstruct anti-Haitianism, the bodies of the victims through passive voice, euphemisms, and digression. To simplify my analysis, I have grouped the works into two major categories: (1) The first category comprises Hispanophile narratives, which often justified anti-Haitianism and minimized the events as a series of simple disagreements between local borderland Dominican peasants and Haitian cattle thieves. In this group we can include the work of Balaguer, Peña Batlle, and Max Henríquez Ureña. (2) The second category comprises the contra*diction* of Literature of Compassion that describes the general state of poverty and desperation affecting Haitians in the Dominican Republic while also rendering Haitians as weak. In this group are such writers as Bosch and Marrero Aristy.

The climate of intellectual ambiguity surrounding the massacre continued to grow throughout the Trujillo regime and well into the late twentieth century as Dominican writers struggled with the trauma of the violence and their desire to produce a cohesive modern nation. In a literary culture where historical novels are prominent, the virtual self-censorship regarding the killings is, at the very least, distressing. This is why Freddy Prestol Castillo's text

El Masacre se pasa a pie (written in 1939 but published in 1973), constitutes such an important, if problematic, historical document. Although Prestol Castillo published his text thirty-six years after the massacre and twelve years after Trujillo's death, it is valuable as a testimonial of the intellectual reaction to the violence. The "testimonial novel" offers a first-person narration from the perspective of a young Dominican writer-lawyer living and working under the Trujillo regime.[52]

The parallel narrative threads in *El Masacre*—Prestol Castillo's life and the young lawyer's account—hint, at times, at a secret conflict that the story resists revealing and that makes the reader question the authority and veracity of this text. Dominican writer and literary critic Diógenes Céspedes considers *El Masacre* to be a suspiciously Trujillo-friendly text in that the tensions between Prestol Castillo's elitist national and racial ideas are contrasted with the author's sense of relief regarding the "Haitian problem."[53] Like many other Literature of Compassion intellectuals, Prestol Castillo sees the "positive side" of the massacre in the imagined repossession of the Dominican frontier. Doris Sommer, who was able to interview the author before his death, finds Prestol Castillo's position to be "a testimony of the author's essential honesty," which, according to the scholar, validates the text as an important historical document.[54] The ambiguity of this work, evidenced in the prologue, in which Prestol Castillo refers to his text both as a novel and as an autobiography, is exacerbated by the many omissions that persist throughout the book.[55] These omissions ultimately made many critics doubt its validity as a historical document.[56]

El Masacre is an apologetic text that struggles to find a way to denounce the injustices committed against rayanos and ethnic Haitians during the Trujillo regime, while respecting the established nationalist discourse that separated the Dominican subject from its Haitian neighbor. The overwhelming ruptures evidenced throughout his writing produce a narrative of silencing that creates a sense of complicity to erase the author's/protagonist's responsibilities under a discourse of national collective guilt:

> ¿A dónde voy? Yo mismo no lo advierto . . . ¿Qué busco aquí?, me dice mi conciencia. . . . Tienes hambre . . . como estos muertos . . . pero el pan que comes está sucio de sangre. . . . Si sigues aquí flotarás también en ese río, río sangriento.[57]

> [Where am I headed? I do not know . . . What am I doing here? asks my conscience. . . . You are hungry . . . like these dead people . . . but the bread

you eat is stained with blood. . . . If you stay here, you too will float in the river of blood.]

The sudden switch from first person (*yo*/I) to second person (*tú*/singular you) not only assumes that the reader is Dominican, but also makes him or her an accomplice, and in turn makes *El Masacre* a project of collective expiation. Like "Luis Pie" and other Compassionate texts of the period, *El Masacre* is inserted within the ambiguity of Dominican nationalist rhetoric while critiquing state-sponsored anti-Haitianism. In that sense, the textual project continues to reproduce the rhetoric of Dominican national identity as one in contra*diction*: to write a Dominican nationalist text in the context of the Trujillo regime is to write an anti-Haitian text. As I see them, these two ideologies are not mutually exclusive, but essentially interdependent. Yet the content of Prestol Castillo's novel gestures, at the very least, at a confrontation with the trauma, guilt, and silences surrounding the killings and his own (Dominican Hispanophile elite) culpability.

El Masacre opens with an autobiographical prologue, titled "Historia de una historia" (History of a History), in which the author explains the reasons behind his firsthand knowledge of the events he is about to narrate. Owing to the loss of his father's fortune to North American industrial expansion in the country, the author/protagonist had to obtain a modest job as a state prosecutor in the borderland province of Dajabón, a less-than-desirable position for any young lawyer. The author describes the experience of moving from his hometown of San Pedro, located forty miles east of the capital, to the distant borderland town of Dajabón as a psychological exile: "Escribí bajo cielo fronterizo, en soledad. Sin darme cuenta, yo estaba exiliado" (I wrote under a frontier sky, in solitude. Inadvertently, I had gone into exile).[58] The narrator's depiction of the area later summarizes the general perception of the elite intellectual class regarding the borderlands. They saw it as a backward, uncivilized area, populated by half-breed peasants who had no notion of what it meant to be citizens of a nation.

Assigned to work in the borderlands, the narrator is suddenly transplanted into what feels like the limits of the nation, a place he considers foreign and untamed. Yet he is more than ever inserted into the nation, for he is "sent" by the dictatorship to be part of a nationalization plan, and in the process becomes an ally of the very system he despises:

El Amalcigo, un paraje lejano agreste, en soledad sin caminos, donde ella, la maestra, es la única persona que sabe eso de que hay una República Do-

minicana. ¿Qué es eso? Dirían los asombrados habitantes del paraje, que
solo tienen una vida mísera, como la de los cerdos, sin noción de patria.[59]

[El Amacilgo, a distant grey village, surrounded by loneliness, without
roads, where she, the teacher, is the only person who knows that there is
something called the Dominican Republic. What is that? the surprised
residents of this village would say—they who had nothing but a miserable existence, like pigs, with no notion of a fatherland.]

Prestol Castillo's assessment of the rayano subject is identical to Balaguer's:
they are subjects that are animal-like and childlike without a nation, savages
living a miserable life, unaware that a nation exists. Unlike Balaguer, however, Prestol Castillo does not see rayanos as a threat, but rather as objects
of pity—their ignorance a testament of their own demise. The Dominican
borderlands have always functioned somewhat independently from the central state, partly because of their geographical distance from the capital, but
also because rayanos had never been incorporated into the nation-building
project. As Richard Turits asserts, Dominicans and Haitians intermingled
and mixed in the borderlands, creating what Homi Bhabha would describe
as a community of neither Haitians nor Dominicans, but a Haitian *and* Dominican community.[60] The existence of such an independent population,
made up mainly of blacks and mulatos, caused major anxiety and discontent
among the elite governing classes, who feared losing their imagined European identity to the potential growth of this hybrid community.

In a 1937 letter to American secretary of state Sumner Welles, literary
critic and historian Max Henríquez Ureña requested an end to the *bracero*
program, which had been implemented by US-owned sugarcane companies
during the US intervention of 1916–24 and continued throughout the Trujillo regime.[61] He stated: "This law seeks to end the importation of black
labor to our country. . . . Because black blood can damage the Hispanic culture and tradition of us Dominicans."[62] Henríquez Ureña, a respected and
internationally renowned intellectual, did not hesitate to offer his support
for the nationalization campaign and the various immigration reforms that
sought to deport all Haitian and West Indian workers in an effort to preserve the imagined Dominican whiteness. Like Prestol Castillo, Henríquez
Ureña saw Haitians as essentially different, culturally and racially, from Dominicans, and so found in Trujillo's campaign a possibility for drawing clear
boundaries to forever separate the two nations.

In the prologue to *El Masacre*, Prestol Castillo speaks of the persecution he suffered because of his dissident thinking during the Trujillo regime. Yet, unlike other antiregime writers such as Bosch, Prestol Castillo remained in the country even when presented with the opportunity to leave.[63] In addition, the author held a position within the state and was, in fact, one of the judges in charge of the proceedings conducted against Dominican peasants in Dajabón after the massacre.[64] That the author does not let the reader clearly see what his role was in the genocide makes his text a narrative of suppression and silencing. A reading of his earlier and extremely obscure essay "Paisajes y meditaciones de una frontera" (1952) offers the opportunity for further understanding the author's self-censorship and narrative of contra*diction* as a desire to express a collective complicity of silence through the partial narration of his autobiography.[65] In "Paisajes" the author adheres to the anti-Haitian, state-sponsored propaganda to show clear "racial" and "innate" differences between Dominican and Haitians, while portraying the rayano as "an obscured hybrid man without a fatherland."[66]

For the intellectuals of the early republic, these incongruities were located in their desire to maintain colonial ties with Spain and thus retain a white European identity while claiming sovereignty and freedom as an independent nation. However, for twentieth-century intellectuals such as Prestol Castillo, the narration of Dominican national and racial identity was further complicated as the peasants and Haitian immigrants began to integrate into the nation (mainly through urban migration), bringing with them Afro-Caribbean cultural traditions. Twentieth-century intellectuals were then forced to reconcile, on the one hand, their project of solidarity with the oppressed and, on the other, their desire to maintain clear national borders that would protect the very elusive idea of the Dominican nation as imagined and narrated by nineteenth-century republican intellectuals. For Prestol Castillo, these contra*dictions* are evidenced in his two very different depictions of Línea Fronteriza.

As the author/character confronts the guilt of his own passive participation in the genocide, *El Masacre* turns to an analysis of the socioeconomic conditions that are shared by the two nations of Hispaniola:

> ¿Qué es esto? Es un balance de conciencia. Y todo esto acontece en una isla antillana dividida en dos países, en cada uno de los cuales existen sendos pueblos azotados por el hambre y por los látigos de los que mandan. ¿Adónde voy? . . . Yo mismo no lo advierto, mientras camina la mula. ¿Qué busco aquí? Me dice mi conciencia ¿Por qué no te vas?[67]

[What is this? It is a balance of consciousness. And all these things happen in an Antillean island divided into two nations, each one inhabited by people haunted by hunger and the yoke of oppression. Where am I going? . . . I do not know where my mule is taking me. What am I doing here? my conscience asks me. Why don't you leave?]

Interpellating "oppression" as a generalized condition of Hispaniola's peoples, the narrator asks himself and the reader about the future of the island and the two nations that share it at the face of "oppression." Prestol Castillo's diction, though loaded with guilt and expiation, is also incredibly vague. What does the author/narrator mean by the "yoke of oppression"? A historicized reading would without doubt point to the political atmosphere of dictatorial Dominican Republic. Yet, the "oppression" of Hispaniola's people can encompass a multiplicity of historical layers dated back to colonial ties. The simplified noun—"oppression"—hides the actor—oppressor—and the specificity of the oppressing action. The ambiguity of Prestol Castillo's diction also blurs the line between author and narrator. Whose tortured conscience does the reader encounter? The author's reluctance to give us an actual depiction of his involvement in the events leading to the massacre in what he claims to be a testimonial novel points to his silent complicity and accentuates his guilt. As a reader, it is difficult to not feel suspicious about the silences this testimony produces and the truths it hides.

The diction of the novel, although empathetic in the spirit of the Literature of Compassion, still shows the vestiges of a strong anti-Haitian sentiment that leaks through as a subtext of what is essentially a nationalist novel: "El haitiano comía de los frutales y tiraba la simiente al llano. Nacían árboles. Muchos árboles. También en las barracas del hato nacían haitianos, muchos haitianos. La tierra se poblaba de haitianos y de árboles" (The Haitian ate from the fruit trees, throwing the seeds on the ground. The trees grew. Plentiful. The barracks also grew with Haitian babies. Plentiful. The land was filled with Haitians and trees).[68] The scatological and violent image gestures at rape or conjugal relations that produce mixed babies. Prestol Castillo's empathy for Haitian immigrants, and the horror he expresses throughout the novel for the racist slaughter to which he was witness, are contrasted almost constantly with the nationalist fear this violent image represents: stereotypical depictions of blacks as hypersexual, overly fertile, and dirty, giving evidence of his loyalty to the ideals of a certain privileged intellectual class. Later in the text, the narrator confirms this hypothesis by naming his position as a writer and intellectual from a more privileged, civilized area of the country.[69]

If *El Masacre* is contrasted with his earlier essay, "Paisajes y meditaciones de una frontera," one cannot help but wonder who Prestol Castillo truly was and which version of his depictions of the borderlands is truthful. We might never find the answer to this puzzling question. However, reading both texts in the contexts in which they were written and published suggests a meaningful point of departure for posing stimulating questions regarding the power of Dominican nationalist rhetoric, as *El Masacre* attempts to recast the events of the genocide and "Paisajes" seeks to protect the borderlands from the Haitians. The dichotomy, however, is not always clear because "Paisajes" grows as an intertext of *El Masacre,* allowing the reader to grasp a more complete picture of Prestol Castillo's understanding of the borderlands and the rayano.

"Paisajes" can certainly seem to be nationalist propaganda that perhaps sought to gain the favor of Trujillo during a time of severe censorship and oppression. In the foreword to his essay, which the author titled "Palabras de explicación" (Words of Explanation), he asserts,

> Allí pensaba en las dos patrias nuestras: la de los *guerrilleros mulatos* olvidados por la crónica, que en aquellas sabanas hicieron pródigos de valor inútil y la nueva patria de Trujillo, que hoy construye una nueva economía y una nueva conciencia cívica en aquellas tierras secas y grises.[70]

> [There I thought about our two fatherlands: that which belonged to the *mulatto guerrillas*, now forgotten in the chronicles, who in this land exercise their amazing yet futile courage; and the new fatherland of Trujillo, which today builds a new economy and a new civic conscious in these dry and gray lands.]

Prestol Castillo disavows mulato historical agency in the construction of the nation: "futile courage." The author then declares Trujillo the true founder of the modern nation for the dictator's "extraordinary work on the borderlands" actually succeeded, in doing what nineteenth-century mulato warriors failed to do: inserting the borderland into the nation-state.[71]

Dominican national identity developed as a slow process of historical interpellation that constantly relied on the history of colonialism and the relationship with a neighboring colony-state. The borderlands existed as an integral part of the Dominican imagination, but not necessarily as a civic partner in the imagined Dominican community. The twentieth century, however, brought new elements that contributed to the development of a border consciousness and to the rise and solidification of anti-Haitian sentiment and xenophobia. Intervention on the island by the United States (1916–24 in the east and 1914–34 in the west) represented key events in the rise of nationalism and anti-Haitianism because the US imperial power brought with it US-centric concepts of race, class, and national frontiers. However, it was not until the emergence of Trujillo's populist nationalist campaign that the frontier was truly established as a division (and not a connection) between the two nations.

The borderlands represented a main concern for the Trujillo regime and his nation-building project because of their fluidity and the lack of police control in the area. The Massacre of 1937 became a quick solution to a long-lasting obstacle for the project of Dominican nation building and modernity. In this context, Prestol Castillo's praise of Trujillo's border policies and his condemnation of the massacre, although seemingly contradictory, are also exemplary of a nationalist ideology sustained by a long process of rhetorical repetition. Haiti was proclaimed, even in the national anthem, as the number-one enemy of the nation. And as such, even when it no longer represented a military threat to the Dominican Republic, the myth of the impending invasion, now embodied in the mass immigration of workers and peasants, continued to haunt Dominican national consciousness.

Lydia Gil's critique of *El Masacre se pasa a pie* posits a view of this text as an essentially valuable historiography that successfully portrays the psyche of a group of people capable of committing terrible atrocities.[72] Both of Prestol Castillo's narratives are valuable in allowing us to understand the mindset of Dominican intellectuals during the Trujillo regime. They shed light on the contra*dictions* those intellectuals were forced to grapple with in the face of an increasing US imperial expansion and the looming threat of cultural hybridization. When juxtaposed with anti-Haitian texts such as Balaguer's, Prestol Castillo's *El Masacre*, as well as Bosch's short stories, demonstrates that the "Haitian problem" was an imminent preoccupation informing the narratives of nationalism undergoing production from both ends of the political spectrum. Although Prestol Castillo undoubtedly wrote Compassionate texts that sought to denounce the violence of 1937, his representation of the Haitian subject was limited as the author dealt with the tensions of living under a dictatorship and negotiating his own position as voice of the nation. In his effort to speak for the victims, Prestol Castillo often rendered Haitians as either primitive or helpless.

Solemn Silences: Toward a Remembrance of the Body

In October 2006 while conducting research in the Dominican Republic, I was invited to attend an Afro-religious cleansing ceremony. The *Despojo* (cleansing) was to take place in the Manogüayabo River, eight miles north of Santo Domingo. Tamara, the *santera* (see figure 3.1), explained the elaborate steps during our long ride north on the congested Autopista Duarte. They needed to find fresh water, she said, adding that "seawater won't do." Upon arriving at Manogüayabo, Tamara set up an altar by a large rock on the riverbanks. She lit three candles alongside three bottles of *refresco rojo* (raspberry soda). When I asked Tamara the meaning of the sodas, she explained, "red soda is important to remember the blood." And then, covering her mouth she added, "but we must not speak of it today." When I asked why not, Tamara responded: "Because it is October."[73]

During the ride home I had to fight the urge to ask Tamara more about the soda, the blood, October. Weeks later I finally got some answers: "October is the month of *El Corte* (The Cutting), a month marked by innocent blood. That is why we must always cleanse at the beginning of October."[74] Tamara is from Dajabón (see map 3.1), the northwestern border town where the massacre began on October 2, 1937. Though Tamara was born in 1957, twenty years after the massacre, and long after a violent blanket of silence had covered La Línea Fronteriza, she carries the pain and trauma of the violence every day. When I asked if she had Haitian origins, Tamara responded, "Don't we all?" I did not ask who, exactly, was included in Tamara's "we," though I assented. A rayana, descendant of a culturally mixed family from the Línea Fronteriza, Tamara grew up in Cristo Rey, one of the most impoverished and violence-stricken neighborhoods in Santo Domingo. Her family moved to Cristo Rey shortly after the assassination of Trujillo in 1961 in search of work. Yet, for Tamara, her home is forever Dajabón, a place where the Massacre of 1937 lingers in a collective trauma she and her family have inherited. Like Tamara, the Afro-religious believe one might be able to quiet the dead, but never to forget them.

The systematic persistence of an omniscient Dominican narrator in Literature of Compassion leaves the curious reader with a desire to see and

3.1 "Dulce Despojo" (Sweet Cleansing). Tamara, a santera, performing a cleansing ritual with honey, in the Manogüayabo River, Santo Domingo. Courtesy of photographer John Paul Gallagher.

hear the body of the victim. To conclude my analysis, I now turn to two novels that I argue attempt to center the Haitian-rayano body in order to remember the victims of 1937, honoring Afro-religious Hispaniola tradition: *Compère Général Soleil* (*General Sun, My Brother*; 1955) by Haitian-Dominican author Jacques Stéphen Alexis and *The Farming of Bones* (1998) by Haitian American writer Edwidge Danticat. Despite their temporal and geographical distance, these two novels establish a fascinating dialogue within themselves while interpellating Dominican narratives by posing a confrontation with memory and history from the perspective of the victims. Read in contra*diction* with Dominican nationalist texts, and within the historical context in which they were produced, they allow for a more complete picture of the events while creating the possibility of building a literary community of healing.

Born in Gonaïves, Haiti, in 1922, Alexis was the son of Haitian ambassador Stéphen Alexis and Dominican dancer Lydia Núñez. A revolutionary leader and communist, Jacques Stéphen Alexis planned a coup d'état against Haitian dictator Francois Duvalier.[75] The plan failed, however, and Alexis was assassinated in 1961, the same year as Trujillo. *Compère Général Soleil*, his first novel, is a peasant, or proletarian, text.[76] It defies the mystification of Haitian subjects who inundated Negrista literature while maintaining certain traditional ideas about Haitian identity: the closeness to the land and the legacy of resistance and struggle acquired through the Haitian Revolution.

Compère Général Soleil narrates the story of an impoverished Haitian couple who migrates to the Dominican Republic to work in the sugarcane fields. Upon arrival in San Francisco de Macorís, Hilarion and his wife, Claire-Herouse, are suddenly confronted with an ongoing racial conflict but find comfort in the kindness of Dominican neighbors. Soon after the move, their first baby is born and so they start to imagine a future on this side of the frontier. The events of October 1937, however, interrupt this new existence, and the couple is forced to run for their lives. The last chapter of the novel describes the horrors they suffer as Hilarion and Claire-Herouse embark on what seems like an impossible journey through the Dominican *montes* (the wilderness) back to the Haitian border. On the way, the couple loses their child to hunger. Although they eventually reach the Masacre River, which divides the two nations on the northern borderland (see map 3.1), a Dominican guard shoots Hilarion as he and his wife attempt to cross it. In his dying moment, Hilarion acquires a revolutionary consciousness, for he has seen "the light when a great red sun lit the chest of a worker named Paco Torres."[77] Paco was a Dominican community organizer who had introduced the couple to militancy and political struggle. As he approaches his death, Hilarion sees the future in the common struggle of the people under the red sun, an emblem of Communism. In a hopeful gesture for Haitian-Dominican solidarity of the oppressed, the text ends in the middle of the Masacre River, halfway between the borders of both nations.

A quick glance at Alexis's characters offers us a good idea of the novel's social aspirations: Hilarion, the protagonist, representing the working class, is driven by hunger to a criminal life. While in jail, Hilarion meets a political prisoner who teaches him about Communism and the struggle for equality. As the novel unfolds, Hilarion encounters many other Communist artists and intellectuals as well as community leaders and, ultimately, converts to the revolution at the time of his death. Claire-Herouse, is a street vendor who lives in extreme poverty and has no formal education but is full of ambition and ideas for their future. She is presented as a simple character whose desires do not go beyond individual material gain. As Hilarion becomes "enlightened" by the socialist movement, the couple grows distant from each other until the birth of their child brings them closer once again. In what Joan Dayan has called the "literature of suffering," Alexis, like many Haitian writers of his generation, uses the body of the peasant to present an image of a Haiti that has been destroyed by imperialism and dictatorships: Hilarion's back was marked by the lesions of many years of labor.[78] In the context of the regime of Duvalier—who, like Trujillo, idealized the peasant as the prototype of the Haitian citizen while endorsing state policies that ex-propriated the land—this novel successfully shows the abject side of Haitian history through the figure of the peasant-proletariat: hunger, fear, violence, illness, and forced migration.

The opening scene of *Compère Général Soleil* summarizes Hispaniola's borders and Haitian-Dominican transnational marginality:

> The tropical night is vibrant, a hustler dressed in black, transparent over parts of her rosy flesh, a stigmata of its vice. The tropical night seems to move. A long light cries out along the street: the red-light district, La Frontière. A maraca laughs in a jazz rhythm. Women are swearing in Spanish and yelling filthy insults: "*¡Coño! ¡Mierda! ¡Hijo de puta!*" A Do-minican whore comes running out of the turbulent Paradise, which is like a castle, exploding with light in all directions through the night. The song echoes between the spasmodic lightning bolts of a musical storm: "*La jicotea no tiene cintura, la jicotea no puede bailar.*" A saxophone moans in an orgasm. Cornets lash the senses with a brutal sexual hurricane. . . . Hilarion is still running. He has relocated his hunger in his stomach—a searing, excruciating wound. He is still running but his numbness is gone. He is speaking and laughing to himself as he walks: "Just because we are beggars with no borders our children have to live and grow up next to noisy brothels. Among drunken whores who go hand in hand next to the corruption and madness of vice. . . ." Three drunken marines arrive in the area arguing angrily with their taxi driver, refusing to pay him. "God damn you!" Hilarion keeps running with determination. He is talking to himself and laughing.[79]

The above excerpt is a striking visual and auditory depiction of the Hispan-iola's borders. The location: La Frontiére is incredibly symbolic of the palimpsestic colonial histories that dwell and occupy the Haiti-DR border. It is a red-light district where the Dominican mulata's body is sold; it is the lo-cation of crime and poverty where the beggar goes hungry and the site where the Yanqui-soldier who "refuses to pay" exercises his privilege and power. La Frontiére is the embodiment of the various underlying realities of the Hispaniola marginal subject, who is black, poor, oppressed, possessed, occupied and, ultimately, very hungry. Like the depictions by Ana Lydia Vega and other contemporary Caribbean writers, Alexis's representation of the border is not solely a critique of colonial oppression. It also encompasses a hopeful proposal for the possibility of a Pan-Caribbean community that, as Yolanda Martínez-San Miguel demonstrates, is eventually created precisely through marginality in the various enclaves of Caribbean immigrants in New York and San Juan.[80] If the nation-state has failed to protect the Caribbean subject against imperialism, Alexis's novel reminds us, the subject has not failed the nation for he carries it on his very body, like a "stigmata." The body of the Caribbean marginal subject, Alexis suggests, contra*dicts* historical oppression.[81]

In his study of Haitian-Dominican borderland relations, literary theorist Eugenio Matibag suggests looking at the island of Hispaniola as a "loosely articulated system" where parallel histories can evoke a pan-insular common identity.[82] Misery, Matibag insists, is one of the commonalities shared by the two people of Hispaniola. Interpellating Hispaniola's history of misery, Alexis's text evokes the multiple psychological borders that regulate Hispaniola subjectivity. If misery is one of the common denominators of Hispaniola's people, Alexis's text questions, why then are the two peoples of this island not fighting *together* against the common enemy instead of with each another? Alexis's narrative offers a thoughtful examination of how nationalist and capitalist interests have been reproduced within the borderlands legitimating the power structures that ultimately separated working peoples who might otherwise have built strong alliances to oppose the oppressing power structures of the nations.

Imperialism on the part of the United States appears in the previous passage in the figures of the marines and later in the novel in the sugarcane plantation manager. As in "Luis Pie," American capitalism is to blame for Haitian-Dominican suffering: "American cars that roll over the body of poor Haiti like enormous toads. . . . The city dweller is the slave of the American, the slave of the state and certain among them would even be ready to sell their wives for that state!"[83] Although the main characters do not seem aware of the significance of US imperialism in the everyday life of the peasants and workers, they are puzzled by this foreign presence on their land. Hilarion, ultimately conscious of the dangers of both imperialism and nationalism, sees them as two partner forces that oppress the people of Hispaniola. His understanding of the complex relationship of these two forces liberates him, for he now knows that his Haitian identity cannot be taken from him, even when his human rights are trampled: "Dawn was making the entire countryside ruddy. He rose up and yelled. General Sun! See him! He is right at the doors of our native land! Don't ever forget, Claire! He slumped back and let out several short breathes. His eyes turned toward the east. . . . He closed his eyes and smiled. She was alone."[84] Hilarion's last words pass on the message of potential liberation to Claire, who is entrusted with the difficult task of surviving so that she may carry the other truth. By entrusting this task to a Haitian woman, Alexis's revolutionary text alludes to the connection between history and storytelling, proposing the latter as a legitimate means for the subaltern's narration of histories. Further, the fact that Claire, a woman, survives to carry on history also summons the Afro-religious sacred traditions in which women, as priestesses, must keep and disseminate truth. Claire survives so that she can bear witness. Her survival is, rather than liberation, a charge to live on, to carry on the remembrance and the truth.

Alexis's novel is an important intertext in Edwidge Danticat's 1998 rendition of the massacre. *The Farming of Bones* was successful in raising awareness about the Massacre of 1937 while provoking a US-Haitian-Dominican interdisciplinary dialogue that allowed for the possibility of Haitian-Dominican solidarity from the diasporic space.[85] Danticat offers us a narration of the events of 1937 from the perspective of an impoverished Haitian woman who survived the genocide. The novel's intertextual interpellation of history can be read as a continuation of Alexis's narrative. Amabelle, the main character, could be Alexis's Claire, who has to go on living with the torturous memories physically inscribed on her battered, marginal body: "The slaughter is the only thing that is mine enough to pass on. All I want to do is find a place to lay it down now and again, a safe nest where it will neither be scattered by the winds, nor remain forever buried beneath the soil. . . . Misery won't touch you gently. It always leaves its thumbprints on you; sometimes it leaves them for others to see, sometimes for nobody but yourself to know of."[86] Interpellating Alexis's poetics of misery, Danticat insists on "misery" as a legacy of Haitianness. Like Alexis's characters, Danticat's have misery inscribed on their bodies, making amnesia an impossibility. If the archive will not recognize the violence and misery bestowed upon Hispaniola's people, the body will. It memorializes violence where History will not. Though Amabelle's "miserable" memory of the Massacre of 1937 haunts her, she does not erase it for it is all she has to remember those who have been silenced. Bodily memory, Amabelle's character demonstrates, shatters silences. Through Amabelle's body, the reader must confront the violence of the present as informed by the historical consciousness of individual and collective identities.

In an interview Danticat stated that what she does with her work is "bear witness," voicing the silences of the victims so that they are not forgotten.[87] Writing about *The Farming of Bones*, Suárez argued that through narrating the memories of violence, Danticat builds a monument "against silenced tragedies," that can serve as a "vehicle to recovery for individuals."[88] To this, I add that Danticat's intervention offers a third side to understanding the triangular construction of Dominican and Haitian narrations of identity, for the novel is written from the diasporic perspective of actors, who may have left their homeland but carry with them the emotional, psychological, and political history of that which engendered their exclusion.[89] Danticat's novel, like Rosario's *Song of the Water Saints*, is then also a texto montado that carries the stories that the Archive of Dominicanidad has silenced. The fact that the novel reached international success also consecrates it as a monument of contra*diction*.

Like Bosch, Marrero Aristy's, and Alexis's stories, *The Farming of Bones* takes place within the context of a Cibao sugarcane town, allowing the reader to experience the complexity of Haitian-Dominican twentieth-century socioeconomic history. The accuracy of historical dates, as well as the author's insistence on the Haitian body as a contact zone for historical encounters, echoes Alexis's narrative project. Danticat's text, however, proposes the necessity to examine the consequences of historical events. Unlike the other texts examined herein, which end with a view of the slaughter or the death of the suffering character, *The Farming of Bones* insists on the contemporary urgency of history as embodied in the memory of the surviving victims and the subsequent generations. Written in English and published in the United States, Danticat's novel seems to take Alexis's proposal a step further by provoking a pan-Caribbean dialogue that looks at the violence of history from outside the geographical and linguistic borders of the island nations. It challenges established historical and rhetorical perspectives. In that sense, the novel reproduces, as Lucía Suárez argues, the possibility of viewing tragedy from the perspective of a potential witness.[90] The characters live as witnesses, if not of the massacre, then of the traumatic effects transmitted through the experience of those who, like Tamara's family, did survive.

A form of interpellation and transnational linkage can be seen in Danticat's *The Farming of Bones*, which examines the structures of nationalism in post-US-intervention Hispaniola, while denouncing anti-Haitianism as a long process of disenfranchisement: "To them we are always foreigners, even if our grandmémes' grandmémes were born in this country."[91] By taking on the role of a witness, Danticat humanizes the victims of the racial massacre, while contemporizing the marginal experience of the Haitian sugarcane workers in the Dominican Republic and insisting on the legacy of violence affecting Haitians in the present.

As in all of the literary texts studied in this chapter, Danticat produces the massacre as a violent event against Haitian migrants rather than as the multiethnic attack on the border community it actually was. Although there is no historical evidence of the killings taking place within the contained sugarcane barracks, Danticat (as did Alexis) locates the violence as part of a more recognizable and persistent rhetoric of Haitian oppression in the Dominican Republic: the batey worker. This recourse, which resonates with the work of Dominican Compassionate writers, situates "the Haitian problem" within a contemporary and ongoing discussion, shedding light on the reality of Haitian immigrants in contemporary Dominican Republic. A contemporary reading of the novel, for instance, will undoubtedly lead to a genealogical reading of the Dominican state's actions of 2013 that lead to the denationalization of nearly 200,000. If in 1937 the Dominican state killed its own citizens in the name of the nation, in 2013 they denationalized their own.

The literature of the US Caribbean diaspora has played an important role in documenting significant historical moments, particularly in reference to the dictatorships, colonialism, imperialism, and migration. As seen through the texts presented in this chapter, writing the history of the Caribbean has been a fluid intellectual project that does not belong solely to historians. Poets, novelists, essayists, performers, and politicians have often claimed — or been granted — historical authority by subsequent generations of letrados. This dynamic is complicated by the presence of such authors as José Martí, Joaquín Balaguer, Fidel Castro, Juan Bosch, and Máximo Gómez, who, in addition to being writers, were actors and subjects in the history of their nations. This Caribbean complexity has produced a rich variety of narratives in which the lines between genres are frequently blurred. There is no doubt that Caribbean historiography has been enriched by literary productions. They served the social function of reconstructing the collective memories of the communities where historical evidence was lacking. In addition, as Pedro Luís San Miguel argues, fictional texts have often been able to reconstruct social reality in times of censorship or strict government control, when history has served the purpose of the state.[92] Writers of the US Caribbean diaspora—such as Julia Álvarez, Edwidge Danticat, Cristina García, Achy Obejas, and Nelly Rosario—often contra*dict* the canon imposed by the paternalistic discourse of national Caribbean narratives by destabilizing history at a very fundamental level. Julia Álvarez and Edwidge Danticat, for instance, have proposed an *other* history from the perspective of women. Achy Obejas and Nelly Rosario queered the foundational fictions of the nation, extending the love to a geographical triangulation that includes the political relationship with the United States and the everyday lives of the exiled/immigrant subjects.

Diasporic interpellations thus insert themselves within the national archives while posing new ways to question official truths. The public discomfort of nationalist historians with the fictionalization of "truths," demonstrated for instance in the publicized exchange between historian Bernardo Vega and Edwidge Danticat, points to the capacity of diasporic literature for destabilizing the national archive.[93] Through the fictionalization of historical interpellations, diasporic writers participate in the debates of two national narratives: the one they evoke (Dominican Republic/Haiti/Cuba) and the one they invoke (United States). Consequently, their work produces transnational bonds that blur the geographies of home and propose a fluid vision that connects wider sociohistorical discussions of dictatorships, US military intervention, imperialism, and economic exploitation to the local experience of their immigrant communities.

The brutality of the Massacre of 1937, as well as other tragedies of the twentieth and twenty-first centuries—such as US military interventions, local dictatorships, and the earthquake of 2010—has affected both Haiti and the Dominican Republic. The process of remembering the specificities of tragic events, as seen through this study, has been marked by silences, omissions, and allegorical representations that, though sometimes summoning an important critique of the colonial, imperial, and dictatorial realities that intervene in the production of Hispaniola's history, often erase the rayano and the black body from the archive. Foregrounding the rayano body in our discussion of the Haitian-Dominican border, this chapter argues, can help us find more than a space of violence and separation in the Haitian-Dominican border; such foregrounding also helps locate embodied memory from which silences can be confronted. My reading thus calls for rayano consciousness—one that acknowledges the border and its people as human subjects rather than as objects of state and colonial control.

The study of the Massacre of 1937 from the perspective of a variety of fictional narrations produced in the three different national territories (Haiti, the United States, and the Dominican Republic) that make up the triangular modern Dominican imaginary presented here can offer a productive point of departure for examining the effects of this violence on Dominican national and racial identities. This study also can bring attention to the persistent silences that inhabit even those dictions that seek to contest hegemony and violence. I chose fiction to study the Massacre of 1937 and its resulting nationalist rhetoric not because it offers the tangible specificities recorded in the often-deficient official documents available in the various Dominican archives, but because of the representation of historical experiences as lived and remembered by those who have been erased from the Dominican national narrative of history. My approach, however, does not posit a contrasting view that places the victims of historical events on one side and the facts regarding the event on another. Rather, this study presents them as two parallel and interdependent ways of remembering or forgetting past experiences.

Narrating the Massacre of 1937 can be perceived only as a historical analysis of a traumatic event. However, in the context of current hostility and oppression affecting immigrants, and especially considering the rise of anti-Haitianism and hatred in the Dominican Republic of the twenty-first century, the "historical" issues currently examined sadly resonate with existing human rights concerns affecting many citizens today. In that sense, my literary examination not only sympathizes with Tamara's efforts to remember the dead, but is also written with a strong desire to keep in mind the living.

II

---

*DIASPORA CONTRA*DICTS

CHAPTER 4

Rayano Consciousness

Remapping the Haiti-DR Border after the Earthquake of 2010

Consider Sonia Marmolejos and understand why, despite everything, I still have hope.
—JUNOT DÍAZ, "Apocalypse: What Disasters Reveal"

In January 2010, as the world coped with news about one of the most le-thal disasters in the history of humanity, Sonia Marmolejos, a Dominican rayana from Bahoruco, became a worldwide celebrity.[1] On January 14, brav-ing the chaos left by the magnitude seven earthquake that shook the island of Hispaniola, killing about 230,000 people, Marmolejos traveled to the capital city of Santo Domingo to seek medical assistance for her two-year-old daughter. The toddler was born with a rare genetic condition and re-quired bone replacement surgery to walk. Marmolejos was hoping to receive aid for her daughter at the public Darío Contreras Hospital, where she had finally been able to secure an appointment after a six-month wait. But when she arrived, the toddler could not be seen because all medical personnel were tending to the hundreds of Haitians in critical condition who had been air-lifted to the Darío Contreras Hospital after the disaster.[2]

While waiting for her daughter to be seen, Marmolejos noticed a baby suffering from cranial wounds among the injured Haitians. The baby cried incessantly and seemed dehydrated and hungry. Marmolejos, who had left her own four-month-old baby in Bahoruco in her mother's care, acted on maternal instinct, picking up the Haitian infant and nursing him to sleep: "Yo lo vi así y actué por impulso, como madre, es lo que podía hacer" (I saw him in that state, and I acted on instinct, as a mother, I did what I could).[3] Days later, Marmolejos continued going to the hospital, eventually nursing twelve injured babies to wellness.[4] The Dominican mother's humanitarian gesture moved people across the globe. The photograph of a smiling Sonia

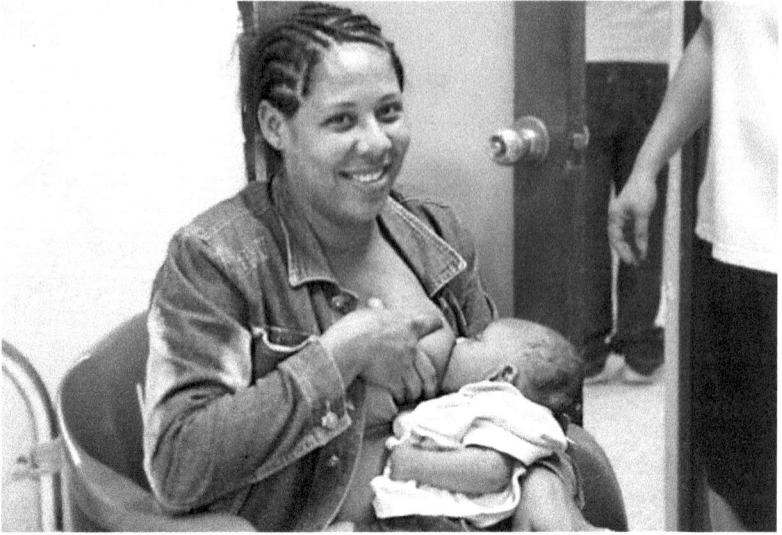

4.1 Sonia Marmolejos smiles while nursing a wounded baby at the Darío Contreras Hospital. Viviano de León, *Listín Diario*, January 17, 2010. Courtesy of Viviano de León.

nursing a wounded baby (figure 4.1) appeared in many publications. She was invited on television programs and was even the subject of a short film.[5] Dominican media and nationalist organizations capitalized on Marmolejos's story, hoping to diffuse the international rage that had escalated over the last two decades as a result of the inhumane working and living conditions of Haitian immigrants in Dominican bateyes.[6] On June 2, President Leonel Fernández awarded Marmolejos a medal of honor in a public ceremony attended by former US president Bill Clinton and former Haitian president René Préval (figure 4.2).

Following the earthquake, international media continuously brought attention to the disparities between the two nations of Hispaniola. A frequent observation among journalists covering the rapid Dominican response to the Haitian disaster was the contrast between impoverished, deforested Haiti with its black, Creole-speaking, *vodou*-practicing population and the relatively prosperous Dominican Republic to the east with its mixed-race, Spanish-speaking, Catholic citizenry. This dichotomist discourse obscured the earthquake-affected Línea Fronteriza, where a Dominican-Haitian culture has existed for centuries and where the rayanos, such as Sonia Marmo-

4.2 Sonia Marmolejos (center) is congratulated by the president of the Dominican Republic, Leonel Fernández (far left), after she was awarded the Duarte y Sánchez Order. She stands next to former president of Haiti René Préval (left) and former US president and special UN representative for Haiti Bill Clinton (right) during the opening session of the World Summit for the Future of Haiti in Punta Cana, Dominican Republic, June 2, 2010. Erica Santelices / AFP / Getty Images.

lejos, experience the same poverty and disenfranchisement journalists and scholars tend to associate with Haiti.

Two photographs of Sonia Marmolejos frame this chapter. The first captures the compassionate image of a happy Sonia nursing the wounded baby. The second shows Sonia in an affectionate embrace with the head of the Haitian state, while representatives of the United States and the Dominican Republic physically surround the couple, exhibiting their approval with gestures and smiles (see figure 4.2). The first photo traveled the world, inspiring writers and activists to highlight Sonia's actions as an example of cooperation and humanity. The second photo also traveled the world, though the focus was different. The second photo served as illustration in news articles about the series of bilateral agreements in which Clinton, as a representative of the United States, was a liaison to the relief efforts.

The second photo of Sonia Marmolejos captures the genealogical borders of dominicanidad this book proposes. The (historicized) body of Sonia appears physically surrounded by the Dominican state (Leonel Fernández), the United States (Bill Clinton) and the Haitian State (René Préval). The image illuminates the ways in which bodies, particularly the racialized body of the rayana Marmolejos represents, reflect the official discourse of the nation because, as Elizabeth Grosz argues, bodies are never natural but, rather, always "marked by the history and specificity of [their] existence."[7] The presence of the state-marked body of Marmolejos in an international political event shows us *how* the three nations that border dominicanidad attempt to co-opt and control racialized bodies through structures of exploitation and social control that continue to sustain economic inequality in Hispaniola.

Returning our gaze to the first photograph, we are also reminded that dominant structures can always be contested through performances of everyday life that often contra*dict* official discourses of the state. Rather than an extraordinary action, nursing another woman's baby is, in Marmolejos's own words, simply "what mothers do."[8] In poor peasant and rayano villages, breastfeeding is a communal endeavor.[9] Poor women often nurse each other's babies, sharing household chores, childrearing, and farming tasks. All of these things are part of the daily strategy for survival in impoverished communities throughout the Línea Fronteriza. Marmolejos's decision to nurse the wounded baby did not result solely from an individual instinct, but rather from an understanding of her responsibility to a community in need. At the hands of the Dominican state, and in the wake of the international media frenzy that followed the quake, Marmolejos's ordinary community performance was depicted as an extraordinary political act of intra-island solidarity. Understood through a dominant Western discourse of childrearing, Marmolejos's nursing body became a site for negotiating state(s) authority, legitimacy, and control over the territory and the people affected by the earthquake of 2010. The rayano episteme—Marmolejos's way of understanding motherhood and community—was silenced to make room for the production of an international narrative of Haitian-Dominican reconciliation that could facilitate state and corporate profit (the Fernández-Préval-Clinton union) in the business of postearthquake Haiti reconstruction.[10]

Through their performances of bodily communion, baby and mother contra*dicted* the bordering enterprise Fernández, Préval, and Clinton represented, for the union of the two bodies symbolized the unification of Hispaniola's people, not the states. The fact that Marmolejos could nourish a "Haitian" baby with her own "Dominican" body proved that Haitians and Dominicans could not be, as Balaguer and others throughout the twentieth century insisted, inherently different. By giving her milk to the child, Marmolejos challenged the Hispanophile rhetoric sustaining Haitian-

Dominican racial antagonism. Her public act of nursing becomes part of a larger performative archive of rayano contra*dictions* this chapter produces through the dialogic analysis of a variety of temporally, linguistically, and formally diverse texts: *Cantos de la frontera*, a poetry collection (1963) by Dominican nationalist writer Manuel Rueda; a series of performances and videos (2005–2010) by David "Karmadavis" Pérez; and "Da pa lo do," a song and music video (2011) by writer and performer Rita Indiana Hernández.

In her influential book *The Archive and the Repertoire*, Diana Taylor argues that performance in the Americas is a "vital act of transfer," transmitting social knowledge, cultural memory, and identities.[11] For Taylor, both the archive (texts and other documents) and the repertoire (so-called ephemeral social practices, such as spoken language, gestures, and rituals) operate as valued sites of knowledge making and transmission. Following Taylor's important theorization of the archive and the repertoire, this chapter proposes Marmolejos's "act of transfer"—the practice of communal nursing—as a framework for understanding what I call rayano consciousness: the multiplicity of performative *dictions* that make up the transnational, interethnic, and multilinguistic borders of dominicanidad.

Through rayano consciousness, artists, writers, and the general public are able to confront anti-Haitianism within and beyond the island territory and find communal ways to create and historicize their own everyday realities. Transcending the conceptual limits of the militarized territorial Haitian-Dominican border, my conceptualization of rayano consciousness remaps Hispaniola's borders on the historicized body of the Dominican racialized subject, bringing attention to the persistent violence of colonial presence, but also to multiple ways of contestations. Rayano consciousness offers the possibility of imagining the rayano body as a site for the performance of political contra*diction*. This process is evident in the works of David Pérez and the music video by Rita Indiana Hernández that I engage in this chapter, as both artists physically embody the genealogical trauma of the Haitian-Dominican border violence in order to contra*dict* it. But *rayano* consciousness also evokes a moment prior to the violence and destruction that has marked the narration of Haitian-Dominican relations since 1937—a moment immortalized in the post-Trujillo poetry of nationalist writer Manuel Rueda. This chapter historicizes the multiple ways in which contemporary artists from different traditions and generations have interpellated the hegemonic version of the Haitian-Dominican border through the figure of the rayano and the Línea Fronteriza territory. The works I engage in this chapter produce an *other* archive of dominicanidad—one that contra*dicts* the violence that has persistently banished rayanos from the Dominican imagination.

Inviting us to think about the rayano experience as one that includes diasporic Dominicans living in the United States, Silvio Torres-Saillant reminds us that the border is a location where the "the transnational, multicultural, transracial and interethnic" interact naturally, "demonstrating what our planet is becoming."[12] Following Torres-Saillant's analysis, we could read the Línea Fronteriza as an anticipation of the future and as an incredibly valuable analytical structure for the development of critical interventions about the pressing concerns of societies across the planet. I invite the reader to think about the possibility of an alternative narrative of dominicanidad in which the *raya*, or borderline, dividing the two nations of Hispaniola can serve as a metaphor for understanding the multiplicity of experiences that make up dominicanidad rather than as a place of constant conflict and political struggle.

Contradicting Hispaniola Borders

One of the earliest examples of rayano consciousness in Dominican cultural production can be found in the poetic works of Manuel Rueda (1921–99). A native of Monte Cristi, a city located on the northern borderlands (see map 3.1) where the atrocious Massacre of 1937 occurred, Rueda grew up surrounded by a multiethnic community of rayanos and ethnic Haitians.[13] Many were integrated into the life of the city, often employed as servants, shopkeepers, artisans, doctors, or teachers. Rueda's poetry was greatly inspired by the multiethnic reality of his native city and by the dramatic landscapes of the northern borderland Artibonito Valley. As an intellectual, Rueda was preoccupied with the environmental, cultural, and political future of the Dominican Republic, as well as by what he perceived to be an "unnatural division" between Haiti and the Dominican Republic.[14] It is in part these preoccupations that gave rise to his collection of poems, *Cantos de la frontera*, which the poet wrote while living in Chile during the early years of the Trujillo dictatorship (1939–51) and finally published in 1963 as part of a larger compilation, titled *La criatura terrestre*.

Rueda's rayano consciousness comes through in the poem "Canción del rayano," in which the lyric voice speaks from the subject position of the borderland subject, summoning a memory of Hispaniola prior to the colonial imposition of territorial borders:

La tierra era pequeña y yo no tenía otro oficio que el de
recorrerla. . . .
y mis espaldas era fuertes como los caminos y las
montañas de la tierra.
A veces sucedíanse juegos y locas carreras a lo largo de la costa,
pero me detenía el mar
Él sólo era mi valla y yo me asemejaba a él en poderío y
ansia de lo libre.[15] (emphasis added)

[The land was small and I had no occupation other than that of
traversing it. . . .
and my back was strong like the roads and the
mountains of the land.
Sometimes games and crazy paths would occur along the coast,
but the sea held me back.
The sea alone was my border, and I took after him in the power and
longing of freedom.]

One of the most intriguing metaphors of Rueda's "Canción del rayano" is
that of the sea as a border. When thinking about borders as a location for
the exercise of colonial and state control, we tend to imagine them as land
between two nations. Yet, in the Caribbean and, more recently, in the Mediterranean, the question of bordering the nation inevitably encompasses the
sea from which potential threats—in the form of colonial forces or, more
recently, undocumented immigrants—can arrive. A contemporary reading
of the sea-border metaphor encapsulates the image of "boat people," to borrow from Mayra Santos-Febres, or *yoleros*, who risk their lives in homemade
rafts to cross the dangerous Mona Canal from Hispaniola to Puerto Rico,
or *balseros* crossing the deathly ninety-mile route from Havana to Florida in
search of a better life.[16]

For Rueda's poetic voice, however, the sea is both a *valla* (fence) keeping
him from leaving the island as well as a symbol of freedom. It is the space
that marks both the end of the insular territory and the beginning of the
endless possibilities of a world beyond. The notion on the Caribbean Sea
as a dichotomist barrier/opening dialogues with a larger Caribbean intellectual and literary tradition defining the archipelago. Édouard Glissant,
for instance, describes the Caribbean Sea as "the estuary of the Americas"
where the three great rivers—the Mississippi, the Orinoco, and the Ama-
zon—flow into the Atlantic.[17] Following Glissant's articulation, the Carib-

bean island can be read as a gateway to freedom and openness, rather than as a separate "insular" entity, as a symbol of globalization and miscegenation: a place where all the waters mix.

Rueda's lyric voice intertextually references Glissant's metaphoric Caribbean global-hybrid sea in all its complexities. The rayano lyric voice recognizes himself in the sea: "Y yo me asemejaba a él en su poderío y ansia de lo libre" (And I took after him in the power and longing of freedom). Such similitude also summons a painful recognition of colonial history—one that resulted in the hybrid nature of the rayano subject. The violence of colonialism, however, the lyric voice explains, is not the cultural-racial miscegenation that engendered rayano subjectivity, but rather the violent imposition of the borderline—la raya—that divided the territory and the humans who inhabit it:

> Pero vino el final y no lo supe. Pero vino el final y yo dormido. . . . Y alguien trazando sobre mí esa línea, diciendo, 'tú serás dividido para siempre.' Un brazo aquí y el otro allá. A mí, al ambidextro, que hacía arrodillar a un toro mientras acariciaba a una criatura.[18]

> [But the end came and I did not realize it. But the end came and I was asleep. . . . And someone drawing that line upon me, saying, 'You will be divided forever.' One arm here and the other there. To me, to the ambidextrous, who brought a bull to its knees while caressing a baby.]

The violence of coloniality, the poem suggests, is present in the state's efforts to define the rayano as a national subject.

Ruben Silié describes the border conflicts between Haiti and the Dominican Republic as constituting "una situación heredada de la dominación colonial, en la que los intereses metropolitanos tuvieron la isla como escenario" (a situation inherited from colonial domination, in which metropolitan interests used the island as a backdrop).[19] Let us remember that the Haitian-Dominican border was defined as a result of a colonial transaction. In 1697, Spain ceded a portion of its colony to France, drawing a line along the Dajabón River in the northwest of the Dominican Republic (see map 3.1).[20] In 1777, the Treaty of Aranjuez, signed between Spain and France after multiple territorial conflicts, attempted to clearly define a border to divide the two colonies, therefore protecting the interests of both colonial powers. By the 1844 independence of the Dominican Republic from Haiti, the frontier as defined in the Treaty of Aranjuez had been redrawn several times through various official and unofficial treaties between the governments of both sides of the island. In addition, Haitians had been living on the western part of San Juan (south) and Artibonito (north) for at least a century after the Aranjuez Treaty was signed, knowingly ignoring colonial laws.[21] During the years following the proclamation of independence, Dominican patriots such as Félix María del Monte and Ángel Perdomo sought to restore the "original line" defined in the Treaty of Aranjuez as the legitimate division of the island, an action that, as Silié reminds us, responded to a colonized imagination.[22]

Critiquing the colonial imagination that dominated Dominican politics in the second half of the twentieth century, Rueda's "Canción del rayano" musters a prepartition Hispaniola, when the rayano inhabited a free (borderless) land. Rueda's rayano world thus precedes the nation(s), and as such exists beyond the nation in a space that is, according to the poem, its own earth—"La tierra era pequeña . . ." (The land [or the earth] was small . . .).[23] This space was thus more than a nation. Rueda's depiction of the rayano as indigenous to Hispaniola is incredibly powerful as it contradicts the official narrative of Dominican racial hybridity that nineteenth-century intellectuals and writers had explained through *indigenismo*.[24] They deployed *indios* as the "ethnic" element of the national racial makeup, and as the true and only natives to the nation. Yet indios were also narrated as extinct, only surviving in an indefinable space of national elite imagination. Substituting the symbolic (decimated) Indian with the (living) rayano, Rueda contradicts the Archive of Dominicanidad while challenging the persistent Hispanophile rhetoric that renders Haitians and Dominicans as ethnic enemies.

In the opening poem of the collection, "Canto de regreso a la tierra prometida" (Song of Return to the Promised Land), Rueda insists on the *raya*—the unnatural division of the land and people—rather than the *rayano*—the people who inhabit the territory now divided by the state—as the evidence of colonial violence:

> Medias montañas,
> medios ríos,
> y hasta la muerte
> compartida.
>   El mediodía parte
> de lado a lado al hombre
> y le parte el descanso,
> parte la sombra en dos y
>   duplica el ardor.[25]

[Half mountains,
half rivers,
and even death
shared.
        Midday divides
man into two sides,
and it divides his repose,
and it divides the shadow in two and
        doubles the heat.]

The visual image the poem depicts is as powerful as it is violent. Everything, even death, is cut in half, except the castigating sun, the suffocating heat that doubles as the mountains and the trees are destroyed. The violent "cutting" of the territory and the people of the Línea Fronteriza in Rueda's poem symbolizes the Massacre of 1937 in which people were attacked using machetes and knives. Yet, in Rueda's poem it is not just bodies that are cut, but bodily actions: death, work, and rest. The symbolic cutting of the rayano body in the violent massacre, the lyric voice reminds us, resulted in the cutting of epistemes and histories, in the destruction of both land and people.

Rueda's depiction of the divided border in "Canto de regreso" laments all that has been lost by the division of the island, while signaling the rayano as a by-product of this unnatural separation. After the first verse, the lyric voice appeals directly to the interlocutor's rayano consciousness, urging her to act or, at the very least, to react to the realities of the border:

¿Sabes adónde vamos? ¿Sabes qué país es el tuyo?
tan fragante y que tiene una línea de resecas miserias,
una pobre corteza resbalando en los ríos
perdidos, bajo los silenciosos cambronales?[26]

[Do you know where we are going?
Do you know which country is yours,
so fragrant and with a line of dried-up miseries,
a poor skin that slips through the rivers
lost underneath the silent cambronales?]

Without directly engaging historical events, Rueda introduces History as an unnatural force that causes the destruction of the island's natural order and breaks the rayano in two halves. The poet, and more specifically, the borderland poet, is thus charged with the difficult task of standing on the border hoping to unite this broken island-person into a whole again:

Oye al pobre poeta,
un corazón entero, ¡tan entero!
—cantar en medio de las heridas
sin comprender la marca de la tierra
sin probar de su fruto dividido[27]

[Hear the poor poet,
a whole heart, so complete!
—sing in the midst of wounds
without understanding the lay of the land,
without tasting of its divided fruit]

Literary critic Homi K. Bhabha defines the border as a Third Space where the cultures and values of both the colonizer and the colonized transform into something new.[28] Rueda's placing of the lyric voice in between Haiti and the Dominican Republic—on the raya—is an important symbolic gesture for transforming and contesting the dominant rhetoric of the nation-state, as suggested by Bhabha. It proposes that borderer, the rayano, has the potential of being both self and other, serving as a translator between languages and cultures. In so doing, the poet proposes rayano consciousness as an antidote to the colonial imagination that dominates and cuts Hispaniola into two antagonistic halves.

Rueda's divided island became a trope celebrated by both anti- and pro-Haitian writers of the second half of the twentieth century because the metaphor encapsulated a clear, if violent, visual of the destiny of the two peoples inhabiting Hispaniola. Yet, contrary to what anti-Haitian writers imagined, Rueda's poem is not a geopolitical manifesto of what has come to be known as the "Haitian-Dominican problem." Rather, the poem visualizes what the rayano, as one who stands in between the two halves of the island, can see from his/her vantage point: "Mira tu paraíso entre dos fuegos, nido de serpientes elásticas" (Look at your paradise between two fires, nest of elastic serpents).[29] The powerful image of the two fires and elastic serpents that destroy the unity of the island poses a strong critique of the political imposition of the two states seeking to control the people and land of the Línea Fronteriza.

Rueda's poetic voice represents the rayano body as a symbol of anticolo-

nial Hispaniola, of "nuestra tierra hasta que el hombre la marcó con el opro-
bio de la raya" (our land until man marked it with the disgrace of the line).[30]
The *diction* "ours" destabilizes the hegemonic rhetoric of dominicanidad,
uniting Dominicans and Haitians, like the island they inhabit, as one body,
a common whole. Though Rueda does not advocate for a political unification of the two nations of Hispaniola, the poet's rayano consciousness is
grounded in what he believes to be a need to acknowledge the history of
political cooperation and the existence of an "ambidextrous" rayano subjectivity. In so doing, Rueda's poetics advocates for rayano consciousness as an
alternative to the coloniality that dominates Hispaniola's politics.

One of the most interesting fundamentals of Rueda's *Cantos de la frontera* is the duality of the border experience it portrays. On the one hand, the
book recovers the landscape, politics, and experiences of the borderlands
through a romantic depiction of the rayano. On the other, the author reminds us of his legitimate voice as a native of the Línea Fronteriza, though
not as a rayano. Carefully identifying himself as Dominican rather than
rayano, Rueda is able to depict the rayano experience without risking back-
lash from the nationalist intellectuals of the post-Trujillo era. A classical musician and self-defined Latin American *vanguardista* poet, Rueda depended
on his ability to work within the Trujillo intelligentsia, avoiding controversial topics while embracing the national intellectual desire for high culture.
Thus, using classic poetic forms recognized as "proper," Rueda secured access
to the elite circles.[31] His decision to publish *Cantos de la frontera* in 1963, two
years after the death of Trujillo, shows an acute awareness of Dominican
politics as linked to the national literary project, while also demonstrating
his concern for the dominant national project he was beginning to represent. Embodying the very contra*dictions* of dominicanidad, Rueda offers the
rayano as both the heart and soul of Hispaniola identity, as well as a tragic
figure caught in the middle of two very different worlds and condemned to
exist outside of both.

Writing thirty years prior to Gloria Anzaldúa, and from a very different
transnational reality, Rueda describes the Haitian-Dominican border as an
open wound, his home located halfway between, "in a highway without
return."[32] But unlike Anzaldúa's border subject, Rueda's is ultimately para-
lyzed, overcome by the horrifying colonial exploitation that after violently
breaking their body in two now dictates the inconclusive future of the two
halves-nations:

Trata de dormir ahora,
de entregar el único párpado a tu sueño
inconcluso.
            Trata de dormir.
Tratemos de dormir
hasta que nos despierten
leñadores robustos,
hombres de pala y canto
que hagan variar el curso de nuestra pesarosa
isla amada,
de nuestro desquiciado
planeta.[33]

            [Try to sleep now,
to surrender the singular eyelid to your
unfinished slumber.
            Try to sleep.
We must try to sleep
until we are awakened by
robust woodcutters,
men of the shovel and song
who will change the course of our sorrowful
beloved island,
of our insane
planet.]

A sense of urgency becomes clearer in the last verse of the poem, warning about the possibility of colonial/imperial intervention, as symbolized by the metaphor of *leñadores robustos*. Responding to a Latin American social consciousness that very much marked the literary production of the mid-twentieth century, Rueda was acutely aware of US political and military interventions in Latin America. His reading of the border locates Haitian-Dominican relations in a global context, while warning about the dangers of US military interventions in a premonitory tone.[34]

Rueda's poetry presents the rayano as a symbolic category for explaining the Haitian-Dominican border. In so doing, the author successfully challenges the anti-Haitian nationalist writing machine that was set into full speed during the Trujillo regime. This contesting position was highly criti-

cized by his contemporaries as "frivolous and without historical consciousness," often raising the suspicion of the dominant political groups.[35] Eventually, Rueda's success as a classical music interpreter earned the forgiveness
and respect of the elite, who ultimately accepted the author's early border
poetry as an important contribution to "Dominican folkloric history."[36]
Rueda's allegiance to national Euro-dominant aesthetics, as well as his impressive accomplishments as a musician, undeniably contributed to his consecration into the elite cultural circles, of which he was a leading figure until
his death in 1999.

Despite writer Héctor Incháustegui Cabral's claims, a careful reading of
Rueda's work establishes that his depiction of the Haitian-Dominican border was historically grounded, though his position differed from that of anti-
Haitian nationalist writers.[37] Rueda's poem "Canto de la frontera" (1945), the
eponymous piece of the collection, comes closest to a critique of nationalism
and hegemony, making clear references to the Massacre of 1937 and the politics of the Trujillo state:[38]

> ¿En dónde estás, hermano, mi enemigo de tanto tiempo
> y sangre?
> ¿Con qué dolor te quedas, pensándome, a lo lejos?
> De pronto vi las hoscas huestes que descendían, aullando
>   y arrasando.
> Vi la muerte brilladora en la punta de las lanzas.
> Vi mi tierra manchada y te vi sobre ella,
> Desafiador,
> La brazada soberbia sobre el cañaveral que enmudece ...
> Y yo supe que nunca habría esperanza para ti o para
>   Nosotros,
> Hermano que quedaste una noche, a lo lejos,
> Olvidado y dormido junto al agua.[39]

> [Where are you, brother, my enemy of so much time
> and blood?
> With what pain do you remain, thinking of me, from afar?
> Suddenly, I saw the unwelcoming armies that descended, howling
>   and destroying.
> I saw death shining at the points of the spears.
> I saw my land stained, and I saw you upon it,
> Defiant,

The proud stroke upon the silencing cane field . . .
And I knew that there would never be hope for you or
    Us,
Brother who stayed for a night, from afar,
Forgotten and asleep beside the water.]

Rueda's lyric voice laments the attack on the multiethnic rayano communities through genocide and border policies, and through the increasing political and symbolic persecution of border subjects at the hands of nationalist thinkers. Writing from exile in the 1940s, the poet appeals to a humanistic rather than a political reaction, lauding what he perceives as the origin and destiny of the island as a whole. Referring to Haitians as "brothers," the author laments the genocide of 1937 not only as a human catastrophe, but also as a spiritual destruction that separated siblings. The Massacre of 1937 destroys hope and the possibility of reconciliation, not only for Haitians but also for *nosotros*, Dominicans. Rueda's interpretation of the massacre is as a destruction of Dominican essence, and not as an event affecting only Haitian immigrants. Contradicting international depictions of the genocide, Rueda asserts that the Massacre of 1937 happened to all of Hispaniola, avowing the rayano as part of the Dominican nation.

Part IV of "Canto de la frontera" is a critique of the complicity of the Haitian and Dominican states in the destruction of the rayano communities:

IV
Era domingo y después de oír los himnos y discursos
después de batir palmas, los señores presidentes se abrazaron. . . .
Luego los dignos visitantes, sin traspasar las líneas,
retiráronse al ritmo de músicas contrarias
reverencias y mudas arrogancias y volvimos a dar nuestros alertas,
a quedar con el ojo soñoliento sobre los matorrales encrespados.
Y volvimos a comer nuestra pobre ración, solos, lentamente,
allí donde el Artibonito corre distribuyendo la hojarasca.[40]

[It was Sunday, and after hearing the hymns and speeches
after clapping our hands, the presidents embraced. . . .
Then the visiting dignitaries, without overstepping their bounds,
went back to the rhythm of opposing music
reverences and mute arrogances and we went back to give our warnings,
to remain with a sleepy eye upon the rough overgrowth.

And we went back to eating our meager portion, alone, slowly,
there where the Artibonito runs spreading the fallen leaves.]

Between 1935 and 1936, Trujillo visited the northern borderlands, riding
his horse around the Artibonito Valley, home of the largest community of
rayanos until 1937. He shook hands with farmers and made many promises
to rayanos about his commitment to the area. During this period Trujillo
also visited Haiti on several occasions, declaring the Haitian to be his "eternal friend" and Haiti, the "other arm of the Dominican Republic."[41] Haitian
president Sténio Vincent returned the favor, visiting the neighboring nation
for various acts and ceremonies throughout the 1930s. On one of these occasions, Trujillo is said to have kissed the Haitian flag. Vincent compensated
such "good faith" by naming one of the main streets in Port-au-Prince after
the Dominican ruler.[42] "Canto de la Frontera" brings attention to the hypoc-
risy of the states—as represented by the iconic memory of Vincent and Trujillo the year before the massacre and the contemporary photo of Sonia Marmolejos, Fernández, Clinton, and Préval during the Summit of 2010—in their
claim to protect citizens from "invasion" and "savagery" in which the invasion and savagery are against its own citizens in the name of the nation. The
poem summons the long colonial history of Hispaniola oppression perpetuated in the present violence of the state in controlling the racialized body.

Unlike Prestol Castillo, who narrated the border as existing outside the
limits of the nation, Rueda's narrative of contra*diction* insists on the border's
liminality as an intrinsic category linked to the nation, rather than opposing
it. In so doing, "Canto de la frontera" locates the Haitian-Dominican border at the center of dominicanidad, as a place that literally marks the end of
the nation while also constituting a barrier to the nation. Perhaps because
Rueda was from a border city and must have grown up seeing the fluidity of rayano culture that existed prior to the Massacre of 1937, his poetry
exhibits a sensitivity that although not devoid of moments of nationalistic contra*diction*, seeks to liberate the rayano from the national stigma and
guilt to which he/she had been relegated throughout the literary history of
the nation. Made the scapegoat of the national project, the rayano was perceived as an indecisive subject who could not be trusted. But unlike the Haitian immigrant, who was viewed as a clear enemy of the nation, the rayano
had the ability to "pass," and therefore constituted a greater threat to the
national project. Turits argues that the bicultural Haitian-Dominican world
that existed in the borderlands had continued to evolve since colonization

despite all attempts to define the borders.[43] As argued in chapter 3, the Massacre of 1937 was an attack on rayano communities as much as it was on Haitian immigrants living on the borderlands.[44]

Rueda's recasting of the rayano as intrinsic to the nation is powerful because it confronts the unmentionable truth of the 1937 genocide: that Dominicans killed Dominicans. The common narration of the Massacre of 1937 as an attack of Dominicans against Haitians does not erase its horrific nature. However, the displacement of the genocide as one of Dominicans against Haitians perpetuates the narrative of conflict and hatred that has sustained anti-Haitianism for over a century. The dominant rhetoric of the massacre also led to the further erasure of rayanos from the history of both nations, a fact that has contributed to the continued obliteration of these communities from the national imagination. Rueda's rayano consciousness reminds the presumed Dominican reader of several points that have been erased by all prior literary depictions of the frontier and of the 1937 destruction: (1) Haiti and the Dominican Republic share the same land, and share a connection that goes deeper than national identity. (2) The rayano is not only Haitian, nor is he only Dominican, but a hybrid subject who is "indigenous" to the borderland and who suffers the great tragedy of having been divided in half, the same way the land was. The rayano's lack of "national allegiance" is, according to Rueda, also "natural," and so he/she must be understood and nurtured rather than alienated and persecuted. (3) Both nations need to cooperate and coexist because the ecological future of the island depends on it.

Keeping the concerns that underline Rueda's *Cantos de la frontera* in mind, one can see strong correlations between the factors contributing to Rueda's rayano consciousness and those contributing to a resurgence of a rayano consciousness in contemporary times. The issues raised in *Cantos de la frontera* illuminate some of the actions and reactions of cultural and political actors in the aftermath of the 2010 earthquake, contributing to the dissemination of rayano consciousness in the public sphere. The 2010 tremor literally shook both Hispaniola nations, though only Haiti suffered massive destruction. Writer Junot Díaz, reflecting on the earthquake, says it shook Dominicans to the core, making them contemplate the vulnerability of the island and the tangible possibility of disaster that Rueda warned his compatriots about in 1963.[45] In the days following the quake, the spirit of interdependence and cooperation symbolized in the figure of the rayano, as imagined by Rueda, overcame the general public. Artists, and scholars, began to work toward a seismic change in attitudes and ideology, destabilizing the structures that have sustained anti-Haitian hegemony for the last few decades.

"Biznis Gouvenman Bénefis Gouvenman"

In his video installation *Línea fronteriza* (*Borderline*; 2008), Dominican artist David "Karmadavis" Pérez depicts the Haitian-Dominican border, as imagined in Rueda's "Canción del rayano," as an unnatural, imposed colonial order. The video installation consists of two maps of Hispaniola outlined by lights (see figure 4.3). The first map shows the island as a whole, without national borders. On the second map, the lights outlining the island are bright and fixed, clearly marking the imagined border that divides land from sea. In contrast, thinner intermittent lights outline the Haitian-Dominican border. Read in intertextual dialogue with Rueda's poetry, *Línea fronteriza* reminds the viewer that the border between Haiti and the Dominican Republic is not static, but rather is a location that exists in a constant state of fluidity, the only "real" border being, as Rueda's lyric voice also suggested, the ocean.

Pérez is a visual artist and performer whose work exhibits an acute concern for what the artist calls *isla cerrada* (closed island): the tensions that have allowed Dominicans to imagine themselves in contrast with Haiti. As an alternative, Pérez's works propose the possibility of an *isla abierta* (open island) where Dominicans and Haitians can imagine themselves coexisting and collaborating in peace and unity. His video action, *Línea fronteriza*, is part of a corpus of over a dozen artistic works in which Pérez's rayano consciousness comes to life, proposing a reflection on daily Haitian-Dominican interactions as part of larger global concerns about equality, migration, borders, and human rights.

Based in Guatemala since 2006, Pérez views himself as a diasporic artist; his social concerns and aesthetics are guided by an acute awareness of the shared challenges facing Latin American nations in a global era. His portrayal of the Dominican experience, and in particular of the Haitian-Dominican conflict, can thus be located within a Latin American sociopolitical context: "We all carry our borders with us, we internalize them, express them in our own body and transplant them to other national territories. Santo Domingo, Guatemala, Latin America, the body exists beyond borders."[46] The artist's ascription locates his work within a growing artistic

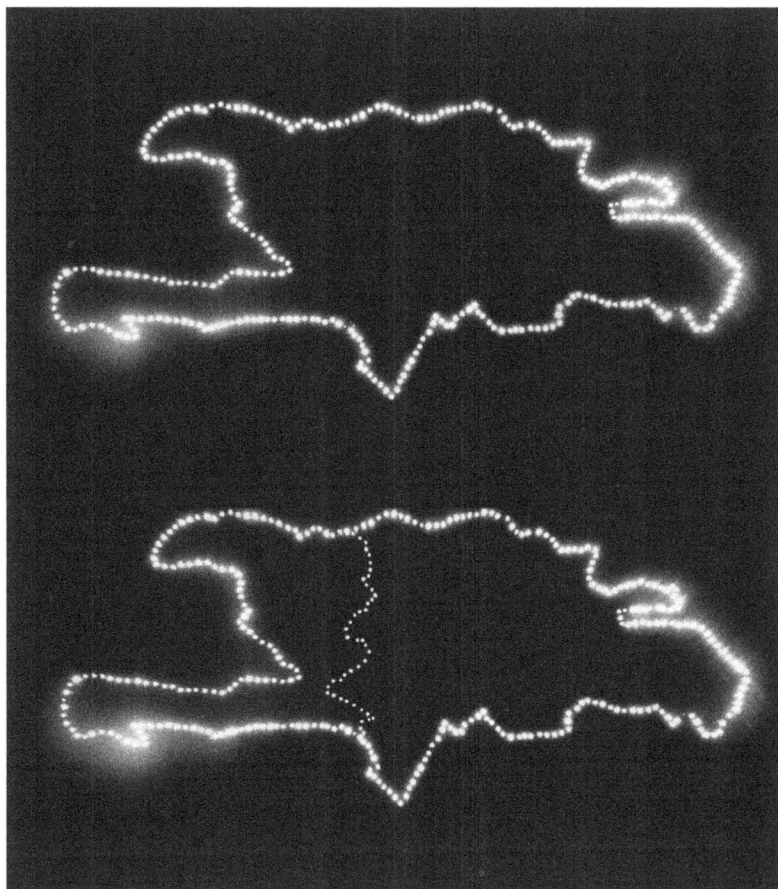

4.3 *Línea fronteriza*. Video still courtesy of David "Karmadavis" Pérez.

tradition that engages the topics of violence, state repression, drug wars, dictatorships, and the presence of coloniality in Latin America. Further, a reading of Pérez's works places the Haitian-Dominican border conflict beyond the island and in the context of the growing global border violence that has marked the beginning of the twenty-first century.

One of the most powerful critiques of border violence is found in Pérez's piece *Lo que dice la piel* (What the Skin Says; 2005). Through a translator, the artist asks an undocumented Haitian immigrant to tell him what he thought was the cause of the Haitian-Dominican conflict. The Haitian man writes his answer on a piece of paper: "biznis gouvenman bénefis gouvenman" (government business benefits governments). The man's words sum-

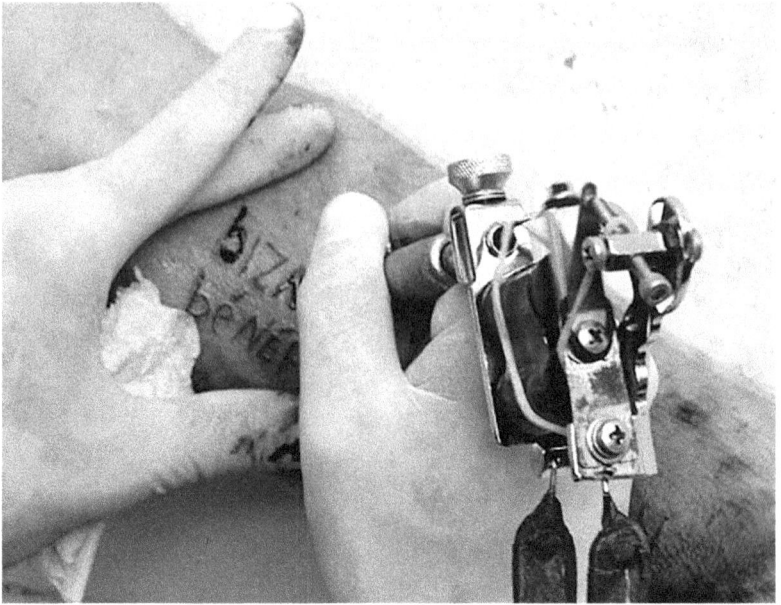

4.4 *Lo que dice la piel*, performance, 2005. Photo courtesy of David "Karmadavis" Pérez.

mon an acute understanding of the colonial imagination that created the raya, dividing Haitians and Dominicans and sustaining Haitian oppression in present-day Dominican Republic. Pérez, without seeking translation from Kreyòl, then proceeded to tattoo the man's words on his arm (see figure 4.4). Bringing to the fore the possibility of cross-border dialogue, *Lo que dice la piel* foregrounds *rayano* consciousness as a possible antidote to anti-Haitianism, internationalized antiblackness, and xenophobia. The use of his own body as the canvas for the Haitian man's untranslated words confirms Pérez's political project, as his skin literally "dice" (says) that "Haitian and Dominican problem" is a conflict of the states; not of the people. What the skin says negates what the states say. The performing body contra*dicts* the archive.

Postmodern feminist theory sustains that tattoos can serve as a way to reclaim the body from the structures that seek to contain it. Becoming a form of text, Elizabeth Grosz argues, the (tattooed) body can be a site of political contestation where messages can be reinscribed. She writes, "This analogy between the body and the text remains a close one: the tools of body engraving—social, surgical, epistemic, disciplinary—all mark, indeed constitute, bodies in culturally specific ways."[47] Grosz's theorization of the body-text is particularly helpful in thinking about the political project guiding Pérez's *Lo que dice la piel*. A light-skinned Dominican from the capital city of Santo Domingo, Pérez's body contains, as Grosz would argue, the historical (if at first invisible) inscriptions of the Dominican state's colonial imagination. His light skin and level of education, as well as his privileged position as an artist, serve as a sort of passport, allowing him free passage in the everyday life interactions of urban Dominican Republic. The decision to mark his skin with Kreyòl is a way of both acknowledging and challenging his own privileged position as an heir to (perhaps unwanted) colonial privilege. The incorporation of pain and blood through the act of tattooing Kreyòl, however, also operates as a permanent reminder of the historical violence of Hispaniola's borders. *Lo que dice la piel* rebukes the ephemeral nature of performance art through the permanent inscription of the Kreyòl message on the artist's skin. The incorporation of pain and blood, in addition to using the body as Kreyòl text, physically summons recognition of the colonial legacy of the Haitian-Dominican border violence while simultaneously challenging the presence of coloniality on his performative body. Pérez's permanent performance of Haitian-Dominican solidarity contains a palimpsest of representations: the violent and the communal, the Haitian and the Dominican episteme, and the presence of the linguistic difference-unity of the Línea Fronteriza.

The notion of an island divided by linguistic difference has been an important thread sustaining anti-Haitianism since the early twentieth century. The nationalization of the Spanish language was the most important tool in the process of Dominican national identity formation since the birth of the republic in the nineteenth century.[48] As language historian Juan R. Valdez argues, Spanish was an important way of differentiating Dominicans from their neighbors during colonial times, allowing *colonos* to maintain cultural ties with Spain.[49] In the period following the Massacre of 1937, the ability to speak Spanish "clearly" became a symbol of national belonging, particularly for dark-skinned Dominicans—a dynamic symbolized in the racist popular phrase "El que sea prieto que hable claro" (If you are black, speak clearly).

During the days of the Massacre of 1937, cultural authenticity—as determined by the ability to speak Spanish—became the deciding factor for survival. One of the methods of identification consisted of asking the potential victim to pronounce the word *perejil* (parsley), the assumption being that

Kreyòl speakers would not be able to reproduce it in "proper Spanish." Failure to produce the Spanish *r* and *j* sounds, often a difficult task for nonnative Spanish speakers, became a death sentence. Thus, the Spanish language, rather than race, was often the deciding factor in the atrocious killings. The necessity for language as a tool of authentication illustrates an acute awareness of Dominican blackness. Pérez's embodiment of Kreyòl functions as a symbolic embrace of both the linguistic diversity of the island and the paradox that places him, an educated artist, in the vulnerable position of not being able to communicate in his own country, an experience common to migrants across the world. Nelson Maldonado-Torres, in his call for the decolonization of theoretical practices, argues that "while theoretical attitude requires detachment and wonder, the decolonial attitude which Du Bois advances demands responsibility and the willingness to take many perspectives, particularly the perspectives and points of view of those whose very existence is questioned and produced as dispensable and insignificant."[50] Pérez's performance approximates Maldonado-Torres's decolonial project as the artist enters the racialized, stigmatized subjectivity of the Haitian worker, introducing him/her to a larger audience where dialogue and criticism can emerge. The Haitian man's acute understanding of the Haitian-Dominican conflict informs the artist's anticolonial project, suggesting the urgent need for rayano consciousness and intra-island dialogue. The actual words inscribed on Pérez's body—*biznis gouvenman bénefis gouvenman*—once understood, opened doors for Haitian-Dominican solidarity outside of the oppressive official position of the states, a project the artist further develops in his award-wining video *Estructura completa* (2010).

A light-skinned blind Dominican man carrying a physically disabled dark-skinned Haitian woman around the city of Santiago de los Caballeros is the only action of the powerful performance *Estructura completa*. The woman cannot walk, but can see the streets and helps the man navigate the chaos of the city. The man cannot see, but has legs and is physically strong, so he carries her around the city. In order to survive in the heavily transited Santiago, the couple must depend on each other, entrusting the other person with their lives. The woman speaks in Kreyòl, the man responds in Spanish. They communicate through touch and sound; the woman taps him on the right or left shoulder to indicate where to step next or how to avoid traffic, potholes, street vendors, and other major obstacles in the chaos of the city.

The photo (figure 4.5) shows the two people forming a single body—her face is turned toward the viewer, covering part of his, while her torso is

4.5 Still from *Estructura completa*, 2010. Courtesy of David Pérez.

superimposed on his torso. The man's eyes are closed, while hers are open. The notion of completeness, of a single structure, comes through quite clearly in the still despite the gender and skin differences. Pérez describes *Estructura completa* as "a complete human structure made of two individuals who form something whole."[51] A strong metaphor for the Dominican and Haitian peoples, *Estructura completa* interpellates the history of Hispaniola as two fragmented territories sharing "tragedies, particularly that of having been guided by deficient mutilated governments that care very little about the people who sustain them."[52] The performance, which first debuted in the León Jiménez exhibition in Santiago, urges the viewer to think about Haitian-Dominican relations from quotidian observations, away from nationalistic rhetoric, devoid of flags and removed from the imposed territorial border. The author appeals to a sense of urgency of the present reality of two peoples who, crippled by the presence of coloniality, can only make headway through cooperation and interdependency, through a rayano consciousness in which Hispaniola can be imagined as a whole island.[53]

In her book *Accessible Citizenships*, Julie Minich examines the role of disability images in the construction of political communities and nations. She argues that national sovereignty is often defined as the nation's right to exclude vulnerable and undesirable bodies (racialized minorities, LGBTQ, and disabled bodies).[54] Metaphoric images of the nation thus tend to imagine it as a healthy, heterosexual, white body; which must in turn be protected from illness and intrusion. Pérez's *Estructura Completa* interrupts the narrative of the healthy Dominican body-nation while building on notions of solidarity and interdependency that has characterized rayano community and subjectivity. Foregrounding the Dominican and Haitian disabled body as the body of hope, *Estructura Completa* enables the viewer to ask different questions about the Haitian-Dominican border and the subjects who inhabit it. But more than a critique of the nations, the performance poses the possibility of hope and citizenship through collaboration. In that sense, Pérez's message is twofold: it critiques the states that refuse to accommodate its citizens and shows how these citizens *could* thrive if they simply worked together.

Minich argues that disability is a social construct that operates to exclude bodies from the nation.[55] Pérez's video brings attention to the relationship between the construction of the disabled body and the construction of the racialized body in the process of bordering the nation. During the United States intervention of the Dominican Republic (1916–24), images of Haitians as decomposing bodies (zombies), disabled bodies, and malnourished bodies began to circulate the world. These images, as I have argued throughout the book, greatly influenced how Dominicans imagined themselves in relation to the neighboring country. After the 2010 earthquake, photos of imperfect Haitian bodies (people who have lost limbs or otherwise showed major injures) proliferated the international media, reminding us all of the disability of Haitian blackness. Pérez's performance embodies those images; turning the attention back to the nation-states by highlighting their neglect and failure. Robert McRuer defines a functional society as "not one that simply has ramps and Braille signs on public buildings but one in which our ways of relating to, and depending on, each other have been reconfigured."[56] Walking as a complete body, the Haitian woman and Dominican man produce, if briefly, the reconfiguration McRuer dreams of.

Building on his artistic commitment to a rayano consciousness, Pérez's *Estructura completa* offers an incisive comment on postearthquake Hispaniola. Though Pérez's corpus had always reflected his acute rayano con-

sciousness, offering meaningful explorations of Haitian-Dominican (mis)
understandings, *Estructura completa* became the climactic piece of his career, earning a place in the Venice Biennale in 2011. The timing, as the piece
was first presented a few months after the earthquake of 2010, was of particular importance at a moment in which Dominicans grappled with their
role as partners in the reconstruction of a partially destroyed island. Following the earthquake, Dominican rescue workers were the first to enter
Haiti. They arrived within hours of the quake, and in the crucial first days
of the crisis, Dominicans offered Haiti urgent aid that saved thousands of
victims. Dominican hospitals, for instance, were emptied in order to receive
the wounded, and all elective surgeries were canceled for three months. The
Dominican government provided generators, mobile kitchens, and clinics
on Haitian grounds. In addition, Dominican communities in the US and
Europe organized to send supplies and money to the victims. While *Estructura completa* was not actually inspired by the earthquake, as the artist conceived the piece before the tragedy, the video performance came to represent an important metaphor for the mindset and concerns of Dominicans
following the tragedy.[57]

One of the most significant actions of solidarity that emerged as a result
of the tragedy came, shockingly, from the Dominican state. President Leonel Fernández, seeing the urgent need of the victims and the slow response
of the international community, declared an "open border" policy, allowing
Haitians to transit freely to the Dominican Republic without need of documentation.[58] The atmosphere, briefly captured in the short film *El seno de
la esperanza* (Milk of Hope; 2012), was marked by a steady flow of wounded
Haitians walking east on the International Highway while Dominican passersby watched with mixed expressions of horror and sadness.[59] Some offered
help, water, or food; others just watched in tears. Though there were anti-
Haitian reactions in the public sphere, as well as in the media, the majority of Dominicans either actively tried to reach out to Haitians, or at the
very least avoided causing them more pain. A few days after the earthquake,
a common scene in Santo Domingo included Dominicans giving up their
seats for Haitians on crowded buses, or passersby asking Haitian street vendors if everyone in their family was safe. Meditating on this significant shift,
author Junot Díaz writes: "In a shocking reversal of decades of toxic enmity,
it seemed as if the entire Dominican society mobilized for relief effort. . . .
This historic shift must have Trujillo rolling in his grave."[60] As if inspired

by Pérez's staged performance of solidarity, the actions of postearthquake dominicanidad contra*dicted* decades of anti-Haitian (disabling) discourse.

The open border policy, as well as the physical presence of thousands of wounded and displaced Haitians in Dominican cities, created a significant rupture in the Dominican anti-Haitian narrative. The presidential decree allowed for symbolic yet tangible contestations of the rhetoric that had sustained anti-Haitianism since the birth of the Republic. In the face of tragedy, Dominicans in the public sphere—particularly those coming from poor social strata—had always collaborated with Haitians. Local NGOs and artists have, since the early twentieth century, expressed the need to reach out to the neighboring country, offering aid in times of hurricanes and other natural disasters. Yet, the resulting narratives of the earthquake, and in particular, the government policies that followed, did more than extend an arm of solidarity. They allowed Dominicans to see the possibility of the island as a whole, without borders, restoring, if only briefly, the natural order imagined by both Rueda and Pérez. The biggest fear sustaining anti-Haitianism—the unification of the island through the opening of the border—had become a reality, and Dominicans at all levels of the population could see that the world had not ended because of it.

The most skeptical critics argued that the actions of Dominicans and the reaction of the Dominican state were fear driven, and as such they would pass soon enough so that the order of business—that is, anti-Haitianism—could be back on its course. Although the borders eventually closed, and three years later we have indeed seen the return of anti-Haitian discourse and practices in Dominican state and media, the event allowed for a significant contra*dictions* of anti-Haitianism at the very core of society. First, if Haitians were indeed monsters, as imagined by del Monte and Penson in the nineteenth century, they would be unworthy of compassion even in the face of an earthquake. Second, if the conflict between the two nations of Hispaniola has been about territorial control, as Michelle Wucker and other US critics have argued, the opening of the border would have posed an incredible risk to sovereignty even in the context of a disaster.[61] Thus, the opening of the borders and the actions of solidarity that sprouted up all over the Dominican Republic demonstrate that the "logic of war" that had sustained anti-Haitianism since the birth of the republic, and had institutionalized it since 1937, was finally broken, giving way for an epistemic shift in Dominican rhetoric that could contra*dict* the hegemonic Hispanophile version of dominicanidad.

Trans-Bordering Rayano Consciousness

I have so far investigated several examples of Dominican cultural production before the earthquake of 2010 that began to question, confront, and destabilize long-held nationalistic beliefs concerning the permanence of the Haitian-Dominican border by invoking a rayano consciousness. The post-2010 era of Dominican cultural production, however, yields several examples of artists and writers who continue to perform rayano consciousness, further pushing the boundaries of even the definition of "borders," going beyond a geographical-cultural understanding. One of the most interesting examples of rayano consciousness in post-2010-earthquake cultural production is the work of Rita Indiana Hernández (1977–). A Dominican writer and musical performer based in Puerto Rico, Hernández engages questions of sexuality, language, nationalism, and (trans)national identities in a contemporary urban language that both embodies and pushes the multiple borders of dominicanidad. This analysis concentrates on the artist's song and controversial music video, "Da pa lo do" (2011), which theorizes the experience of Haitian-Dominican border conflicts, engaging the multiplicity of contra*dictions* and borders of the Dominican experience by deconstructing the traditional gendered and racialized narrative of the nation.[62]

The opening scene of the video performance portrays a majestic ceiba tree, also known in the Caribbean as the tree of life.[63] The ceiba sits in the middle of an arid landscape that resembles the Artibonito Valley. Following this scene, a dark-skinned black man wearing a nineteenth-century Haitian military uniform appears. The Haitian soldier holds a rifle. He is in search of something or someone, but, yielding to the hot sun, stops to rest and drink water from a nearby river. The next scene shows another man, this time a dark-skinned mulato, wearing a Dominican military coat. The Dominican mulato soldier, also feeling the castigating sun, takes off his coat to refresh himself by the river.

The historical (nationalist) scene recalled in the image of the two soldiers is interrupted fifty seconds into the video by the appearance of a *motoconcho* (motorbike taxi), a contemporary referent for everyday urban life in Hispaniola. Riding on the back of the motoconcho is a brown-skinned Madonna, played by Hernández. She wears a blue, gold, and pink robe: the colors of both the vodou deity Mambo Ezili Freda and the Catholic Vírgen de las Mercedes. The Madonna has a large gold chain with a letter M pendant, resembling a *vévé*, the ornate religious symbols used in Haitian vodou.

Hernández's skin, which is naturally light, has been painted golden brown. The mulata Madonna is revealed as an apparition to each of the men, her vévé bling reflecting a beautiful shade of pink and blue on their faces.

At the end of the music video, the two men, convinced by the message of solidarity the Vírgen brings, strip off their uniforms and national colors, keeping on only their white pants.[64] The half-naked men then walk toward each other, meeting face to face in front of the ceiba tree (see figure 4.6). The music video ends with the men dropping their weapons and embracing while the Madonna sings and swings her hips, accompanied by a chorus of black and mulato children. A powerful transhistorical allegory of Haitian-Dominican relations, "Da pa lo do" is packed with symbols and imagery that contra*dict* anti-Haitianism in a language capable of reaching multiple audiences. The richness of the lyrics and video images demand a careful analysis aimed at unpacking the nuances of the five-minute performance.

Literary, intellectual, and public discourse on Haitian-Dominican relations usually looks at the two nations of Hispaniola as irreconcilable enemies. Michelle Wucker's celebrated book *Why the Cocks Fight* (2000), for instance, introduces the metaphor of the *gallera* (cockfighting pit) as a useful tool for understanding Haitian-Dominican conflict. The gallera is suggestive, particularly given that cockfights occupy such an important space in the cultural history of both Haiti and the Dominican Republic and act as symbols of their struggle.[65] However, it is a heavily problematic symbol because it perpetuates two of the most questionable ideologies about Haiti and the Dominican Republic: that Dominicans and Haitians hate each other and that they are fighting for control over the territory. [66]

Overemphasized and repeated in official Dominican history, nineteenth-century Haitian interventions in the east have been reiterated as justification for the harsh border policies and immigration laws of the twentieth and twenty-first centuries. Hernández's music video acknowledges the history of Haitian "invasions" on Dominican soil, allegorized in the Haitian soldier, while presenting us with the counterpoint image of the Dominican peasant-soldier. A powerful and traumatic symbol, the Dominican peasant-soldier carrying a machete alludes to the Massacre of 1937, when the killers were said to have used machetes in order to simulate a conflict among locals, hiding the fact that the killings were orchestrated by the state.[67] But Hernández's intervention acknowledges these traumatic moments of Haitian-Dominican conflicts in order to let them go rather than to dwell on the fear they often evoke. The video seems to suggest that while both states—symbolized in the soldiers—have sponsored death and pain, when stripped of their uniforms and flags, the peoples of both countries simply love each other.

Caribbean scholar M. Jacqui Alexander proposes memory as an "antidote to alienation, separation, and the amnesia that domination produces."[68] Hernández's video performance recalls the painful historical moments that have marked the narrative of Haitian-Dominican relations, while seeming to pose the questions: "But where are we now? And more importantly, where do we go from here?" Hernández's answers to these interrogations, I argue, materialize in the contra*dicting* narratives that the song and video offer. These narratives of contra*diction* fill in the gaps perpetuated by the dominant scholarship on Haitian-Dominican relations, while also shattering the long silences sustained by the Hispanophile hegemony of the Archive of Dominicanidad. In so doing, the memories created in "Da pa lo do," as Alexander would suggest, have the potential to be become an antidote to the coloniality of power that engendered and sustained anti-Haitianism for over a century.

The first and most significant contra*diction* to the hegemonic version of dominicanidad "Da pa lo do" presents us with is the metaphor of the Dominican Republic as an orphaned child. Nineteenth-century Dominican intellectuals, battling with their desire for sovereignty and their yearning to maintain a link to "Mother Spain," lamented the loss of Hispanic cultural values, blaming the challenges of their republican enterprise on that loss.[69] Hernández rescues the metaphor of orphanage that nineteenth-century lettered men repeated, but rather than apply it only to Dominicans, she recasts both siblings as colonial "orphans."

Without a mother, the two sibling-nations must depend only on the care of an abusive and brutish father: "Habían dos hermanitos compartiendo un pedacito porque eran muy pobrecitos y no tenían ni mamá" (There were two little brothers sharing a little piece because they were so poor, and they didn't even have a mother).[70] By making both brother-nations orphans, Hernández deconstructs the foundational myth of the Dominican Republic that persisted in casting Haiti as a colonizer-invader, replacing it with a memory of the shared colonial history of the two nations:

Siéntelo
el abrazo del mismo abuelo
Desde Juana Méndez hasta Maimón
Y desde ahí a Dajabón[71]

[Feel it
the embrace of the same grandfather
From Juana Méndez to Maimón
And from there to Dajabón

In so doing, the artist asserts that Haiti is not the enemy of the nation, and that perhaps the problems these nations face were caused by another (foreign) force and not by each other. In this whole-island imaginary, the rivalry between Haiti and the Dominican is equal to a dispute between two loving siblings: "y cuando los dos niños se metían a la mordía el papá le decía la verdá" (and when the two children would get into it, the father would tell the truth).[72] As such, the song suggests, the dispute should end as children's fights often do: in a loving embrace.

With the mother (Spain) gone, the law of the father, who symbolizes the United States, ruled over the two brother-countries. But the father (US) was too busy making money and had no time to deal with the two boys' constant quarreling: "Su pai se la bucaba trepao en una patana repartiendo plátano y patá y trompá" (Their father worked as a truck driver, delivering plantains, kicks, and punches).[73] When the children fought, he would order them to get along and share, unless they wanted a whipping:

Agárrense de ahí, que no hay ma ná
Pónganse a jugá o la correa voy a sacá
Uno por alante y el otro por atrá
Dio me lo mandó juntico pero utede na de ná.[74]

[Be happy with what you have, that's all there is
Go play or I'm going to get the belt
One in front and the other behind
God sent you both together, but you two do not get it.]

Facing the threat of colonial punishment, the children eventually agree to sharing, affirming "da pa lo do": there is enough for both of us. The orphans must contend with their inherited colonial violence ("pata y trompá") and the persistence of state violence that forces them to share the territory of Hispaniola.

Historicizing Dominican and Haitian encounters with the US Empire, "Da pa lo do" evokes Roosevelt's "Big Stick" policies and Wilson's paternalistic discourse, which resulted in the early twentieth-century interventions in both Haiti and the Dominican Republic.[75] Going beyond the shared colonial/imperial history, "Da pa lo do" reminds us that the US continues to be a force in deciding the fate of the two nations. Hispaniola's survival depends, as Pérez's performances also suggest, on the two nations' willingness to work together as one:

Una puerta para do comenjé
Dos números pa juga palé
Un mar de sudor pa to eto pece
alé, alé, alé.[76]

[One door for two termites
Two numbers to play the lotto
One ocean of sweat for all these fish
alé, alé, alé.]

If left unaddressed, the inherited violence, Hernández suggests, will turn destructive as the two sibling-nations will slowly, like termites, destroy the island, leaving behind only more violence and dust. Hernández's historical interpellation of Haitian-Dominican conflicts contra*dicts* the dominant discourse of difference sustaining anti-Haitianism by insisting instead on the two siblings as abandoned orphans living in poverty under the tight grip of an abusive and dominant father.

The image of Haiti and the Dominican Republic as two (contrasting) parts of a whole has been a recurring trope in Dominican Narratives of Solidarity of the twentieth century, as seen in the work of Bosch, as well as in US public and intellectual discourses of difference regarding the two nations of Hispaniola. In the aftermath of the 2010 earthquake, for instance, contrasting views of Haiti and the Dominican Republic resurged in US media. Almost every mention of Haiti in the press reiterated that it was "the poorest nation in the western hemisphere," in comparison with its "prosperous" brother/neighbor.[77] Words such as "chaos" and "dysfunction," as well as a recounting of Haiti's historical struggle for democracy, almost always accompanied the images of destruction. Through a discourse of pity, Haiti's misfortunes were racialized as results of the country's African religiosity and as signs of "barbarism" and "incivility," a view exemplified in the now-famous broadcast by televangelist Pat Robertson. Robertson opined that Haitians were suffering because "they had made a pact with the devil" and turned their backs on God.[78] A few days after Robertson's remarks, David Brooks published a column in the *New York Times* in which he explained Haiti's poverty as a by-product of "progress-resistant cultural influences . . . including the voodoo religion."[79] Both Robertson's and Brooks's interventions returned to the colonial/imperial discourse of Haiti that, as demonstrated in this book, was used to justify military interventions throughout the twentieth century.[80]

Since the birth of the republic in 1804, Haiti has occupied an important space in the US imaginary. Fear of Haiti overtook the slave-driven US nation, and thus myths were constructed and disseminated in order to propagate fear and hatred in the public sphere.[81] US intervention in the Dominican Republic has been, for lack of a better term, more discreet. Although Dominicans are incessantly aware of US influence in national politics, culture, and economy, many US citizens do not know the Dominican Republic exists outside of baseball. In the critical media and US scholarship, Dominicans are mentioned inasmuch as they offer a helpful comparison for explaining "What is wrong with Haiti?" Though in this problematic dichotomy, Dominicans are depicted as prosperous, civilized, and educated, these adjectives are only used in comparison to what is imagined to be the less prosperous, less civilized, less educated Haiti. Like the forgotten sibling in a dysfunctional family, the Dominican Republic thus exists within the US imaginary because of its relationship to Haiti, one that has been narrated as marked only by rivalry and conflict.

Hernández's song and video performance engage the most prevalent and pervasive discourses of Haitian-Dominican relations—as produced in United States as well as on the island—appealing to the urgent need for a rayano consciousness through which the inherited colonial violence ("patá y trompá") that is slowly destroying Hispaniola ("do comejé") can be contra*dicted*. The Madonna on a motoconcho seems to appeal to a rayano consciousness that extends beyond the internal borders of the island. She interrupts the memories of conflict that have dominated the public perception of the island, bringing the audience face to face with the urgency of the present. The image of the Madonna suggests the spirit, not politics, as an antidote to the traumatic memories sustained in the official narratives of the nation. Alexander, pondering the relationship between memory, trauma, and the role of African spirituality, argues that "sacred knowledge comes to be inscribed in the daily lives of women through an examination of work—spiritual work—which, like crossing, is never undertaken once and for all . . . knowledge comes to be embodied and manifest through flesh, an embodiment of the Spirit."[82] Hernández's Madonna comes to remind Dominican and Haitian peoples, allegorized in the two soldiers, that rather than being at the service of the state, their loyalty should be to the spirit, which resides in the soul of the land and the bodies of the people.

Traumatic memories are often marked on the body as the result of state impositions of the colonial order. To get rid of such trauma, the Afro-religious believe, the body must be stripped and washed of traumatic inscriptions so that that it can heal, once again becoming a canvas onto which new narratives of truth can be inscribed. In Afro-Dominican religious rituals, *despojos* (cleansings) are often practiced on people living through hardships and sorrows. The *despojado* (person being cleansed) must wear only white clothes during the ritual so that the body can successfully absorb light and goodness, ridding itself of all spiritual ailments. Hernández "transfers," to borrow from Taylor, the religious performance onto the political realm through the image of the two soldiers who, stripping their uniforms and wearing only white pants, proceed to wash in the river (see figure 4.6). The two men then receive the cleansing from the Madonna, embracing in brotherly peace.

The image of the mulata Madonna (figure 4.7) is the richest and most provocative one in the music video, yet I found it the most difficult with which to engage. Though Hernández's performances and literary works are known for their stylistic irreverence, the artist's decision to appear in what, from a US perspective, may be perceived of as "blackface" made me terribly uncomfortable at first. I decided to study the song as soon as I first heard it on the radio. Once the video launched, however, I was drawn to its symbolic richness, and in particular to Hernández's engagement of Afro-religiosity as an anticolonial praxis. Yet the performance of the mulata Madonna brought me closer to a confrontation with my own contra*dictions.*

Though I am a light-skinned Dominican like Hernández, my encounter with US racism, particularly outside the urban area in which I grew up, led me to identify as black. Still, I am aware—and often reminded—of the fact that in the Dominican Republic, my light complexion and my acquired middle class make me a racially privileged Dominican.[83] My own racial contra*dictions*, combined with my engagement in US race/ethnicity struggles, provoked a discursive dead end in my analysis (commonly known as "writer's block") when confronting the mulata Madonna. In order to escape this crisis, I began to ask myself questions about my own discomfort with the image: Why did the Madonna bother me so much? Was I examining the video within its historically specific context? How did the image of the Madonna

4.6 Two soldiers wearing white pants to receive a cleansing. Still from "Da pa lo do." Photo by Máximo del Castillo, 2011. Courtesy of Engel Leonardo.

4.7 Rita Indiana Hernández as the Mulata Madonna. Screenshot from music video "Da pa lo do" (2011). Courtesy of Engel Leonardo.

change my analysis of the song? Was I influenced by the comments and re-actions of other viewers? Asking these and other questions allowed me to confront my own contra*dictions*, an exercise that brought me closer to a new pedagogical and investigative approach: one in which the specificity of the experience being examined superseded my own ontological bias.

Partly as a reaction to the prevalence of anti-Haitian discourse in the Dominican Republic, US scholarly perception of Dominican racial iden-tity often condemns Dominicans for what is perceived as a denial of their African roots, and a resulting racial hatred toward Haitians.[84] In contrast with the demonizing view of Dominicans, race scholars in the United States often portray Haiti as a source of African identity in the Americas, a place where one can locate the roots of black authenticity. In a recent film fea-tured on PBS, for instance, African American scholar Henry Louis Gates Jr. highlights the Massacre of 1937 as a product of "Dominican black denial."[85] Applying a US racial lens, Gates sees all Dominicans as black or, rather, as what would be considered black in the "one-drop" US racial system.[86] This mode of analysis obscures the possibility for a fruitful comparative analysis of race at the same time that, as social historian Wendy Roth reminds us, it perpetuates an obsolete way of understanding what the racialization process looks like in present-day United States: "The United States no longer has economic or political incentives to enforce such classifications. Even its cen-sus has increasingly shifted toward monitoring racial self-identification over classification by enumerators or one's community, indicating that identifi-cation and physical appearance are becoming more important to American classifications than ancestry."[87]

The question of Dominican racial identity has also dominated current intellectual debates among diasporic Dominican scholars. Silvio Torres-Saillant and Ginetta Candelario, for instance, have been concerned with how migration can shape the way Dominicans view themselves racially. Over the last few years, the topic has also transcended the academic sphere, gain-ing significant visibility in the mainstream media.[88] In the summer 2007, for instance, important diasporic Dominican scholars found themselves in the middle of a major controversy after being misquoted in an article entitled "Black Denial," published in the *Miami Herald*.[89] The article, which was part of the newspaper series "Afro-Latin Americans," argued that the practice of hair-straightening, which is popular among Dominican women, was proof of the population's "historical rejection of all things black which makes the one-drop rule work backwards, so that to have one drop of white blood makes even the darkest Dominican feel like she or he is other than black."[90]

A couple of weeks after the publication of "Black Denial," another controversy emerged when a flyer with a picture of Juan Pablo Duarte—the most celebrated Dominican independence leader—with the words "Padre del Racismo" (Father of Racism) written across the page and the caption "Juan Pinga Duarte" (Juan Dick Duarte) appeared posted all over the #1 train, which goes from downtown Manhattan to Washington Heights, the largest Dominican neighborhood in the United States. The flyer was part of a publicity campaign for the upcoming release of a film about Dominican independence from Haiti. The producer, Taína Mirabal, stated that her film *Father of Racism* (2007) seeks to open eyes and make people understand that "nuestra historia ha sido escrita por las mismas personas que cometieron genocidio en contra de los indios y que esclavizaron a los africanos" (our history has been written by the same people who committed genocide against the native peoples and who enslaved the Africans).[91] The flyer, as well as the film, created a heated debate among Dominicans and Dominicanyorks in which even the descendants of Duarte stepped into the public light to defend the image of the father of the nation. Many Dominicans protested, and some even demanded that the US conduct an investigation, as they considered the flyer to be "a critical offense to the Dominican people."[92]

Dominican racial identity is rife with contra*dictions*; a fact that often dominates US scholarly and public debate about race in the DR. "Da pa lo do" engages and confronts these racial contra*dictions* with humor. The artist's irreverent gesture sanctions the so-called Dominican black denial while bringing attention to the intellectual dominance of US scholarship on the island. The video's director, Engel Leonardo, conceived the mulata Madonna as a political, rather than aesthetic, representation of dominicanidad.[93] Leonardo sought to visually contra*dict* the dominant representation of Dominicans, which, privileging whiteness, means most television programs feature European-looking actors.[94] The prevalent standards of beauty for both Dominicans and Haitians demand the Europeanization of women, a practice evidenced in the use of whitening creams, plastic surgery, and hair straightening. Likewise, Christian religious iconography depicts white deities—a white Virgin Mary, white saints, white Jesus—on an island where the majority of the population is black and mulato. In contrast, Afro-Hispaniolan religiosity is inclusive of the racial and cultural diversity of the island, including emblems that encompass all cultures, races, and heritages of Hispaniola.

Leonardo's virgin was intended as a representation of the racial majority of the population. However, read outside the intended cultural context and through a US-mediated racial lens, the video resulted in another controversy that further condemned Dominicans for what was perceived as a lack of racial consciousness.

Reading multiple reactions to the video posted on YouTube and Facebook, though paralyzing at first, also pushed me to confront my own contra*dictions* about the mulata Madonna in "Da pa lo do." A culturally specific reading of "Da pa lo do" would not cast Hernández as a performer in "blackface," as many of the commenters suggested. Instead, it points to the artist's embodiment of the mulata Madonna as an attempt to make Afro-Hispaniola religiosity an alternative way for understanding the island's cultures and histories. Arguably, Hernández was not in "blackface"—a term specific to US racial history—but in "brown skin," a counterhegemonic action in the context of Dominican national ideology and cultural dominance.

The controversial reactions to the video that inundated cyberspace shortly after its international debut raise concerns regarding how scholars, writers, and cultural producers understand and disseminate information regarding sociopolitical and historical processes and their effects on communities. A more just approach thus necessitates the constant and often difficult exercise of entering the cultural specificity of the subject as part of larger transnational intellectual dialogues. While difficult, this practice is the only fruitful way of understanding and engaging complicated topics, such as race, without falling into a "colonizing trick" in which that which we are seeking to deconstruct is reproduced in our work.[95] After pushing through my own contra*dictions*, I was able to approach the mulata Madonna within the cultural context in which she was produced, a process that in turn allowed me to unpack the various meanings she embodied, finding multiple layers of significations beyond the oversimplification of US black-white racial understanding.

The mulata Madonna is also Mambo Ezili Freda, the deity of love and discord, herself an image of contra*diction*. Ezili Freda is powerful and sensuous, emanating life and beauty, yet she can be vengeful and can be used to divide lovers. Ezili is mulata; her mixed-race ancestry represents power and wealth while also symbolizing the hybrid nature of the island after the colonial encounter. She is a native of Hispaniola and a <u>rayana</u>. In addition to her many attributes, Mambo Ezili Freda is known for her love of jewelry, a sign of her delicate femininity and upper-class status. Leonardo's version of Ezili sports a large "M" bling on a gold chain, a marker for an *other* form of Hispaniolan hybridity.

Blings, or large gold chains, are associated with *cadenuses*, Dominican migrants returning on vacation from the US who often wear large gold jewelry as a sign of success.[96] Made the scapegoat for the rise of crime, the fall of *cultura*, and the prevalence of what were perceived as "corruptive practices" (drug use, long hair, afros, rock-and-roll music, foreign fashion) on the island, Dominicanyork cadenuses became a target of Dominican and US media during the 1980s.[97] The symbolic mulata Bling Madonna bridges the various borders of Dominican alterity that dominate Hernández's literary and musical corpus—Dominicanyork, rayano, ethnic Haitian or black—an action that is further clarified in the song lyrics:

> Si esta tierra da pa' do' y hasta para diez
> Tira ahí el hoyo en un do' sale una mata de block
> Si es que ellos tan bien aquí
> Aunque tú no seas de ahí
> Tu no tiene doce tíos en otro país?[98]

> [Yes, this land is enough for two and even for ten
> Plant a seed there and soon it'll grow into a cement tree
> They are fine here
> Even though you are not from there
> Don't you have twelve uncles living in another country?]

Hernández is an accomplished writer whose work has been published and translated widely, yet she was virtually unknown in mainstream popular culture until the launch of her music album *El Juidero* in 2010. The innovative style of her music, which draws from merengue and other popular rhythms to create a new fusion, as well as the imaginative lyrics of her songs and the use of current urban Dominican slang, earned her immediate success among the youth. Contra*dicting* national rhetoric, Hernández's music— and in particular, the *cadenú-mulata* Madonna she embodies in the "Da pa lo do" video—presents a head-on critique of the structures sustaining the dominant notions of dominicanidad: Hispanic cultural values, whiteness, national frontiers, and heteronormativity.

Through the use of irreverent symbols, such as the mulata Madonna, the artist disidentified—to borrow from performance studies scholar José Esteban Muñoz—with the majoritarian discourse, while also intervening in mass media forms.[99] The Virgin Mary, in all its variations, is often offered as a sacred image of the nation, as the mother watching over a country. Instead of giving us La Vírgen de la Altagracia, the white, pure image of Dominican Christianity, Hernández presents us with a virgin in drag, as Rachel Combs puts it — one that is African, brown, Dominicanyork, irreverent, and sexual.[100] Similar to the appropriation of the Vírgen de Guadalupe by the Chicana feminist artists Combs explores, Hernández's mulata Madonna crosses a multiplicity of borders, becoming a contact zone for the marginal subjectivities of dominicanidad. Rather than a virgin mother, offering unconditional yet passive love, Hernández's virgin comes across as a *tíguera* (woman with street smarts) — a matron whose knowledge is both spiritual and immensely mundane. She understands it all, as she is both the spiritual mother and the immigrant-mother-returnee who has come back to care for her (abandoned) children.

The Dominicanyork returnee virgin is an important metaphor for the social reality of present-day Hispaniola. Migration continually forces the separation of Hispaniola families, as mothers are often obligated to leave their children behind in the care of extended family to go abroad to work caring for children of the privileged. Referred to as *los dejados* (those left behind), these children often experience feelings of abandonment and resentment. Los dejados are a recurring theme in Hernández's literary and musical work through which the artist insists on the impact of migration on those who never travel but are as affected by the process. In Hernández's novel *Papi* (2004), for instance, the main character, an eight-year-old girl, fantasizes about the return of her father from New York. Though her father's absence is compensated for by gifts from abroad, the girl's yearning for her father's presence drives her into a fantasy world to which she retreats when her father is killed in the Bronx.[101]

A rayano consciousness, as articulated through Hernández's work, demands an understanding of the triangularity of Hispaniola's borders and the tangibility of the diasporic rayano experience. Haitians migrating to the Dominican Republic must often leave their children behind to work; Dominican migrants must do the same. Meanwhile, children and loved ones left behind experience the violence of migration in different and complicated ways. Abandonment and the orphanage are both symbolic and real experiences affecting both peoples of Hispaniola. The only way to bear the pain of the reality is, as Hernández insists, through a very tangible form of solidarity and interdependency — one that requires a return to the communal way of life sharing that Marmolejos's nursing of the Haitian baby embodies. There is only, after all, one door for two termites:

> Una puerta para do' comején
> Dos números para jugar pale
> Un mar de sudor para to' esto peces
> Alé, alé, alé, alé
> Vinimos todos en el mismo bote.[102]

> [One door for two termites
> Two numbers to play the lotto
> One sea of sweat for all of these fish
> Alé, alé, alé, alé
> We all came in the same boat.

Sharing the load is the only way to survive the pain. Like Pérez's proposal for the creation of a complete structure out of two imperfect halves, Hernández's rayano consciousness proposes communal love, forgiveness, and interdependency as the only possible option for confronting the violent oppression of the state(s)—Haiti, the Dominican Republic, and the United States—that continue to separate people on Hispaniola.

Bearing in mind Torres-Saillant's invitation to think about the border as an anticipation of the future of our world and Hernández's depiction of an all-inclusive dominicanidad rayana that comprises Haitian-Dominican and the diaspora(s), let us return to the image of Sonia Marmolejos nursing the Haitian baby. In a television interview a few days after the earthquake of 2010, Marmolejos was asked why she nursed those Haitian babies.[103] Perplexed, Marmolejos stayed silent for nearly one long television minute, finally responding: "I don't understand the question."[104] Inspired by the interview, Dominican American filmmaker Freddy Vargas made *El seno de la esperanza* (Milk of Hope), a short film that debuted at various international festivals in 2013. The film contextualizes Marmolejos's actions within the borderlands' cultures, showing Bahoruco as an impoverished town that, devoid of opportunities, survives only through its commerce with Haiti. Presenting Marmolejos as a heroine and a model Dominicans should strive for, the filmmaker hints at the need for intra-island rayano solidarity. Arguably, the filmmaker locates the rayano experience, embodied in the character Sonia, as the anticipation of the future Torres-Saillant suggests, rather than as the fading memory of a lost glorious past Rueda imagined in his poetry.

Moved by Sonia's actions, Vargas, a Dominican American whose career was launched in the United States, returned to the island to make the film. In the process, the story the film narrates became intertwined with the film-maker's experiences, providing a metaphor for understanding how rayano transnational consciousness is evolving as an integral part of dominicanidad. Though the rayano community that existed in the borders prior to 1937 was indeed violently attacked and destroyed by the Trujillo dictatorship in 1937, rayano consciousness—as exemplified in Marmolejos's actions, and theorized in this chapter through the analysis of the artistic works of Rueda, Pérez, and Hernández—has survived, gaining strength through the experience of migration(s) and diasporas. The reactions of Dominicans such as Marmolejos following the earthquake allowed for an important epistemic break that inspired cultural, literary, and artistic production, in addition to a heightened sense of awareness at every level of the population. Has anti-Haitianism, xenophobia, discrimination, and intolerance ended in the Dominican Republic? Sadly, it has not. But a more inclusive, fair, and constructive dominicanidad in which the multiplicity of borders, experiences, and identities can be represented has begun to be imagined, allowing for the visualization of a dominicanidad inclusive of a multiplicity of borders, through which more than 150 years of oppression, silences, and hatred can finally be contra*dicted*.

CHAPTER 5

Writing from El Nié

Exile and the Poetics of Dominicanidad Ausente

This is her home. . . . This thin edge of barbwire.

—GLORIA ANZALDÚA, *Borderlands/La Frontera*

A few years ago during my presentation of a version of this chapter at Facultad Latinoamericana de Ciencias Sociales (FLACSO) in Santo Domingo, a young Dominican scholar asked me why it was that so many of "you people" insisted on studying race and identity in the Dominican Republic. Puzzled by his question, I asked him to please elaborate on what he meant by "you people." The scholar said, "You know, you, the *dominicano ausente* [absent Dominican] scholars. It is like you become obsessed with race and the Haitians when you go abroad, like there is nothing else that can be studied here, like there is nothing more important."[1] The comment originally made me feel terribly uncomfortable, especially considering that I did not define myself as *dominicana ausente*, a term that reminded me of Christmas music and airport posters. However, I later thought that perhaps the Dominican scholar had a point. After all, the question of Dominican racial identity has dominated the emerging field of Dominican studies in the diaspora, especially in the United States, perhaps because, as Silvio Torres-Saillant has argued, Dominicans in the United States are confronted with a binary racial system that forces them into one category, which for most of us is "black."[2] I then wondered why it bothered him so much that "we people" were talking about race.

The dynamics reproduced in the "you people" in the young scholar's question respond to a rhetoric popularized during the 1980s that proposed a view of the dominicanos ausentes as corruptors of the "national essence": criminals, drug addicts, and uneducated "powerful trash." This antimigrant rhetoric excluded those of us who did not live on the island, los dominica-

5.1 "Rabia" by Juan Pérez-Terrero, April 28, 1965. Santo Domingo, Dominican Republic. This photo was awarded a Pulitzer Prize in 1966. Courtesy of photographer Juan Pérez Terrero.

nos ausentes, or more commonly, Dominicanyorks, to protect the version of the nation that dominated the twentieth-century nationalist discourse. The young scholar's dismissal of Dominicanyorks as intrinsic to dominicanidad is an interesting contra*diction* in which the cultural capital of migrant dominicanidad is disavowed at the same time that the economic infusion, the remittances of migrants, sustains and improves the quality of life for many Dominican citizens. The economic power of Dominicans living in the United States, in addition to the increasing transnational status of the Dominican community in New York City, has allowed for a powerful and influential interpellation of these very discourses, persistently changing the cultural and political reality of the island by asserting a dominicanidad that, rather than ausente, has a strong presence through what Yolanda Martínez-San Miguel calls "another DR in the Diaspora."[3]

The term *dominicanos ausentes*, which broadly refers to Dominicans living overseas, has permeated both popular and official discourse on the island since the 1980s. Although the expression creates a distinction between "us" (Dominicans who reside on the island) and "them" (Dominicans who migrated), it is generally perceived as positive, particularly when compared to the pejorative "Dominicanyork." The term "Dominicanyork" was originally coined in the early 1970s by young Dominican men who played sports on US teams, particularly basketball. However, in the early 1980s, following a transnational media campaign that portrayed Dominicans living in the United States as drug dealers and criminals, Dominicanyork became synonymous with undesirable, lower-class, criminal, sellout, and corrupt. Lately, many diasporic artists have begun to reappropriate the term.[4]

I opt for the term *dominicanos ausentes* to refer to diasporic Dominicans for the inclusive, even if still problematic, meanings the term emits. On the one hand, *dominicanos ausentes* points to the transnational nature of Dominicans who are not living on the island yet still presumed to be part of the nation—perhaps due to the political and economic power they are able to exercise precisely because they are abroad. On the other hand, the word *ausente* serves as a metaphor for the complex position Dominican migrants occupy within both national territories that define them. They are absent—that is, excluded—from accessing full citizenship and representation in the United States as well as in the Dominican Republic. Finally, the term *dominicanos ausentes* is fruitful in a study of the ever-growing Dominican diaspora that is rapidly extending outside the Caribbean and the United States, therefore allowing for a comparative way to analyze the experiences of migration and marginality of diasporic Dominicans in the twenty-first century.[5]

Torres-Saillant defines diasporic Dominicans or dominicanos ausentes as exiles:

> Sépase que la gente normalmente no abandona su tierra de manera voluntaria. Se desgaja de su cálido terruño, sus paisajes familiares, su lengua, su cultura y sus amores compelida por la urgencia material. Emigra quien no puede quedarse. . . . Nuestra emigración es una expatriación.[6]

> [Let it be known that normally people do not abandon their homeland voluntarily. They uproot themselves from the warmth of their cradle, their familiar landscapes, their language, their culture, and their loved ones only because of material urgency. Those who emigrate do so because they cannot stay. . . . Our emigration is the same as expatriation.]

Torres-Saillant's revisionist definition of Dominican migration blurs the terms "exile," "diaspora," and "migration" while pointing to the failure of these terms to accurately capture the experiences and conditions of the subject(s) they attempt to define.

A further analysis of Torres-Saillant's enunciation necessitates a critique of the performative element of the dictions migration, exile, and expatriation as linked to questions of representation, legality, and national belonging or acceptance. That is, these terms are more than mere descriptions, for they can function as speech acts that could grant the exiled person, for instance, certain legal rights and opportunities not usually available to the immigrant. This disparity of meaning often extends from the statutory realm—as in the ability to obtain a work permit or a social security number—to the symbolic—as in cultural representations of migrants as unwanted subjects or invaders—because migration, unlike exile, is often perceived as voluntary, an act of desire and will rather than an escape from oppression and desperation. Torres-Saillant's theory of Dominican migration as exile or expatriation is the premise for this chapter. To Torres-Saillant's contribution I add that in the United States, Dominicans and their US-born descendants encounter another form of exile as they become racialized into a US minority and are thus excluded from full US citizenship, inhabiting the dual border space of marginality. Dominicans who migrate to the United States are "racexiles"; they are expunged from the Dominican nation because of their race yet they remain inadmissible in the United States for the same reason.

Paradoxically, the dual marginality occupied by racexiled Dominicans has resulted in an interstitial space of belonging that, borrowing from artist Josefina Báez, I will call El Nié: literally neither here nor there.[7] Like Anzaldúa's metaphor of the borderlands as a barbwire in the epigraph of this chapter, El Nié is an uncomfortable place that hurts and makes the subject bleed, creating an open wound of historical rejection: "una herida abierta."[8] Yet this discomfort also offers the possibility of finding a poetics of dominicanidad ausente, from which to interject both US and Dominican histories. It is in El Nié that the contradictions of dominicanidad are embraced and redefined, allowing the Dominican subject to emerge as an agent of his or her own history and identity/ies, finding hope, harmony, and even bliss within this very uncomfortable space of contradiction.

The image at the beginning of this chapter, titled "Rabia" (figure 5.1), symbolizes the complexity of Dominican racialization as linked to the ever-present role of the United States in the nation's culture, politics, and economy. Photojournalist Juan Pérez Terrero took the photo during the second US military intervention in the Dominican Republic that began

April 28, 1965. The intervention of 1965 arose four days into La Guerra de Abril, a civil revolt in response to the coup d'état that deposed the democratically elected president Juan Bosch in 1963. The military and the Catholic Church opposed Bosch's democratic reforms, which included a space for labor unions and socialist reforms in education, health care, and other services. Pérez Terrero's photo captures the *rabia* (rage) that the occupation of 1965 caused among the *combatientes* (revolutionaries) who found themselves in another David and Goliath confrontation with the strong oppressing alliance of US Empire and the Dominican elite against Dominican citizens. Frustrated and angry, the man in the photo fights back against the US soldier using nothing but his own body.

The multiple layers of inequality that the powerful Pulitzer Prize–winning photo depicts encapsulate the complexity of the US relationship with Hispaniola. The soldier, a large white man, carries a rifle—a symbol of the state(s) he represents. The combatiente, a black man, has only his body, his own fists to resist the powerful imposition. Yet, he still fights, though by looking at the marine's body position the viewer can predict the violent consequence of the combatiente's presumed transgression. The marine will strike him with his rifle. The black Dominican combatiente will bleed.

Historically rooted in the 150 years of unequal relationship between the United States and the Dominican Republic, and particularly the trauma of the US Occupation of 1965, the poetics of dominicanidad ausente breaks away from the nostalgic trope of migration narratives in order to propose a transnational critique of the relationship between power, the production of history, and the construction of (trans)national citizenship and identities. The poetics of dominicanidad ausente is rooted in rayano consciousness, the multiplicity of borders that make up dominicanidad. Exploring the various ways in which the poetics of dominicanidad ausente has emerged as a dialectic process of transnational interpellation of the Archive of Dominicanidad, this chapter analyzes Josefina Báez's performances *Dominicanish* (2000), *Comrade, Bliss Ain't Playin'* (2007), and *Levente no. Yolayorkdominicanyork* (2011), in dialogue with twentieth-century Dominican narratives of exile as exemplified in the seminal works of Juan Bosch and Pedro Vergés.

Though seen as a recent development, dominicanidad ausente has existed since the beginning of the twentieth century as an alternative to the hegemony of the Dominican state and, even if it seems like a contradiction, as a result of the imperial impositions of the United States on the Dominican Republic. Although there is a clear difference between the narratives of exile exemplified by the work of Bosch and the diasporic literature of Dominican-york writers such as Josefina Báez, this chapter traces the trajectory of both authors linked by an ancestral notion of national identity in which writing away from the national territory has allowed Dominicans to confront colonial and state violence. The major difference between the exilic and diasporic writings of *dominicanos ausentes* is the desire and/or possibility of returning—clearly expressed in Bosch's exilic literature—that are absent in the diasporic writings of El Nié, where there is no desire to return. The latter embodies an active voice that contra*dicts*, confronts, and revises the passivity that dominates the hegemonic Archive of Dominicanidad.

Writing from Exile: Toward a Poetics of Dominicanidad Ausente

Caribbean literature has traditionally played an important role in documenting significant historical moments, particularly in reference to dictatorships, colonialism, imperialism, and migration. Antillean writers have often claimed historical authority, or been granted it by subsequent generations of letrados.[9] This dynamic is complicated by the presence of authors such as José Martí who, in addition to being writers, were actors and subjects in the history of their nations. Caribbean literature has produced a rich variety of narratives in which the lines between genres are often blurred because, as Pedro San Miguel argues, fictional texts have often reconstructed the social reality in moments of censorship or strict government control, when history has served the purpose of the state.[10]

Juan Bosch is a great example of the Caribbean paradigm. A writer, thinker, and the founder of two of the three dominant political parties in the country, Bosch was one of the most influential political figures in the twentieth-century Dominican Republic. In addition to his political thought, his short stories and essays influenced Dominican letters, creating a distinctive literary style that challenged the nation and the rhetoric of oppression imposed by the various US military occupations of the twentieth century and the Trujillo regime. Yet, most of Bosch's influence in Dominican culture and politics was exercised from exile, where he spent a large part of his productive life (1938–62, 1963–78).

Knowing that Trujillo wanted to buy him off with a position in Congress, Bosch managed to leave the country in January 1938, settling in Puerto Rico. There, Adolfo Hostos—the son of Puerto Rican thinker, educator, and independence leader Eugenio María de Hostos—welcomed Bosch and gave him work.[11] A year later, Hostos asked Bosch to oversee the edition and publication of his father's complete works in Havana. It was during his time in Cuba, following the ideals of the Confederación Antillana, that Bosch's desire for social justice matured into a strong political thought.[12] He was inspired by the principles of solidarity and freedom that the elder Hostos had envisioned at the end of the nineteenth century:

> Si mi vida llegara a ser tan importante que se justificara algún día escribir sobre ella, habría que empezar diciendo: Nació en La Vega, República Dominicana el 30 de junio del 1909, y volvió a nacer en San Juan de Puerto Rico, a principios de 1938, cuando la lectura de los originales de Eugenio María de Hostos le permitió conocer qué fuerzas mueven y cómo la mueven, el alma de un hombre al servicio de los demás.[13]

> [If my life would ever become so important as to justify writing about it someday, one should begin by saying: He was born in La Vega, Dominican Republic on June 30, 1909, and was born again in San Juan, Puerto Rico, at the beginning of 1938, when the reading of the original works of Eugenio María de Hostos allowed him to learn the forces that move, and how they move, the soul of a man who is serving others.]

With the support of Enrique Cotubanamá Henríquez (Pedro Henríquez Ureña's brother), Juan Isidro Jiménez, and many other important Dominican and Latin American thinkers, Bosch took on the difficult task of organizing the very dispersed Dominican exiles into a multinational community in order to create a revolutionary party that could potentially fight the Trujillo regime and return peace and democracy to the country:

> Yo no aceptaba posponer la tarea de proceder a organizar a los dominicanos exiliados. . . . Me dediqué a pensar en la manera de solucionar el problema causado por la dispersión geográfica de los llamados a ser miembros de la fuerza política que el pueblo dominicano quería para librarse de la sanguinaria tiranía que los oprimía.[14]

> [I could not postpone the tasks of organizing the exiled Dominicans. . . . I began to think about a way to solve the issue caused by the geographical dispersion of those called to be part of the political force that the Dominican people wanted in order to liberate themselves from the bloody tyranny that oppressed them.]

This is how the Dominican Revolutionary Party (Partido Revolucionario Dominicano, PRD) was created in 1942.[15] Traveling to the various countries where Dominicans had gone during the Trujillo regime—Cuba, Puerto Rico, the United States, and Venezuela—Bosch was able to form small sections of *perredeísta* supporters under the leadership of local juntas, a method that would later become the basis for the Dominican party system. New York and Havana became the two most important enclaves of dissidence for Dominicans, while the technology of writing—the use of writing as a mobilizing machine—functioned as the medium for the creation of this transnational community and for the drafting of a unique narrative of social justice.

Upon his arrival in Puerto Rico in 1938, Bosch realized that he was known as a writer because some of his short stories had been circulating in literary magazines. Through Bosch's literary works, many readers—including important writers and thinkers—befriended Bosch, imagining, to borrow from Benedict Anderson, a new form of nation.[16] Bosch wrote:

> Cuando llegamos a Puerto Rico tenía solo 90 dólares pero encontré que allí me conocían; por lo menos me conocían en los círculos literarios y a los pocos días tenía amigos que hicieron todo por ayudarme, antes del mes estaba trabajando en la trascripción de todo, casi todo lo que había escrito Hostos, y puedo afirmar que Hostos fue para mí una revelación, algo así como si hubiera vuelto a nacer. Es curioso que un maestro pueda seguir siendo maestro 33 o 34 años después de muerto, pero en el caso mío, Hostos hizo su obra de formador de conciencia un tercio de siglo después de su muerte.[17]

> [When we arrived in Puerto Rico I had only $90, but I found out that they knew me there, at least within the literary circles, and so within a few days I had friends that did everything to help me out. Within a month I was working on the transcription of everything, or at least almost everything, that Hostos had written, and I can say that Hostos was a revelation to me, something like a rebirth. It is interesting that a teacher can continue teaching thirty-three or thirty-four years after his death, but in my case Hostos completed his work as conscious builder a third of a century after his death.]

Much like the ideological closeness that Bosch developed with Hostos while working on the edition of his works, many Caribbean literary circles had also embraced Bosch and his ideals. He soon found himself part of a much larger community and greater social project. The writer had left his homeland in search of the freedom to write because he recognized that "lo que primero tuve no fue conciencia de lo que quería decir, sino la angustia de no poder decir lo que debía decir" (the first thing I had was not awareness of what I wanted to say, but the agony of not being able to say what I should say), and while in exile, this search became the basis for Bosch's narrative and the backbone of his revolutionary project.[18] With the anxiety of censorship gone, Bosch was able to reconcile his memories of the Dominican Republic with his desire for a democratic future. While many of his stories were inspired by his life in La Vega as a young man, it was not until he was in Cuba, during long and multiple periods of exile, that he externalized these experiences into a coherent narrative of social justice that was later linked to the democratic rhetoric of his political party.

When examining Bosch's life, most scholars concentrate on either his political work or his creative writing. But Bosch's literature and politics, as he saw them, were two complementary passions that could not be separated from one another. Despite the fact that it was through his participation in Dominican politics that Bosch was known among all segments of the population, it is important to remember that writing was Bosch's first political act, as he himself expressed in an interview in 1965 with journalist Mateo Morrison:

> Yo empecé a escribir porque había que decir cosas del pueblo dominicano. No sabía bien qué cosas eran, eso no lo podía determinar aún. . . . Por eso los proyectos literarios como tal no me interesaban. . . . Para mí la literatura por definición debía servir un propósito social."[19]

> [I began to write because there were things that needed to be said about the Dominican people. I was unsure as to what those things were. That, I could not figure out just yet. . . . This is why literary projects per se did not interest me. . . . To me, literature had to serve a social purpose.]

Bosch was unwilling to accept literature—and other forms of art—that did not reflect the social reality of his nation, a fact that marked his political path. One of Bosch's most articulate examples of his socially committed narrative written in exile can be located in his collection of short stories *Cuentos escritos en el exilio* (1962). The title of this collection alludes to the geographical distance of the writer at the moment of conceiving each of these stories, as well as to a sense of legitimacy through the forced displacement of the narrator from his homeland. It is important to note, however, that most of the stories that appear in this collection had already been published as individual texts or as shorter compilations under different titles. The decision to employ the word "exile" in the title demonstrates Bosch's awareness of the significance of his condition as dominicano ausente. That is, Bosch was aware that his story of forced migration would allow him to establish his political persona as a patriotic leader who, despite being abroad for many years, was very much part of the nation. In addition, Bosch's exiled persona functions as a performative contra*diction* that led the author to exile.[20]

In exile, Bosch was able to maintain an impressive closeness to the history and to the present political situation of the Dominican Republic, a task he admitted was difficult yet rewarding: "Los efectos del exilio en un escritor pueden ser muy malos; desarraigan al escritor. Lo que ocurre es que yo no me desarraigué. . . . Es decir, iba viviendo, minuto a minuto, la vida de la República Dominicana" (The effects of exile can be devastating for a writer; they can uproot him. But what happens is that I do not become uprooted. . . . That is, I continue to live, minute to minute, the life of the Dominican Republic).[21] Arguably, Bosch's rooted consciousness constitutes one of the most significant traits of the exile experience because, as Torres-Saillant insists, those who leave never forget.[22] The very condition of physical absence has allowed diasporic Dominicans a consciousness evident in the prominence of historical novels within the Dominican American literary corpus.[23]

Without attempting to, Bosch was able to draft the blueprints for the poetics of dominicanidad ausente, which, as he eloquently describes during his interview with Morrison, was largely present in the construction of the modern Dominican nation. Thus, during his long and multiple exiles, Bosch became the first thinker to articulate and promote a dominicanidad that could extend outside the geographical borders of the nation. He did this by believing in the likelihood of a community alliance of Dominicans living abroad with those who resided on the island, and by insisting on the possibility of staying rooted in the nation while being physically forced out by the regime.

Bosch's absence from the national territory is presumed, in the titles of his books, as a necessity, an involuntary and temporary circumstance caused by the persecution of a dictatorial regime. However, as Torres-Saillant argues, all diasporic Dominicans are living in exile because they have been forced out of their nation by hunger and desperation.[24] Following Torres-Saillant's argument, we should read Bosch's discourse of exile as the earliest beginnings of the poetics of dominicanidad ausente that eventually made contemporary works such as Junot Díaz's novel *The Brief Wondrous Life of Oscar Wao* (2007) worthy of a Pulitzer Prize.

Singing *Rabia*: Bolero and Post-Trujillo *Desamor*

On April 28, 1965, the US military landed in Santo Domingo with the excuse of protecting American investment in the island during the civil war that had begun a few days earlier. The purpose of the war was to restore the democratically elected president, Juan Bosch, who was then in exile.[25] A little over two years prior to the intervention, an overwhelming majority had elected Bosch president of the republic, only for a military coup headed by Colonel Elías Wessin y Wessin to overthrow it seven months later on September 25, 1963. A triumvirate was established shortly after, but dissidence and the desire for democracy produced a series of social upheavals that ultimately gained the support of the liberal faction of the military that favored a return to the Constitution and the elected president, Juan Bosch. After three days of battle, however, the United States invaded the island and sided with the coup leaders, preventing Juan Bosch from occupying the presidential position that he had earned during the elections of 1962. The presence of the marines led to frustration among Dominican rebels, who found themselves with nothing but their fists and anger to fight a giant and powerful force. The Pulitzer Prize–winning photograph by Juan Pérez Terrero that opens this chapter accurately exemplifies the impotence felt by the people as the efforts of 1965 were crushed by the giant fist of the US intervention forces, ultimately destroying the democratic dreams embodied in the figure of Juan Bosch.

Demoralized by their loss and with the country in the hands of the right-wing Trujillistas once again, many Dominicans began to look at migration as their only alternative to repression and hunger. Soon it became clear the ideals of freedom and democracy Bosch embodied would never materialize in his country as long as the United States continued to intervene in the matters of the nation: "Creo que en la República Dominicana Latinoamérica ha recibido una lección . . . que no es posible establecer democracia con la ayuda de Estados Unidos, y que tampoco es posible establecer democracia contra los Estados Unidos" (I believe that with the Dominican Republic, Latin America has learned a lesson . . . that it is not possible to establish democracy with the help of the United States, nor is it possible to establish democracy against the United States).[26]

The intervention and ultimate trauma of 1965 led Bosch to a different type of exile than his first one in 1938: he stopped writing, became disillusioned, lost faith in his party, and ultimately became much more radical in his political views. Never again would he be president of his country. Ironically, for many of his followers, this disillusion marked the beginning of a massive migration to the United States, which has continued to today, as well as the emergence of prominent diasporic Dominican literary production.

The unequal relationship between these two nations, and in particular the role of the United States in Dominican politics after the assassination of Trujillo, opened many doors through which Dominicans could emigrate. During the Trujillo dictatorship, it was extremely difficult to travel outside of the country. Passports were virtually unaffordable to anyone but the rich, and government control made travel difficult. In 1950, the Dominican community in New York numbered about thirty-nine thousand. By 1965, this number had quadrupled, as the first demands of Dominicans after the assassination of Trujillo were the right to travel, the opening of the borders, and access to passports and US visas. Historian Jesse Hoffnung-Garskof argues that due to public pressure the United States granted Dominicans ten thousand resident visas per year through the 1960s, in addition to thirty to forty thousand tourist, transit, and student visas.[27] Dominicans left the island en masse in search of opportunities and a better life after the regime or to escape persecution in an uncertain political climate. For many, the United States, particularly New York, represented the only possible way to better their lives amidst the economic and political climate of the Dominican Republic in the 1960s.

Pedro Vergés, in his novel *Sólo cenizas hallarás (bolero)* (1980), depicts the brief historical moment (1961–62) following the death of Trujillo and before the first democratic elections won by Bosch in which migration to the United States became a possibility. Using a premonitory tone, the author unpacks the complexity of the moment as Dominicans, particularly the young, feared the failure of a democratic government and looked to emigration as their only possible path to freedom and citizenship. Despite the hopes embodied in Juan Bosch after the death of the dictator, the characters in Vergés's novel appear as characters in a bolero searching for love but finding nothing but disillusion in the pre-1965 revolution political climate.[28]

The title of the novel proposes bolero as an allegory of post-Trujillo dominicanidad. A ballad-like romantic style born in Cuba and popularized in Mexico at the beginning of the 1920s, boleros usually tell a story of love or disillusion (*desamor*) from the heterosexual male perspective. In his important historical analysis of bolero as a transnational cosmopolitan genre, Alejandro Madrid argues that in early twentieth-century Mexico, boleros encapsulated a form of worldly desire that opposed the regionalism and autochthonous rhetoric other genres, such as *son*, symbolized.[29] In the post-Trujillo Dominican Republic, one of the first priorities of the emerging urban class was to be connected to the world through travel, economic enterprise, and access to cultural products previously banned by the regime (music, film, books). Bolero, a transnational product of the Spanish-speaking free world, offered a cosmopolitan alternative to merengue, which Trujillo had co-opted throughout his regime. As Paul Austerlitz and Deborah Pacini Hernández have argued, merengue became a tool for Trujillo's totalizing nationalization project. The dictator owned merengue orchestras and promoted the genre as a "high-class" national dance. In the wake of his assassination, radio and television opened up to foreign music and film industries—particularly to the Spanish-language production of Mexico's media giant Televisa. Bolero, a genre older Dominicans were familiar with, experienced a new boom in the postdictatorship Dominican Republic, particularly among the lower-middle-class and poor city dwellers who began to participate, for the first time, in the consumption of international media.

Lucila, one of the main characters in the novel, is the first to introduce the readers to this romantic and seductive bolero of post-Trujillo dominicanidad. A representative of the farming class, which found itself free to move to the city in search of the new "progress" that promised to emerge in the post-Trujillo nation, Lucila secures a job as a maid in the home of some powerful Unión Cívica Nacional (UCN; National Civic Union) allies.[30] The novel recounts:

> Ella vivía feliz en el patio, haciendo la comida, planchando la ropa, lavando y escuchando el radito de pilas que ponía unos boleros chéveres de Vicentico, de Daniel y de Lucho. . . . En eso demostraban las doñas que buenas que eran, en cuanto ella llegó le dijeron toma este radito para que te entretengas y se lo pusieron encima de la mesa.[31]

> [She lived happily on the patio, making the food, ironing the clothes, washing, and listening to the little battery-powered radio that played some great boleros by Vicentico, by Daniel, and by Lucho. . . . In this way the ladies of the house showed how gracious they were; as soon as she arrived they told her, "take this little radio to entertain yourself," and they put it on the table.]

The ladies of the house—the emerging Dominican bourgeoisie—give Lucila (the peasant) a radio to entertain her with bolero. Lucila is quickly seduced by the political rhetoric of progress and is swept up in the arms of the UCN: "Que gane la UCN, y ya se veía en el futuro la señorita Lucila, encargada de tal o cual, con un sueldito chévere" (Should the UCN win, she could already see her future as Miss Lucila, in charge of this or that with a pretty nice salary).[32] Though Lucila is very interested in national politics, she sees it as a quick way to attain social mobility and escape the stagnation in which her family had been forced to live during the Trujillo regime. The bolero Lucila hears is not about the creation of a collective, freer country, but rather about the new possibilities for economic progress in the booming capital city. Yet, like a bolero of desamor, hers ends up being a disappointment as Lucila finds herself back in the *campo* (countryside), poor, pregnant, and disillusioned. There, she begins to hear another bolero that would take her far away to New York, where she could finally have a better life.

The bolero in *Sólo cenizas* facilitates a symbolic engagement with what the author, using the allegorical and passive voice that characterizes nationalist literature of the twentieth century, calls the "forces of history"—that is, the violence that the union of the Dominican state and the US corporate interest perpetrate against the Dominican citizenry.[33] The forces of history, as it were, would make it impossible for the Dominican Republic to become a democratic state, as the majority of the people were prevented from gaining political representation, economic mobility, and equality. Yet, like a bolero, the political rhetoric of the emerging parties would seek to seduce and entice the citizenry with the promise of progress, freedom, and cosmopolitanism in order to exploit them. Many, like Lucila, continue to participate in the political process, amidst the violence and corruption that continuously benefits the almighty alliance of US corporate interests and the Dominican Hispanophile elite.

Vergés's allegorical bolero tells the dysfunctional fiction of post-Trujillo dominicanidad through which the romantic story sustaining the myth of national unity turned sour, leaving visible a generalized disillusion and desamor with the national project. Trujillo's nationalism, as I have argued thus far, sustained the Hispanophile hegemony of dominicanidad—a process Doris Sommer linked to the nation's "foundational fictions" of love and desire.[34] In the post-Trujillo Dominican Republic, this fiction crumbled, turning into *cenizas* (ashes) as Dominicans faced the impossibility of democracy and progress in a country dominated by the "forces of history." In such a climate of desamor and dysfunction, migration—whether to the cities or to New York—became, for the majority of the population, the only possibility for economic mobility and political enfranchisement.

In *Footsteps in the Dark: The Hidden Histories of Popular Music,* George Lipsitz calls for "reading popular music as history and interpreting history through popular music."[35] As Lipsitz proposes, music, particularly trans-national popular music, can often encapsulate political desire, particularly as linked to ethnically oppressed or marginalized groups. Though Wello Rivas's international hit "Cenizas" (1952) is a song about falling out of love (desamor), in the climate of the postdictatorial Dominican Republic, it also summons the past and present violence that the Dominican state has imposed on its citizens: "Después de tanto soportar la pena de sentir tu olvido" (After putting up with the sorrow of knowing you have forgotten me).[36] It also calls to mind the detrimental consequences of violence on the national psyche as people lose faith in the state: "Solo cenizas hallarás de todo lo que fue mi amor" (You will find nothing but ashes of everything that was once my love).[37] Reading the song beyond its literal meaning, as Lipsitz urges us to do, and in parallel to the historical and the rhetorical archive that Vergés's characters embody, "Cenizas" becomes emblematic of the political desamor period that emerged after the fall the Trujillo Regime and just before the revolt and intervention of 1965. This process is best understood through the main character of the novel, Freddy Nogueras.

Freddy struggles with his dreams of progress and the uncertainty that emerged after the death of Trujillo and before the elections of 1962. An idealist and a dissident during the last years of the regime, Freddy loses all hope in the democratic project after realizing that his beloved father had not been assassinated by the regime as he had believed, but rather was killed in a drunken fight. This ideological parricide leaves a huge void in Freddy's life. In the end, the uncertain political climate and the evidence of continuous corruption make Freddy decide to migrate to New York in hopes of finding a new way to imagine his national identity:

> Yo creo que me fuera de todas formas, con muertos o sin muertos. Yo creo que uno no entiende este país hasta que no se aleja de él. . . . Lo malo, contestó Wilson, es que después lo comprende tan bien que ya no hay quien te haga regresar.[38]

> [I think I would leave no matter what, with or without all these deaths. I think you just do not understand this country until you are far away

from it. . . . The thing is, Wilson said, once you leave you understand it so well that no one can make you return.]

Freddy's awareness of the "forces of history" leads him to predict that Bosch will not last long in power, that democracy will not succeed, and that he will never be able to simply exist within the oppressive walls of the nation:

> En los últimos días, en efecto, Freddy había tenido en todo momento la sensación de que . . . la Historia, los demás, lo que estaba más allá de sí mismo—acabaría agarrándolo por los pelos y arrastrándolo por toda la ciudad con los ojos abiertos y asombrados. . . . [S]abía de sobra que nunca sería hoy, que jamás surgiría semejante oportunidad y que los que eran como él no tenían más remedio que largarse o joderse o pegarse un plomazo en la cabeza.[39]

> [Recently, in effect, Freddy had constantly felt the sensation that . . . History, others, those forces larger than himself, would end up grabbing him by the hair and dragging him throughout the whole city with his eyes open and amazed. . . . [H]e knew all too well that neither today nor ever would there arise a similar opportunity, and that those who were like him had no recourse other than to leave or fucking put up with it or put a bullet through their heads.]

In the midst of his exasperation, Freddy finds comfort in the possibility of exile from which he hopes to return, eventually, with a deeper understanding of his own country. But the reader imagines that it will be many years before Freddy can return and, as predicted by his friends, he will never be able to stay. Like Bosch in 1938, Freddy recognized that he could not do any more from within the nation; he becomes aware of the possibility of being Dominican from outside. However, unlike Bosch, Freddy's absence ends up being marked by the "forces of history" that eventually turn him into a Dominicanyork, an unwanted subject in official late twentieth-century Dominican narration.

The lives of these two characters—the fictional Freddy and the historical Bosch—intersect in Vergés's text through a disillusionment narrative that ultimately separates both men from their homeland and their political dreams. As predicted by Freddy, the same historical forces that attacked him end up destroying Bosch's possibility of governing the nation, sending the writer and revolutionary back into exile and condemning the country to what seems like an eternal crisis of democratic values. Vergés's novel ends with exile as an alternative to the failures of Dominican democracy. Absent from the island himself, Vergés could not imagine the possibility of writing beyond the experience of departure, even if that departure was necessary for the survival of Dominican historical understanding. Thus, Freddy must leave. Yet Freddy's emigration is seen as conflictive and almost tragic, as he will forever lose the possibility of returning and with it, his sense of home.

Vergés, writing from Spain and undoubtedly watching migratory phenomenon develop, attempted to articulate "the impossibility of a return" that he assumed those who left, whether by force or will, must have felt. Earlier, writing in the 1940s from exile, Juan Bosch's articulation of dominicanidad ausente highlighted the importance of staying rooted even when "return" seemed impossible. Bosch could not have imagined that in a few decades 10 percent of the Dominican population would emigrate, and that many of those who remained on the island would put their hopes and dreams in the future possibility of emigration or in the hands of those who left. Neither Bosch nor Vergés could have dreamt of the emergence of a dominicanidad without return, or that Dominicans in New York would come to imagine themselves as both Dominican nationals and New York natives, deconstructing the idea of the nation that twentieth-century intellectuals had sought to solidify. Interestingly, New York had become, as Martínez-San Miguel argues, "the other Caribbean."[40] It was a place where the Latin American and Caribbean solidarity imagined by Bosch, Bolívar, Martí, and Hostos would finally materialize, albeit in a space of marginality and disavowal. The final part of this chapter turns to the narratives of dominicanidad ausente that, emerging out of the margins of US histories and the silences reproduced in the Archive of Dominicanidad, I argue offer an alternative dominicanidad; one belonging to racexiled others.

Dominicanidad Ausente-Presente: Migration and Race in El Nié

The stage is dark. A trumpet plays a slow melody while a timid orange color lights the back of the stage. The sun has risen. A woman enters the stage, her hands placed together above her head, body contorting so as to re-create slow waves (see figure 5.2). She is a boat crossing the ocean at sunrise. She has arrived. The dominicana ausente is born. In the opening scene of her performance piece *Dominicanish* (1999), Josefina Báez re-creates the arrival scene of the soon-to-be immigrant.[41] Like many other immigrants, the main

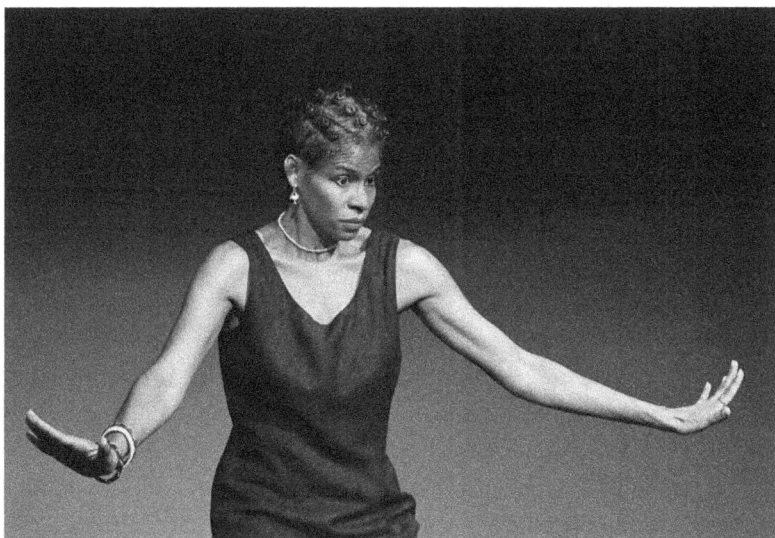

5.2 Josefina Báez performing *Dominicanish* at Ay Ombe Theatre in New York, 2007.
Courtesy of photographer Jorge Vismara and performer Josefina Báez.

character, Josefina, arrives in New York with a suitcase full of hope and the
determination to attain the "American Dream." But unlike in fairy tales, the
"American Dream" does not come true.[42] Instead, a series of dislocations
and disruptions are presented throughout the forty-five-minute one-woman
performance, as Báez re-creates the Dominican racexile migrant's difficult
encounter with the binary US racial system, the English language, and the
city of New York.

Upon her arrival in the United States, the character Josefina, like many
other Dominicans, was forced to confront questions of political and cultural belonging and to choose ethnic alliances in order to survive on the
streets of New York: "Hablo con el pájaro del barrio. Craqueo chicle como
Shameka Brown. Hablo como Boricua y me peino como Morena" (I talk
with the neighborhood fag. I crack gum like Shameka Brown. I speak like
a Puerto Rican, and I do my hair like an African American girl).[43] Defying
the norm, Josefina embodies the multiplicity of the New York City underground while searching for a place of belonging. But as sociologist Ginetta
Candelario demonstrates, these alliances require one to navigate a palimpsest of contra*dictions* that are intersected by a long history of colonialism and
oppression.[44] Moreover, the liberal political thought of the United States in

the mid-twentieth century advocated for immigrants' assimilation. This process required that the subject deny the very historical processes that formed his or her particular experience in order to become part of the American Nation. For Dominicans such as Josefina, this process posed a contradic-*tion,* as it required US Dominicans in exile to forget the previous years of US-Dominican relations that have in great part provoked their immigration.[45] But the very logic of US citizenship also marked Dominicans by their national origin, class, culture and, most important, race. Therefore, they are never able to fully participate as citizens of the United States, no matter how much history some manage to forget.

Dominican mass migration to the United States coincided with the 1965 Immigration Act, which is often cited as the single most important event shaping US immigration history in the second half of the twentieth century. The Immigration Act ended visa quotas, allowing a new and diverse flow of immigrants to the United States. However, the Dominican exodus happened in spite of, rather than as a result of, the legendary act. Prior to 1965, there were no established visa quotas for Latin Americans traveling to the United States. This lack of limitation allowed for a tremendous growth in the US population of Latin Americans, particularly those originating from Mexico. In addition, the Jones Act of 1917, which granted US citizenship to Puerto Ricans, facilitated their travel to and resettlement on the mainland.[46] As a result of these events, as well as a series of postcolonial encounters between the United States and Latin America, by the time Dominicans began to migrate en masse to New York City in the 1960s, there was already a large Hispanic presence in the nation, which was reflected in the workforce as well as the popular culture and politics of the time.

Latin American presence in the United States also resulted in a strong anti-immigrant sentiment, particularly after the Great Depression in the 1930s and in the Cold War climate of the 1950s. In California, for example, the Zoot Suit Riots herded many young Mexican Americans to prison during World War II, after tensions rose between stationed marines and young Mexican Americans who were portrayed as "unpatriotic" or "foreign" by the dominant nationalist discourse disseminated in the media.[47] In 1954, "Operation Wetback" sent over eighty thousand ethnic Mexicans to Mexico, about half of whom were US citizens. In 1964, the Bracero Program, which sanctioned the hiring of seasonal workers from Mexico, was terminated due to pressure from the conservative Right and union labor advocates. Although these events appeared to be measures to control immigration, particularly Mexican immigration to the United States, they actually allowed for a much larger flow of illegal immigration and for the racialization of Mexican and other US Latino/as as "illegal immigrants" or foreign—that is, as unwelcome subjects.

Literary scholar Lisa Lowe reminds us that the modern nation-state forms "abstract citizens ... disavowing the racialization and gendering of noncitizen labor in the economic sphere through the reproduction of an exclusive notion of national culture."[48] Immigration policies enforced in the second half of the twentieth century, in addition to "protecting" the borders of the nation, also contributed to the construction of Latina/os as foreigners, strangers, exotic, and objects of fear, a dynamic that anthropologist Arlene Dávila warns us is still very much in place today.[49] On the east coast of the United States, the dynamics of Puerto Rican migration complicated this Latina/o racialization process by introducing questions of citizenship, national belonging, and coloniality to political thought. As a result, and in the context of the Civil Rights Movement and a widespread climate of social dissidence, the 1960s became an important decade for the creation of a Chicano-Nuyorican-Latino cultural citizenship that interjected itself into the national consciousness through cultural, political, and social representation.

When, in heavily accented English, the character Josefina states: "Black is Beautiful," Báez confronts this complexity of racialization and dual invisibility Dominicans face while bringing attention to the contra*dictions* of race that have dominated both cultural and academic dialogues on US Dominican identities.[50] This short line in the performance brings attention to the significance of racial politics in the United States of the 1970s and to the binary racial system encountered by the newly arrived Dominicans who become labeled in two significant ways: as foreigners (with accents) and as blacks. Being black and being Dominican appear, at the moment of Josefina's arrival to the United States, as contra*dictions*.

Despite the fact that the majority of Dominicans are mulatos (of African and Spanish descent), the Dominican nation, as we have seen throughout the book, has been historically constructed as a mythic mestizaje of white and Indian blood, with some minor African influence.[51] The Dominican racial vocabulary uses terms such as *indio* or *moreno* (Indian or brown) to describe blackness, reserving the latter term for the enemy of the nation: the Haitian immigrant. Let us remember that in its formation, the Dominican Republic was conceived as a hybrid nation where there could only be one race: the Dominican race. This construction privileged Hispanic language, history, and culture and claimed the long-lost Taíno indigenous heritage. In this context, to claim one's Dominican and black identities represents a contra*diction* to the Archive of Dominicanidad.

Silvio Torres-Saillant and Ramona Hernández consider Báez's performance an act of confrontation against the violence of Dominican hegemonic ideologies: "A black woman whose ancestral line links her directly to the African-descended sugarcane workers of the bateyes of La Romana, Báez draws on the mental transformation set in motion by migration to peruse many of the social, political, and cultural myths of the Dominican Republic. The linguistic, racial, religious, and ethnic diversity of New York fuels the discourse of her performance texts, which ingeniously indict the negrophobia, conservatism, misogyny, homophobia, Eurocentricism, and upper-class bias that characterize the official Dominican discourse of Catholic Church leaders, mainstream politicians, and state-funded intellectuals in the sending society."[52] Thus, Báez's work becomes an active narrative of contra*diction* that challenges the passivity and violence that perpetually silenced black histories from the Archive of Dominicanidad while creating an active diction, a new language from which the experiences of the human being who confronts oppression can be narrated.

Báez's *Dominicanish* illuminates the complex experience of Dominican blackness in a diasporic context. I call this "translating blackness," referring to the experience of the Dominican migrant who navigates between various systems of racial identification, disidentification, and oppression. For Báez, race—or more specifically, Dominican blackness—is always a transnational, transitory, and translingual experience.[53] Upon her arrival, Josefina found herself confronted with these seemingly mutually exclusive identities: "Higher education took me to places of pain and pleasure. History in black and white."[54] Amidst this contra*diction*, Josefina opted to embrace her blackness while maintaining dominicanidad. This "double consciousness" was produced mainly by an encounter with African American culture and black political movements.[55] It constituted, at first, a strategic alliance for surviving in the new host nation and confronting the binary black-white history now imposed on her: "In that cover I found my teachers . . . The Isley Brothers. Distinguished teachers: Pearl Bailey, Earth Fantasy, Wind September . . . and the dearest of all, Ms. Billie Holiday."[56] Báez's pedagogical soundtrack in *Dominicanish* summons an *other* history of political struggle because, as Lipsitz remind us in *Footsteps in the Dark*, music, particularly soul and jazz, often contains a political message and a "hidden history" of mourning and renewal.[57] Báez's teachers brought her closer to an understanding of what Vergés called the "forces of history." Further, it gave her a language to confront the colonial legacy of white supremacy that silenced her racexiled body from the historical archives of her home and host nations.

The complexity of Dominican racialization is precisely linked to the fact that "black," as an ethnically differentiated segment of the population, does not exist in the Dominican imagination.[58] What does exist is a series of social injustices and inequalities that are in large part the result of the economic exploitation of the majority of the population, which is black and mulato, by the international corporations and the local government. Or as Torres-Saillant explains: "To measure the living conditions of Dominican blacks and mulattos would mean no more than to assess the social status of the masses of the people, which would correspond more fittingly to an analysis of class inequalities and the social injustices bred by dependent capitalism than to a discussion of ethnic oppression."[59] In what is now a famous quote, historian Frank Moya Pons argued that in the United States, Dominicans "realize they are black."[60] Critiquing that provocative idea, Torres-Saillant argues that Dominicans in the United States are confronted with new forms of racism and are therefore forced to make ethnic alliances with other racialized minorities.[61] Though I find Moya Pons's analysis simplistic, I concede that in the diaspora Dominicans are indeed confronted with a different type of discrimination from the one they faced at home. In the United States, it is not just class, but also skin tone, hair texture, accent, education, level of cultural assimilation, and ability to participate in the purchase of cultural commodities that define one's race. Thus, in the diaspora, confronted with a US racialization that is very much linked to the open wound of slavery and Jim Crow as foundational experiences of the American Nation, diasporic Dominicans find that blackness provides a language for confronting their new place in the host nation while interpellating historical oppression back home. It is not that Dominicans "find out they are black" when they migrate to the United States, as Moya Pons suggested, but rather that in the United States Dominicans find a political language from which to articulate their own experience of racialization, oppression, disenfranchisement, and silencing—a process that allows them to build alliances with other oppressed communities around the world.

In the United States, and through her new soul "teachers," the character Josefina finds a diction from which to translate her oppression and racialization to a larger transnational community. Her teachers thus became an important part of Josefina's new life as a black Dominicanyork: "Discos del alma con afro. Con afro black is beautiful. [Soul records with an afro. With an afro, black is beautiful.] Black is a color. Black is my color. . . . Repeat after them, my teachers the Isley Brothers."[62] The speech act, "Black is a color, black is my color," challenges Dominican and US monolithic ideas of race and ethnicity by proposing the possibility of converging multiple and seemingly contradictory identities in relation to national and transnational identifications. Thus, Báez's performance of translating blackness resignifies dominicanidad, problematizing the national narratives that dominated Dominican thought throughout the twentieth century. This dynamic is in large part possible due to the hybridity of New York City as a space of palimpsestic interactions and transethnic encounters.

Underground City: Dominicanyorks and the Creation of El Nié

Para conocer el país dominicano en sus bordes más intensos hay que tirar una hoja a la izquierda y advertir el otro corazón de la creatividad local. Estaremos frente a Nueva York. Si buscamos un nombre que sintetice la variedad de nuestros colores, que nos tense más que la mejor tambora, hay que caer en un nombre: Josefina Báez.

[In order to know the Dominican country to its most intense limits, one must turn the page and take note of the other heart of local creativity. We would thus find ourselves facing New York. If we look for a name that synthesizes the variety of our colors, that tightens us more than the best drummer, you have to fall on one name: Josefina Báez.]
—MIGUEL D. MENA, "Y con ustedes, Josefina Báez: De la Romana al Infinito"

Like many underprivileged Dominicans, Josefina Báez migrated from La Romana to New York in the 1970s in search of economic opportunities and progress. As a political act, Báez opts to identify herself as "Dominicanyork," a derogatory term used to identify dominicanos ausentes living in the United States: "I am, like many people, from the very local and the plurality of places, from New York, from La Romana and from everywhere. But I think the nationality that best fits me is that of Dominicanyork."[63] Insisting on her Dominicanyork nationality, Báez illustrates the specificity of her alterity because, as Torres-Saillant explains, the Dominicanyork must be poor, black, lower-class or all of the above, so that "hablar como Dominicanyork presupone el reconocimiento de una marginalidad intrínsica" (to speak as a

Dominicanyork presupposes the recognition of an intrinsic marginality).[64] Following this reasoning, it is safe to argue that Báez's work embarks from the premise that the Dominicanyork condition does not secure access to, but rather the erasure from, both nations. But, as she asserts, "You see there is no guarantee. Ni aquí ni allá. Not even with your guiri guiri papers. Here, there, anywhere. There is no guarantee without accent or PhD."[65] This condition of in-betweenness that constitutes Dominicanyork subjectivity accentuates the idea that once a person is an immigrant, she will always be an immigrant, defined only by the action of leaving, moving, and never fully belonging to a location. Or, as Báez better describes it in her text *Comrade, Bliss Ain't Playin'* (2007): "From too many places I have arrived. From many places I have left. . . . All ask the same questions: Where are you from? When are you leaving?"[66] For Báez, however, this condition of in-betweenness, rather than a loss or a reason to lament, creates alternative forms of enunciation and representation liberating to the Dominican subject who now has the ability to create his or her own nation, a "Flagless nation. A nation with no flag."[67]

Báez's New York City is the underground location from which the poetics of dominicanidad ausente emerge as a result of contact with the violence, multiplicity, and "crookedness" this place embodies: "Crooked Cupid a woman named city hips swing male or female. Hips swing creating our tale. . . . No one to blame or complain but go. Just go let go go fast but go. *Crooked City*. A woman named cupid. City glorifying the finest brutality in blue. City nuestro canto con viva emoción. City a la guerra morir se lanzó. City. Suerte que la 107 se arrulla con Pacheco. . . . Me chulié en el hall. Metí mano en el rufo. Craqueo chicle como Shameka Brown. City. *I pulled the emergency cord*" (emphasis added).[68] In New York, the immigrant is confronted by the "crooked" city, the place where police brutality is the norm and marginality reigns. Yet it is also a place from which solidarity can emerge through contact with other marginalized ethnic groups, a place where the music of Johnny Pacheco and Spanglish can mix in a comfortable crookedness that the immigrant can navigate with ease. In the crooked city, the immigrant becomes a powerful subject by performing small acts of resistance in her daily activities: speaking Spanglish in the public sphere—"metí mano en el rufo" (I messed around on the roof)—interpolating Dominican oppression by singing a verse from the national anthem—"A la guerra a morir se lanzó" (Launched into war to the death)—and making the city stop and listen to her voice—"I pulled the emergency cord." Thus, New York City, or at least its underground, is converted into a home for the immigrant, the marginal, and the poor through these daily and mundane actions that resist the seductive and oppressive narrative of assimilation, which is also a narrative of erasure. Most important, New York can become a place for rewriting history and creating a new voice, a poetics, through the very body of the Dominican immigrant woman: "hips swing, creating our tale."[69]

In her performance, Báez's "crooked city" is paralleled to the racexiled Dominican female body that carries it, quite literally on her hips. Queering both the geographical location—New York City—and the sexualized figure of the Afro-Dominican woman, Báez's crooked dominicanidad contra*dicts* the hegemonic rhetoric that persistently casts Dominican women as either virgins or whores. The image of a woman who swings her hips is typically associated with *mulata cabareteras,* like the iconic Iris Chacón, who performed a sexual fantasy for the viewers' enjoyment. Báez's text owns the image of the *levente/cabaretera*'s sexual body while simultaneously queering it as a site of historical contestation: "creating our tale." The tale, which can also be understood in the performance as "the tail" (the butt) summons a revision of the historical and rhetorical narrative that persistently casts the mulata/black body as either a site of corruption or a tragic object of consumption. Neither a whore nor a virgin, Báez's hip-swinging woman summons the Afro-Dominican religious episteme, which, as explored in chapter 2, is physically carried on the woman's body through songs (*salves*) and dances (*atabales*). Afro-religious women's dancing and singing is a performance of remembering with the body as a site of historical contestation. The hips that swing thus perform *dominicanas*' sexual agency and archival contra*dictions*.

In his text *The Practice of Everyday Life* (1984), Michel de Certeau argues that marginality has become universal because people who are oppressed have developed tactics that lend political dimensions to everyday practices: "The formality of everyday practices is indicated in these tales which frequently reverse the relationships of power. . . . This space protects the weapons of the weak against the reality of the established order. It also hides them from the social categories which 'make history' because they dominate it. . . . Both rhetoric and everyday practices can be defined as internal manipulations of the system."[70] When Báez juxtaposes the Dominican national anthem with her description of New York City, she builds El Nié as an imagined space inhabited by the immigrant where memories and the present are intertwined with the experience of oppression. Furthermore, as she uses her middle finger to symbolize the placement of a bindi on her forehead, while saying, "glorifying the finest brutality in blue," she makes history as de Certeau proposes (see figure 5.3).[71] The language of her body, juxtaposed with the rhetoric of her speech, creates a space for manipulating the official discourse and stating a new "truth" in a nonofficial language. Her speech act, "I pulled the emergency cord," is a performance of power.[72] It is a form of authoritative speech that puts the interlocutor in the role of the actor. By "pulling the emergency cord," Josefina brings the audience into the crooked city, making the audience, even if only for the forty-five minutes of the performance, feel exiled, while she is clearly at home in her "crooked city."[73]

Báez's New York includes Dominican politics, Caribbean history, and particularly all the contra*dictions* that had been denied in the official narration of the Dominican subject in the United States and the Dominican Republic. Although her work departs from the specificity of the individual experience of Josefina, the immigrant from La Romana, Báez successfully performs an immensely collective experience of dominicanidad that at times, because of New York, becomes a larger Caribbean, immigrant, marginal, universal subject experience of identification: "I write about the very mundane, common experience of being from La Romana and New York, which turns out to be not so specific but rather a common experience of you and me."[74]

Much like Juan Bosch's encounter with the Confraternidad Caribeña during his exile, Josefina Báez imagines the possibility of being Dominican once she is surrounded by caribeños in New York because, as Martínez-San Miguel asserts, New York is transformed through migrations into another Caribbean space from which national identities are renegotiated.[75] By becoming part of something larger—Caribbean peoples, immigrant subjects, blacks, Dominicans, exiles—Báez interjects national narratives. Doing so redefines her own notions of dominicanidad and proposes collective ways of being, a process that is most clearly exemplified in her latest piece, *Levente no. Yolayorkdominicanyork* (2011). In it, through a voice the author calls "Ella-el-Pueblo(s)," and in the multiplicity of characters that live in the island-nation building of El Nié, solidarity becomes the norm and the only way of survival:

> Como en nuestro edificio-barrio-pueblo-país-isla-continente-mundo conversemos con la única regla de que podemos estar en desacuerdo y ser amigos. . . . Somos personajes del *Levente no.* Un poema con grajo. Un comentario sin visa, ni ningún sueño. La llamada no literatura. . . . Tú, yo, o alguien a quien conocemos.[76]

[Like in our building-neighborhood-town-country-island-continent-world, let's converse with the only rule being that we can disagree and be friends. . . . We are characters of *Levente no*. A poem with body odor. A comment without a visa or any dreams. The so-called not literature. . . . You, I, or someone we know.]

Through the imagining of the collective experience of El Nié, Báez's performances raise questions about her black-Dominicanyork identity while embodying a larger Pan-Caribbean identity. She reconciles the tensions produced by the hybridity of the Caribbean region through the simultaneous performance of African and Indian races/cultures and the use of English, Spanish, and Hindi.

The contra*dictions* that Báez once viewed as her own individual tribulations represent, in the performance of Caribbeanness, a collective contra*diction*: being Caribbean already implies living in constant negotiation between races, languages, and cultures. The multiplicity of identities that make up the Dominican experience in New York creates a possibility for negotiating a position within the national spaces because hybridity, as cultural theorist Shalini Puri states, does not necessarily imply a dismantling of national identity, but rather a strategy for resisting hegemony from within the nation(s): "Although the refusal to recognize national borders in much liberal and leftist post-nationalist discourse undoubtedly stems in part from a genuinely utopian declaration of solidarity with the nation's others, the strategic wisdom of the refusal is questionable. . . . A more productive transnationalism that could both attend to the politics of location and de-essentialize it would ask: 'How do I, even as a dissident, participate in nationally mediated structures of power and oppression?'"[77]

Báez's use of Kuchipudi (a dance from India), Hindi, and Indian cultural practices in her performances and writing allude to the reclamation of an oft-forgotten part of the Caribbean identity Puri examines. In the mid-1800s, thousands of East Indians were brought to the Caribbean as indentured servants. Many stayed, forever changing the dynamics of racial and cultural identities in the Caribbean (more specifically in the English-speaking islands). However, as Puri argues, Indo-Caribbean legitimacy as "truly Caribbean" is often questioned, even as tensions between Afro- and Indo-Caribbean people continue to escalate.

As black and Dominican identities are negotiated through linguistic representation, Báez's corporeal language, as exemplified in *Dominicanish*,

5.3 "Bindi" by Jorge Vismara, 2007. Báez mimes the placement of a bindi using her middle finger. Courtesy of photographer Jorge Vismara and performer Josefina Báez.

seems to contradict her speech. The apparent disjunction between body and speech is accentuated through the use of Kuchipudi, which further challenges the official discourses of national identity, race, and ethnicity. Báez's incorporation of East Indian language and culture opposes Dominican racial codes (Indian, Brown) through transgression and humor. Báez, while performing her own version of Dominican identity, dances Kuchipudi to Merengue and uses South Asian cultural references, embodying not the Native Indian myth that was imposed on her by the Archive of Dominicanidad founded by Galván and others, but a South Asian Indian identity that seems, in the Dominican context, strange and out of place, yet common and normal in the Dominicanyork experience. Furthermore, her use of the middle finger (see figure 5.3) to place the bindi, adds to the political humor of the piece. The use of a bindi usually marks a woman's marriage, her binding to man through a state-sanctioned performance. For Báez, who has chosen not to marry, the bindi performs both her bodily ownership— being married to herself—as well as a political act of feminist contra*diction*: the refusal to be controlled by hegemonic forces, whether they be the state, a language, or a man.

Báez's performance is an act of "playing Indian."[78] It renders Dominican claims to a Native American identity as silly and unreal, while proposing a more realistic encounter with East Indian culture through her Caribbean and New Yorker identities: "Forgotten deities looked at me recognized me in the process they became turmeric yellow I jet black . . . unleash the starched sari let its prints and colors play wild ragas foreplaying the juiciest kalankhan foreplaying the juiciest dulce de leche."[79] To be Indian in *Dominicanish* can also mean to be black, American, and Caribbean. At the same time, *Dominicanish* proposes that all the other identities can be subverted so that to be American may also mean being Caribbean and/or Indian. Báez's work privileges the infinite possibilities that a multiplicity of experiences can create in a subject, while challenging the ideas of clear national, racial or ethnic identities through her own literary diction: "I dentity. I dent it why? A prioritized feeling that photographs a nation. Identity. Flagless nation . . . Identity. A mere feeling . . . Countless I, I, I, I . . . Again. Nothing new under the sun."[80] Taking apart the word "identity," Báez disavows identity politics and represents a more complex subjectivity than the narrow categories emerging in relation to colonial legacies and the state. The "I" in repetition summons a head-on confrontation with the passive "one" or "they" that characterizes Dominican literature. Her fearless "I, I, I" is a performative diction that reminds, remembers, and recenters the subject in the history while rejecting the constraints that strip her of the ability to name herself and her desires. Her proposal suggests a collective history that rather than based on the erasure of the subject for the creation of the community, is grounded in the individual experiences of the subject from which then the collective I can emerge. In the multiplicity of individual experiences it is possible, Báez's performance suggests, to create collective empowerment.

Caribbean contra*dictions* staged throughout *Dominicanish* establish the relationship between colonization, imperialism, and migration, the last being, of course, the direct result of the former two. The Dominicanyork as performer of contra*dictions* is a subject in *vaivén*, in constant search of freedom from the systems of oppression that persist in denying her access to full citizenship. She is a subject that is only acknowledged through the actual act of moving (migrating, performing). This argument illuminates the relationship between marginality and illegality. The act of migrating, as understood in this framework, carries with it the implicit notion of becoming an "illegal alien." Dominican migration, like most current Latin American migration to the United States, and as historian Mae Ngai argues, has been deemed unlawful, thereby criminalizing immigrant subjects.[81]

The Dominicanyork as presented in *Dominicanish* is a subject in transit, constantly running from the yoke of the states that persist in enslaving her: "No way to blame of complaint but go. Go fast, go slow, but go."[82] The exilic condition is a handicap to active political life within the nations: having an accent, for instance, is often perceived as a handicap to US citizenship; in the Dominican Republic, those who live abroad are often seen as traitors or not "Dominican enough" to be allowed to make social or political contributions. Thus, the dominicana ausente is not accepted on the island because she is seen as poor, black, and uneducated. She does not find a place in her new nation for the same reasons. Yet the body of the immigrant becomes a means for representing history in the underground of New York and in El Nié. Báez's invented language, Dominicanish, emerges as a means of contradicting the archive.

Finding Language Is Finding Home

And here I am chewing English and spitting Spanish
—JOSEFINA BÁEZ, *Dominicanish*

A reading of Báez's corpus—which includes poetry, prose, acts, happenings, and dances—resists the traditional classification: "Todos mis textos son lo que son. . . . yo los escribo con la idea de ser representados. Son siempre textos en movimiento, textos que están ligados a la experiencia corporal" (All of my texts are what they are. . . . I write them with the idea of acting them out. They are always texts in motion, texts that are linked to the corporal experience).[83] The richness of her artistic and literary production is a perfect example of the poetics of dominicanidad ausente because it rejects all essentialist forms of nationalism while embracing a multiplicity of experiences, locales, and languages as the true nation-self. Staging the complex negotiation dominicanos ausentes must endure, Báez's corpus presents us with three sites from which dominicanidad can be (re)imagined and embraced in the United States: (1) body, (2) location, and (3) language. The body depicted is the Dominicanyork subject in vaivén—to and from geographical, imaginary, and historical spaces. The location is always El Nié, the invented space that exists in the New York underground at the margins of the Dominican Republic and the United States. The language is Dominicanish, a form of Spanglish that integrates English and Spanish syntax while using Dominican linguistic codes and cultural references to describe US experiences. With it, Báez imagines her home-island-nation of El Nié and interjects both historical and rhetorical narrations of dominicanidad.

The challenges of writing in a language other than one's own are many. But which tongue is native for an immigrant whose mother tongue is Spanish and whose language of instruction was English? How can she articulate the multiplicity of her experiences in the host language without losing part of her own history? Grappling with similar questions, Danny Méndez locates the work *Dominicanish* within the framework of "minor literature" as defined by Gilles Deleuze and Pierre Félix Guattari.[84] That is, as an "assemblage of enunciations" that construct a collective voice. For Deleuze and Guattari, minor literature constitutes the deterritorialization of a major language through a minor literature written in the major language from a marginalized or minoritarian position.[85] Minor literature thus, according to Deleuze and Guattari, must be written in the language of the colonizer. A reading of Báez as a deterritorialized subject, and her work as an emerging form of minor literature, can indeed highlight the political urgency of Báez's works within the framework of the poetics of dominicanidad ausente. However, given that Báez's position as a citizen of El Nié locates her at the margins of both the Dominican Republic and the United States, and therefore outside of both English and Spanish, I would argue that *Dominicanish* exists at the margins of even minor literature. Unlike diasporic Dominican authors such as Julia Álvarez and Junot Díaz—both of whose work appears in literary anthologies published by powerful presses, is sold in commercial bookstores, and is therefore part of the mainstream—Báez is self-published, understudied, and excluded from the Latino/a canon. Thus, Báez's work exists only within El Nié and as a direct confrontation of what Chicana writer Gloria Anzaldúa called "linguistic terrorism": the imposition of dominant languages—English and Spanish—on the border subject.

As defined by Anzaldúa, linguistic terrorism is an act of violence against not only the mind but also the body as it keeps border subjects from fully expressing themselves:

> For a people who are neither Spanish nor live in a country in which Spanish is the first language; for a people who live in a country in which English is the reigning tongue but who are not Anglo; for a people who cannot entirely identify with either standard (formal, Castillian) Spanish nor standard English, what recourse is left to them but to create their own language? A language which they can connect their identity to, one

capable of communicating the realities and values true to themselves—a language with terms that are neither español ni inglés, but both. So we speak a patois, a forked tongue, a variation of two languages . . . *language is a homeland.*[86] (emphasis added)

Báez's confrontation with linguistic terrorism is highly corporeal: "I thought I would never learn English. No way, I will not put my mouth like that. No way. Jamás ni never. Gosh. To pronounce one little phrase, one must become another person, mouth all twisted. Yo no voy a poner la boca así como un guante."[87] The acquisition and resignification of language as performed by Báez serves as an antidote to "linguistic terrorism" because it represents the corporeal, subjective, and highly individualized experiences through the enunciation or writing of words. Historically grounded, Báez's "border language" is constantly becoming through the performance of the very condition of absent/immigrant/exile that it re-creates. This is evident in the different ways and forms in which Dominicanish, the language, is depicted in performance texts. Thus, Báez's *Dominicanish* emerges from El Nié as a performative lexicon that embraces the multiplicity of experiences of the immigrant who confronts the contra*dictions* and oppression of linguistic terrorism and the historical silences of US-Dominican exclusion, or as her character Kay explains: "I am pure history."[88]

Soon after the stage lights up at the beginning of *Dominicanish*, the artist's mouth starts to move, fast and abruptly, talking about itself, as if it existed apart from the body that stands immobile. The first few minutes of the monologue employ the Brechtian alienation effect, a theatrical technique that produces confusion and anxiety in the audience.[89] Words in a semifamiliar language seem to flow without any obvious connection: "Every sin is vegetable. Begetable. Vege tabol."[90] The audience seems confused yet interested in what this mouth is molding as it produces unfamiliar sounds. The performer's strategy is powerful because she "invests what (s)he has to show with definite gesture of showing."[91] Furthermore, she persuades the audience that her experience is authentic in order to lead them to a conclusion about the entire structure of society in this particular historical time. Báez's initial performance of speaking Dominicanish grabs the audience's attention at the same time that it creates a feeling of alienation for the monolingual subject.

This initial alienation allows for a dramatization of an everyday life reality: immigration, assimilation, and oppression, shedding light on the significance of cultural representation in creating the possibility for political questioning. The antagonism presumed by the monolingual subject embodies an underlying conflict between the nation's rhetoric of inclusion and multiculturalism and the impossibility of assimilation for some immigrant subjects. This impossibility, as we have seen throughout the chapter, has the potential to create an *other* contra*diction* for Dominicans who are expected to integrate into US culture, aesthetics, and language but are excluded from national representation. However, Báez's intervention subverts these contra*dictions*, making them part of her island-nation-home-language: "Now I don't care how my mouth looks, I like what I am saying."[92] Her act of subversion is also one of joy: her contra*diction* pleases her. In this joy she also finds a way to be that points to the inclusiveness of the discourse of solidarity that Bosch drafted between 1938 and 1961, while insisting on her marginal belonging to the US through the very visceral experiences that produced el Nié: "and here I am chewing English and spitting Spanish."

Dominicanish concludes with a deconstruction of the homogenous and normative ideas of the immigrant identity. In addition, Báez's work embraces the contra*dictions* that the politics of location, nationality, ethnicity, and race create for the immigrant in a hopeful gesture toward shattering the silences of the marginal communities in the United States and in a successful exercise of talking back. Rooted in the discourse of solidarity that Bosch drafted in the early twentieth century and in the long history of Dominican migration and exile, the poetics of dominicanidad ausente drafted by authors such as Báez successfully blurs the lines of "here" and "there" often drawn by the state and citizens living on the island, thus allowing for a more participatory and transnational citizenship of dominicanos ausentes. Dominicanidad ausente destabilizes the official discourse of the Dominican nation, and the canon of cultural and literary production in both territories, leading to a more democratic dialogue based on rayano consciousness. This new rayano consciousness is also contributing to intrasolidarity dialogues that confront the trauma of violence and division that has marked the relationship between Haitians and Dominicans. Thus, in El Nié and through the marginal language of Dominicanish, the kind of solidarity Bosch imagined is finally becoming.

Anti-Haitianism and the Global War on Blackness

My name is María. This is my country. The only one I have ever known. Here I learned to walk, to talk, and to write my name, María. My parents came here to give me a better life. I have broken no laws. Yet I am treated worse than an animal, like a goat, like a cow brought up to exist without identity. I have no papers. Yet here I am, belonging to no other nation than this one. Why do they do this to us? My only crime is that I was born to poor black immigrants who followed the route to work and survival.

—MARÍA PIERRE, 19, ethnic Haitian born in the Dominican Republic

My name is Elizabeth. I am undocumented. I was brought to this country when I was five years old. . . . My parents made a choice to move here in an effort to provide a better life for their children. . . . I was enrolled in American elementary school. I take all AP classes. I play violin for the youth symphony. I get good test scores and I participate in my community. Yet my opportunities get slimmer and slimmer due to recent legislation. . . . This reminds me of Jim Crow when customers were turned away with cash in hand . . . all because they were a different race. . . . How could someone who doesn't know me judge and reject me? . . . My name is Elizabeth. I am a high school senior. I was brought here when I was five. I broke no laws. I am not a criminal. Please don't let them treat me this way.

—ELIZABETH GARIBAY, 19, ethnic Mexican, raised in Athens, Georgia

On September 23, 2013, as many people prepared to commemorate the anniversary of the Massacre of 1937, the Dominican Constitutional Court reinstated a piece of citizenship law from 1929 that condemns ethnic Haitians to another form of obliteration. Ruling 168-13, better known as La Sentencia, dictates that all persons born to "illegal immigrants" or "persons in transit" since 1929 will not be entitled to Dominican citizenship and are, therefore, subject to deportation.[1] The Dominican Government claimed La Sentencia was part of an "expansive immigration reform aimed at controlling undocumented immigration from Haiti which increased by about twenty percent since the 2010 earthquake."[2] But because it is retroactive to 1929, this "immigration reform" means that people such as María Pierre, whose testimony opens this final section, become stateless, as neither Hispaniola nation acknowledges them as citizens.

The ruling of the Constitutional Tribunal came in response to a lawsuit brought against the Dominican state by Juliana Deguis in 2008 after the Central Electoral Board refused to issue her a *cédula* (state ID). Deguis, who was born in 1984, appealed the state decision for at the time of her birth, jus solis was applied to all except people in transit, a category that until 2000 pertained only to tourists or visitors who stayed in the territory for no more than ten days. In 2000, legislation changed Haitian laborers' legal status to "persons in transit," which made them ineligible to register their Dominican-born children. In 2004, the constitutional designation of "in transit" was once again redefined to include all persons without legal residency. La Sentencia was the climax of two decades of legal actions aimed at disenfranchising ethnic Haitians and divesting them of civil liberties and citizenship rights.

La Sentencia is part of the troublesome history of Hispanophile anti-Haitianism institutionalized during the Trujillo regime. Though politicians and the general public coincide in their condemnation of the Trujillo dictatorship (1930–61) as the most violent period in twentieth-century Dominican Republic, his legacy continues to guide the political horizon of the nation. One of the most pervasive bequests of the Trujillato is the production of black bodies—which, as we have seen throughout the book, are imagined as Haitian—as foreign. Politicians, journalists, and state-serving intellectuals use the term "Haitian" to refer to Dominican citizens of Haitian descent, rayanos, immigrants, and seasonal cane workers. The conflation of *haitiano* has two equally pervasive results: the symbolic and civic exclusion of ethnic Haitians from the nation, and the perpetuation of the notion of the Dominican Republic as a monolithic Hispanic nation. Though this dominant diction of *haitianidad* has historically excluded ethnic Haitians and Afro-Dominicans from the national imaginary, the recent passing of Law 168-13 converted the symbolic into action, effectively legalizing the expulsion of black Dominican citizens of Haitian descent from the nation's territory.

The arguments of supporters of La Sentencia rests on a series of myths about "Haitians."[3] These myths include that Haitians are trying to "recover" the Dominican Republic's territory to unify the island as they did in 1822, that Haitians are murderous rapists coming to pillage and destroy the Dominican Republic, that Haitians will contaminate the Hispanic language and culture of Dominicans, and that Haitian migrants take away jobs and resources from Dominican citizens. These myths resonate with nineteenth-century nationalist literature (del Monte, Galván, and Penson) and with ideologies dating from the mid-twentieth century and promulgated by the Trujillo intelligentsia (Balaguer, Peña Batlle, and Max Henríquez Ureña). They also echo global present-day conservative rhetoric that presents migrants as economy drainers (they are coming to take our jobs) and moral corruptors (they bring drugs and violence). Historical anti-Haitianism has thus merged with contemporary anti-immigrant xenophobia, demonstrating *how*, as Trouillot warned us, the past can persist in sustaining structures of power that create oppression.

In the Dominican Republic the structures of power behind anti-Haitianism materialize in the continuous exploitation, erasure, and destruction of black bodies for the benefit of national and foreign corporations (such as the Vicini family, Citibank, Nike). Dominican-Haitian human rights leader Sonia Pierre declared that "the community of poor Haitians and poor Dominican-Haitians is the poorest and most vulnerable, subjected to the cruelest denial of their rights."[4] Perpetuating poverty, Pierre reminded us, ensures the continuity of exploitative working conditions that made "the rich richer and the poor more vulnerable."[5] To Pierre's reasoning, I add that the profitability of corporations operating in the Dominican Republic is dependent upon the successful antagonism of Hispaniola's poor blacks. Transethnic alliances can facilitate, as they have in the recent past, the successful contestation of oppressive economic regimes.[6] La Sentencia is at least partly a response to the rising rayano consciousness that, as demonstrated in chapter 4, has matured since the earthquake of 2010. Rayano consciousness strengthens political and economic collaboration among poor Dominicans and poor Haitians living in the borderlands and the bateyes, as the recent film by Loré Durán documents.[7] Rayanos and the organizations that support them understand that the future of the borderland region lies neither in the hands of the state that excludes them, nor in the corporations that exploit them, but in the mutual cooperation of the communities that inhabit the region.

It is precisely because of the expanding rayano consciousness that La Sentencia has been contested. Contrary to the silence and passivity that characterized mid-twentieth-century intellectual and public response to the Massacre of 1937, for instance, the present wave of anti-Haitian nationalism and xenophobia has met a strong political opposition on the island and abroad. Critics from across the globe denounced the ruling as a violation of human rights, some going as far as comparing it to the Holocaust.[8] Among the most vocal Dominican opponents of La Sentencia are the organizations Reconicido (Recognized) and Participación Ciudadana (Citizen Participation); the journalists Marino Zapete, Juan Bolívar Díaz, and Patricia Solano; scholars Quisqueya Lora and Edwardo Paulino; and writers Junot Díaz and Rita Indiana Hernández. Their political actions include several efforts to obtain humanitarian visas to the United States, Canada, and Europe for denationalized youth, conducting "know your rights" workshops in ethnic Haitian communities, building intra-island community structures, and raising global awareness about the human rights violations.

Individuals who voice opposition, however, have been subjected to harsh criticism, cyber-bullying, and even death threats. In June 2015, for instance, after participating in a roundtable discussion with Haitian American writer Edwidge Danticat, Junot Díaz became the victim of a vicious attack. Journalist Daniel Rivero erroneously reported that the author called for a boycott of the Dominican Republic.[9] The reactions to the misquote were rapid and clearly divided among those who sided with the author and those who condemned him and deemed him "anti-national" and a "traitor." The spiteful critics went as far as calling for the denationalization of Díaz, claiming the author's emigrant condition as the main cause of his "betrayal." The negative reactions continued even after Rivero retracted and after the author issued a public statement clarifying his position.[10]

The disavowal of Díaz and other Latino/a Dominicans who oppose La Sentencia demonstrates the persistent and often similar ways in which dominicanos ausentes and ethnic Haitians are racexiled from the Dominican nation through claims of authenticity, linguistic competency, and cultural assimilation that are rooted in the long history of Hispanophile hegemony. In an open letter published by the digital journal *7 Días*, a group of nationalist writers including Eduardo Gautreau de Windt, Pura Emeterio Rondón, and Efraim Castillo cite Díaz's "lack of command of the Spanish language" as evidence of his estrangement from dominicanidad.[11] The letter goes on to insult Díaz, calling his interest in the country of his birth "feigned," "unnecessary," and "offensive." Taking the attacks to another level, the executive director for the Dominican Presidency's International Commission on Science and Technology, José Santana, called Díaz a "fake and overrated pseudo-intellectual" who "should learn better to speak Spanish before coming to this country to talk nonsense."[12] But the "linguistic terror-ism" to which Díaz was subjected is not a rare experience for US Latinos/as, as Gloria Anzaldúa reminds us in her seminal essay "How to Tame a Wild Tongue."[13] Bilingualism, Spanglish, and the emerging variations of Latino/a languages in the United States have been a source of anxiety for both US and Latin American nationalists since the 1970s. In the Dominican Repub-lic, the linguistic bordering of the nation, exemplified in the case of Díaz, is entangled with the gruesome anti-Haitian violence of 1937, when "proper use of the Spanish language" was often used as a marker of national belong-ing. Díaz's interpellation of nationalist politicians and the attacks that fol-lowed led to a widespread condemnation of La Sentencia among US Latinos and ethnic minority activist groups. The Haiti-Dominican border, as I have argued, is present in the United States through the body of the Dominican racexile. The Latino/a critical reaction to La Sentencia further avowed this reality, enabling a more nuanced critique of the Haitian-Dominican border as a product of US Empire.

Since the independence of 1844, the United States has influenced the construction of dominicanidad in opposition to *haitianismo*. This process intensified during the military occupation of 1916–24, when the United States introduced the concept of border patrol and implemented the bracero labor system that brought cheap Haitian labor to cut cane in the US-owned sugar corporations. The most recent example of the role of the United States in bordering Hispaniola is the creation in 2008 of the CESFRONT, a special-ized border security police, trained by the US Border Patrol as part of the American Empire's effort to promote "strong borders" abroad.

Enforcement of the US border, particularly in the context of the Global War on Terror, is shaping actions and dictions, defining national sovereignty in a post-9/11 world. The international expansion of the War on Terror is evi-dent in the policies and legislation shaping present day Hispaniola's borders and in the nationalist rhetoric that seeks to define citizenship and belong-ing. Yet, as the Latino/a response to Díaz's case demonstrates, while physical and ideological borders are erected across the world, they are also contested in unprecedented ways. Immigrant and racialized communities are finding new ways to collaborate and contest oppression through social media and international activist networks. They are producing a lingua franca of con-tra*diction* ("Black lives matter," "No human being is illegal") aimed at dis-mantling the structures of power producing immigrant and black bodies as a criminal mass.

Racialized Immigrant Citizens

Two testimonies open this final chapter of the book. The first is by María Pierre, a Dominican woman born to undocumented Haitian parents and who has recently become stateless, and Elizabeth Garibay, a Mexican-born undocumented high school senior who has lived in the United States since age five. Though the legal structures surrounding immigration in the United States differ significantly from the 2013 actions of the Dominican Constitutional Court, the similarities in the testimonies of both women point to the violent consequences of the global process of bordering nations that police and control immigrant bodies. In 2011 Elizabeth spoke in front of the Georgia State House against two rulings: Georgia HB 87, a copycat of the infamous 2010 Arizona SB 1070—which was, at the time, the broadest and strictest anti-immigrant legislation in US history—and Policy 413, which banned undocumented students from access to the top state public universities.[14] Georgia HB 87, like its predecessor, required law enforcement officers to inquire about immigration status during routine stops for minor traffic violations and to hand over any undocumented suspects to federal authorities. The bill also required most employers to check immigration status through the federal "E-verify" database, and stipulated possible prison sentences for those convicted of knowingly harboring or transporting undocumented residents. The actions effectively legalized racial profiling, marking black and brown bodies as suspiciously foreign. While the "show-me-your-papers" provisions of Georgia's HB 87 and similar laws have resulted in civil liberties lawsuits and preliminary injunctions by federal judges ending in the eventual dismissal of the provisions, insufficient attention was given to the move by the Board of Regents to deny undocumented students access to state universities and colleges. Clearly, the state of Georgia did not expect a loud response from the population. The unintended result was, however, the emergence of a new movement that employs tactics similar to those used during the civil rights struggles of the 1960s to combat present-day segregation.[15]

Employing those "old tactics," Elizabeth reminds her audience that it is not her immigrant condition but her race that renders her foreign. Referencing Jim Crow at the Georgia State House, Elizabeth demonstrates her historical awareness and asserts her belonging to the nation that seeks to expel her. Angela Davis, speaking at Spelman College in Atlanta in 2011, a few weeks after Elizabeth, further avows the Georgia immigrant struggle as a civil rights struggle: "Anti-immigration draws from and feeds on the racisms of the past, the racisms that have affected people of African descent."[16] The struggle for immigrant rights, Davis concluded, "is the key struggle" of our times.

In her powerful address against HB 87, Elizabeth repeats her name twice. Her speech act, "My name is Elizabeth," contra*dicts* anti-immigrant rhetoric that seeks to render her part of a criminal mass. Insisting on her innocence—"I was brought here when I was five"—Elizabeth also reminds listeners of the unconstitutional cruelty of the Georgia legislation that penalizes her for an act committed at age five. Similarly, María appeals to an audience of fellow citizens asserting her belonging to the nation at the face of state disavowal: "This is my country." Also repeating her name twice, María proclaims her individuality while asking the collective dominicanidad to recognize her as one of their own. Community recognition, María and Elizabeth seem to suggest, can contra*dict* the states that persistently push them out of their home.

María and Elizabeth's stories, read in tandem, illustrate the sordid consequences of present-day racialized anti-immigration policies on the everyday lives of people. The striking similarities in the racialized ethnic Mexican experiences in the United States and the racialized ethnic Haitian experiences in the Dominican Republic are not coincidental. Rather, as this book highlights, they are part of the centuries-old unequal and complex relationship between the United States and Hispaniola. Elizabeth's and María's public speeches are unequivocally rooted in their understanding of the links between economic exploitation, racism, and anti-immigrant prejudice. Their words, uttered in two very different geographical spaces and two years apart, show that as global oppression expands, immigrant and ethnic minority struggles also transcend borders—a fact that in turn allows for transnational coalitions of contestation. In particular, the comparative reading of the two testimonies crystallizes the significance of US ethnic and immigrant political diction in shaping transnational justice and democracy struggles. Both young women's speech acts respond to broader anxieties about race, immigration, and citizenship in our present world. Further, María's assertion "My only crime is that I was born to poor black immigrants who followed the route to work and survival" appeals to the vast Hispaniola diaspora and the international immigrant population.

Knowing and Doing

I am constantly confronted with my own place as a US Latina-Dominican scholar amidst the growing war on black and brown bodies that is affecting my birth and adoptive homes. Throughout the book I have insisted on the genealogy of anti-Haitianism as a global force that is strongly linked to the dominant structures of power and oppression that sustained colonial slavery and racist legislation such as Jim Crow. I have also argued that physical violence, particularly the destruction of black bodies at the hand of the state or in the name of the state, is intrinsically linked to the hegemonic discourse of white supremacy that sustains economic inequality and political disenfranchisement across the globe. In the case of the Dominican Republic, anti-Haitian discourse allowed the elite to silence Dominican blackness from the nation's archive. Anti-Haitianism also facilitated US persecution of Afro-religious communities such as the liboristas and Trujillo's violence against rayanos, Haitian immigrants, and ethnic Haitians in the borderlands.

But the Massacre of 1937, as I argue in chapter 3, did not happen randomly and in isolation. Rather, it occurred within a global context of xenophobia. The ideology justifying the massacre was sustained by the same eugenicist philosophy that led to the Rape of Nanking and the Holocaust. Likewise, La Sentencia and the denationalization crisis that followed were born in the context of a global war on blackness, amidst the rising climate of the criminalization of migrants, and within the structure of corporate-state union. These factors continue to divest the poor (particularly the racialized poor) from the so-called underdeveloped countries. Migration and exile, as my study of Josefina Báez demonstrates, become the only option for survival.

In the United States, the second decade of the new millennium has brought forth a series of terrorist acts against black bodies, particularly young black men, and black communities. In August 2014, the shooting of Michael Brown in Ferguson, Missouri, by a police officer, made visible the presence of institutionalized racism in law enforcement. In April 2015, Baltimore, Maryland, became the site of a series of protests after another black man, Freddie Gray, died at the hands of the police. As I write these last lines, nine black members of the historic Emmanuel Methodist Church in Charleston, South Carolina, have been murdered at the hands of a white supremacist killer. The climate of antiblackness in the United States seems to have gotten worse with the presence of black and brown bodies at the center, rather than the periphery, of the state, as exemplified in the presidency of

Barack Obama. Meanwhile in Europe, anti-immigration and racism have also increased. During the first half of 2015, 1,300 black and brown bodies washed up in the Mediterranean while politicians discussed how to shoot boats carrying immigrants as a way to deal with the immigration and refugee crisis.[17] All these tragedies take place as the global economy rests on the backs of racialized immigrants.

This book is in many ways my way to respond to the growing anti-immigrant and antiblack violence devastating our (my) present world. Speaking about the need for a more conscientious scholarship that engages in actually dismantling oppression rather than simply critiquing it, Barbara Tomlinson and George Lipsitz argue that scholars need to "know the work we want our work to do" and how our scholarship can serve to accompany positive changes in our society.[18] The myths sustaining white supremacy, and its particular Hispaniola brand (anti-Haitianism), are linked to a long scholarly tradition. In Latin America, for instance, lettered men such as Domingo Faustino Sarmiento and César Nicolás Penson constructed intellectual projects—historical and literary projects—that shaped the racial ideology, national archive, and intellectual history of generations.

Letrados such as Penson and Sarmiento *knew* what they wanted their work to do for the nation they were helping to build. They were effective in shaping the nation's archive, psyche, politics, and ideology. The aftershocks of their scholarship are still destroying lives. Paradoxically, Penson and Sarmiento are widely read and studied in schools and universities across the world. Their literary and intellectual contributions are widely acknowledged and praised. There are monuments, streets, and libraries named after men such as Penson all over the world.

I am acutely aware that my book will not change the painful experiences of people like María Pierre and Elizabeth Garibay, nor will it erase the trauma of the violence that forces them and many more to live in their own country as exiles. But I am hopeful that the work I want my book to do—to shatter silences and uncover other archives of knowledge—will get us closer to a dialogue about the ways in which scholarship can dismantle the intellectual legacy sustaining systems of oppression.

Humanity continues to search for ways to make sense of our violent history—slavery, colonization, and the Holocaust—and its legacy on our present world. Yet, as drug violence, gun violence, racial violence, and anti-immigrant violence grow, it is clear that we do not yet have the answers. My book argues that in order to truly understand the present we must examine the systems, rhetoric, and stories that sustained the violence of the past. Such reasoning, however, can only succeed if we are open to reading in contra-*diction*, against our own "truths." Reading in contra*diction* brings us closer to our own individual and collective discomforts, traumas, fears, and losses. But the act also brings us closer to justice. I hope this book accompanies new interdisciplinary dialogues about race, immigration, nationalism, and borders seeking to shatter the long historical silences that have persistently sustained state violence, exclusion, and oppression of a large part of our humanity for far too long.

NOTES

Introduction

Unless otherwise noted, translations of foreign-language quotations are my own.

1. I use the Spanish version of the term "dominicanidad" without italics and in lowercase to name both the people and the ideas related to Dominicanness. When "Dominicanidad" appears capitalized it refers to hegemonic and official versions of Dominicanness (as in the Archivo of Dominicanidad or the Archive of Dominicanness). See "Note on Terminology" at the beginning of the book.

2. Torres-Saillant, *El retorno de las yolas*, 18.

3. The military base of Barahona and San Juan became operational once again following the closing of the Vieques US Navy Post in Puerto Rico in 2001.

4. US Bureau of the Census, 2000.

5. Dávila, *Latinos Inc.*

6. I choose not to give an exact date of independence here as the very argument of my book suggests that the birth of the nation is a process of contra*diction*. In chapter 1, I explore the three possible dates for Dominican independence: 1821, 1844, and 1865.

7. The term *rayano* comes from the word *raya* (line) and alludes to people living on the dirt line that for centuries divided the two territories that make up Hispaniola.

8. Báez, *Levente no.*, np.

9. Anzaldúa, *Borderlands/La Frontera*, 25.

10. Luis Rafael Sánchez, *La guagua aérea*.

11. Gustavo Pérez Firmat, *Life on the Hyphen*.

12. Anzaldúa, *Borderlands/La Frontera*, 25.

13. Báez, *Levente no.*, np.

14. M. Jacqui Alexander, *Pedagogies of Crossing*.

15. Anzaldúa and Moraga, *This Bridge Called My Back*.

16. Mignolo, *Local Histories/Global Designs*, and Nelson Maldonado-Torres, *Against War*.

17. Grosz, *Volatile Bodies: Toward a Corporeal Feminism*, xiii.

18. In Marxist theory "interpellation" refers to the process by which an ideology is embodied in major social and political institutions, informing subjectivities and social interactions. My use of the term follows Althusser's argument that the situation always precedes the subject. Individual subjects are thus presented principally as produced by

social forces, rather than acting as powerful independent agents with self-produced identities. Althusser, "Ideology and Ideological State Apparatuses," 11.

19. Renda, *Taking Haiti*, 15.

20. Renda, *Taking Haiti*, 15.

21. See Fischer, *Modernity Disavowed*.

22. Treudley, "United States and Santo Domingo," 112.

23. Fordham, "Nineteenth Century Black Thought in the United States," 116.

24. Treudley, "United States and Santo Domingo," 112, 113.

25. Treudley, "United States and Santo Domingo," 113; Fordham, "Nineteenth Century Black Thought in the United States," 175.

26. Fordham, "Nineteenth Century Black Thought in the United States," 120.

27. Fordham, "Nineteenth Century Black Thought in the United States," 120.

28. Douglass, *Life and Times of Frederick Douglass*, 410.

29. Brantley, "Black Diplomacy and Frederick Douglass' Caribbean Experiences," 197–209, 203.

30. Douglass, *Life and Times of Frederick Douglass*, 398.

31. Welles, *Naboth's Vineyard*, 77–78.

32. In his PBS documentary airing in 2012, race scholar Henry Louis Gates Jr. introduced the topic of Dominican racialization, avowing Dominicans' denial of their blackness. I further explore this subject in chapter 4.

33. Here I capitalize Dominicanidad for two reasons: to follow Spanish grammar and to highlight the hegemonic/official nature of term as different from dominicanidad (in lowercase) which is more fluid and inclusive.

34. See Anzaldúa, *Borderlands/La Frontera: The New Mestiza*; Lazo, *Writing to Cuba*; Ortíz, *Cultural Erotics in Cuban America*; Saldívar, *Trans-Americanity*; and Sanchez, *Becoming Mexican American*.

35. Coronado, *A World Not to Come*, 34.

36. Guidotti-Hernández, *Unspeakable Violence*, 12.

37. Foucault, "Nietzsche, Genealogy, History," 64–139.

38. Trouillot, *Silencing the Past*, 4.

39. Trouillot, *Silencing the Past*, 23.

40. An unofficial collective annual commemoration began in 2013 organized and led by Edwardo Paulino, a Dominican American historian: the Border of Lights, an event in which artists and community activists stage a memorial of the massacre in Dajabón and Ouanaminthe.

41. Trouillot, *Silencing the Past*, 26.

42. Trouillot, *Silencing the Past*, 34.

43. Taylor, *The Archive and the Repertoire*.

44. Guidotti-Hernández, *Unspeakable Violence*, 12.

45. The Dominican migration to the United States has been mostly caused by economic crisis. See Torres-Saillant, *El retorno de las yolas*; Hoffnung-Garskof, *A Tale of Two Cities*; and Duany, *Quisqueya on the Hudson*.

Chapter 1: The Galindo Virgins

1. The exact location is not clear, though there is a reference to the "catedral" and "muros" from which I draw the conclusion that the posters were indeed hung on the cathedral and surrounding walls of Calle Las Damas in the colonial city. See Archivo de la Época Haitiana (1822–44), Legajo 2, Folder 1, AGN, Santo Domingo, DR.

2. Guerra Sánchez locates Galindo in the northern outskirts of the city walls, while the official record book indicates the hacienda was about nine kilometers east of the city. I was unable to locate the original records Guerra Sánchez cites. I have reconstructed a map following the record book and the court transcripts I was able to consult at the National Archives between 2005 and 2006 to guide the reader through a timeline of the crime. The significance of the location is its isolation. Both versions (the record book and Guerra Sánchez's article) describe Galindo as an isolated *monte* (wilderness). See Guerra Sánchez, "Toponomía y genealogía Galindo o barrio Mejoramiento Social," 11, and "Venta de Hacienda Galindo," in Protocolos, *Libro de asiento 1818–22: Época Haitiana*, Legajo 2, AGN, Santo Domingo, DR.

3. See "Sentencia de los reos de Galindo," in Sentencias Penales de la Época Haitiana (1822–31), Boletín 83, 1954, AGN, Santo Domingo, DR.

4. During the Haitian Unification of the island (January 1, 1822, to February 27, 1844), the territory of what is now the Dominican Republic was officially identified as Spanish Haiti. Informally, many referred to this part of the island as Eastern Santo Domingo. The term "Spanish Haitian" refers to residents of the east who self-identified as Spanish or Dominican.

5. "Sentencias de los reos de Galindo," 335.

6. Given that all citizens of Hispaniola were Haitian, ethnic distinctions or sometimes linguistic distinctions such as Spanish Haiti or French Haiti were also used.

7. "Sentencia de los reos de Galindo," 334.

8. There is discrepancy in the ages and names of the girls between the historical records available for consultation and Guerra Sánchez's findings. The court transcripts state that the ages of the children were six, ten, and fifteen. Águeda appears as the eldest. These records are contradicted by Guerra Sánchez's genealogical research (based on baptismal records), in which the children's ages are recorded as two, five, and eleven. See Guerra Sánchez, "Toponomía y genealogía Galindo o barrio Mejoramiento Social," 11; Archivo de la Época Haitiana (1822–44), Legajo 2, Folder 1, AGN, Santo Domingo, DR; and "Sentencia de los reos de Galindo," 335.

9. "Sentencia de los reos de Galindo," 334.

10. "Sentencia de los reos de Galindo," 335.

11. "Sentencia de los reos de Galindo," 335.

12. "Sentencia de los reos de Galindo," 335.

13. "Sentencia de los reos de Galindo," 335.

14. Also known as "las mariposas" (the butterflies), Patria, Minerva, and María Teresa Mirabal were assassinated on November 25, 1960, for opposing the Trujillo regime. They have become a symbol of bravery, feminism, and dominicanidad. Domini-

can American writer Julia Álvarez raised their popularity with her novel *In the Time of the Butterflies* (Chapel Hill, NC: Algonquin Books, 1994), which was adapted into a Hollywood film in 2000. See also Vallejo, *Las madres de la patria y las bellas mentiras*.

15. Franco, *Historias de las ideas políticas*, 76.

16. I use the Spanish "criollo" here to refer to the descendants of the Spanish colonial caste whose ancestry is white European—not to be confused with the Creole definitions of racial and cultural mixing.

17. Penson, *Las vírgenes de Galindo*, 245; Balaguer, *Discursos*, 45.

18. Nicolás Ureña, "Mi patria," 1835, AGN, Santo Domingo, DR.

19. Del Monte, *Las vírgenes de Galindo*, 6.

20. Demorizi writes about the painting in his book *Pintura y escultura en Santo Domingo*, 47. However, I have not been able to locate the painting in the Dominican Republic nor to see any photographs of it. In my quest for the whereabouts of this painting, I found that it was last seen in the Museo de Baní circa 1950. I venture to guess that it hangs on the wall of an elite and wealthy Dominican family.

21. *Costumbrismo* (sometimes anglicized as *Costumbrism*) is a nineteenth-century literary or pictorial style that developed in Spain and Latin America. It depicts local everyday life and customs. Costumbrismo is related both to artistic realism and romanticism, sharing the romantic interest in expression as opposed to simple representation and the romantic *and* realist focus on precise representation of particular times and places rather than of humanity in the abstract.

22. Penson states that he was able to "interview people who knew the victims" and who were alive during the event. However, given that he writes in 1891, almost seventy years after the murders, it is unlikely he found witnesses. Further, he does not provide interview transcripts, nor does he name the witnesses. See "Notas del autor," in *Cosas añejas*, 309–20.

23. Penson, *Las vírgenes de Galindo*, 314.

24. The Conspiración de los Alcarrizos was one of the first plots against the Haitian government after the unification of the island. Its organization began in January 1824, in the house of Father Pedro González, in the municipality of Alcarrizos (see map 1.1). The plot was discovered fairly quickly, and its main leaders were tried and executed. See García, *Compendio de la historia de Santo Domingo*.

25. The national rhetoric of Dominican whiteness is complicated because it always includes mulatos—particularly educated, elite mulatos. African American scholar Henry Louis Gates Jr. has called this racial phenomenon "the backwards one drop rule." See *Black in Latin America* (PBS, 2011).

26. In 1853, Nicolás Ureña published a poem entitled "Mi patria" in which the incident is briefly mentioned as "el crudo martirio de las vírgenes de Galindo" (the crude martyrdom of the virgins of Galindo). See *El Progreso*, July 17, 1953, in Documentos de la República (1844–60), Legajo 7, Folder 4, AGN, Santo Domingo, DR.

27. Gregorio Luperón was an important leader in the Restoration War of 1863–65 that reestablished independence to the Dominican Republic after its reannexation to Spain. Luperón also sought to redefine Haitian-Dominican border relations, a fact

that often caused discontent among Haitian leaders. See Moya Pons, *Manual de historia dominicana.*

28. See del Monte, "Advertencia," in *Las vírgenes de Galindo*, ii.

29. As I discuss in chapter 4, there was a large population of people who recognized themselves as neither Haitian nor Dominican and who had little investment in a national identification process. This is particularly true for rayanos, or border subjects, who were used to living freely and crossing the borders on a daily basis.

30. Balibar and Wallerstein, *Race, Nation, Class*, 87.

31. A blunderbuss, or Trabuco, is a rare type of short-range rifle.

32. See Moya Pons, *Manual de historia dominicana.*

33. Martínez-Vergne, *Nation and Citizen in the Dominican Republic*, 109.

34. Liberal Party leaders came from the elite European-educated criollo class. They lived in the urban centers (Santo Domingo, Santiago, and Puerto Plata) and controlled the printing and publishing industries, the schools, the university, and the press. Radicals, on the other hand, were mostly mulatos belonging to the emerging hatero (cattle rancher) and merchant classes. They had little access to institutions of learning and to print media.

35. Renda, *Taking Haiti*, 16.

36. See Moya Pons, *Manual de historia dominicana* and *La dominación haitiana.*

37. Fischer, *Modernity Disavowed*, 133. See also Moya Pons, *La cuestión haitiana*, and Sagás, *Race and Politics in the Dominican Republic.*

38. Kazanjian, *The Colonizing Trick.*

39. Alejandro Tapia y Rivera (1826–82) was a Puerto Rican poet and essayist whom many consider the father of Puerto Rican literature. Tapia dedicated a lot of his work to recovering historical documents about colonial sixteenth- and seventeenth-century Puerto Rico. Nicolás Heredia (1855–1901) was born in Baní, DR, and migrated to Cuba as a child. He was the founder of El Diario Matanzas (1881) and El Álbum (1882).

40. Rama, *La ciudad letrada*, 23.

41. Del Monte, *Las vírgenes de Galindo*, 16.

42. Del Monte, *Las vírgenes de Galindo*, 16.

43. Article 1 of the 1805 Constitution of Haiti.

44. Duarte, "Unidad de las razas."

45. Arroyo, *Writing Secrecy in Caribbean Freemasonry.*

46. See Moya Pons, *El pasado dominicano*, and Turits, *Foundations of Despotism.*

47. One of the most important of these rebellions was the one led by mulato cattle rancher Hernando Montero in La Yaguana in 1606, known as the Guaba Rebellion.

48. There were many causes of the Devastaciones, including economic causes. Spain was trying to maintain a monopoly on commerce with the colonies, and contraband affected this plan. Additionally, Spain understood contraband as a source of economic power for its enemies.

49. Sánchez Valverde, *Ensayos*, 46.

50. Bonó, "Apuntes para los cuatro ministerios de la república."

51. Moya Pons, *Manual de historia dominicana*, 197.

52. Duarte, *Apuntes*, 43.

53. Duarte, *Apuntes*, 146.

54. Duarte, *Apuntes*, 43, 147.

55. Artículo 1, Constitución de la República Dominicana de 1844, Archivo General de la República.

56. Félix María del Monte, "Canción dominicana," in Lloréns, *Antología de la poesía dominicana*, 42–44.

57. At the beginning of the eighteenth century, some criollos began to call themselves *dominicanos españoles* in an effort to distinguish themselves from Haitians, who were subjects of a French colony. During the independence movement, Hispanophile writers like del Monte began to use the term as a way to assert cultural and racial identity as Hispanics while insisting on a separate nationality from Spain as Dominicans.

58. Lloréns, *Antología de la poesía dominicana*, 42–44.

59. Lloréns, *Antología de la poesía dominicana*, 42–44.

60. See Liberato, *Joaquín Balaguer, Memory, and Diaspora*.

61. Balaguer, *La realidad dominicana*, 39.

62. *Facundo: Civilization and Barbarism* (original Spanish title: *Facundo: O, civilización y barbarie*) is a book written in 1845 by Domingo Faustino Sarmiento, a writer and journalist who became the seventh president of Argentina. The book helped define the parameters for thinking about the region's development, modernization, power, and culture. Subtitled *Civilization and Barbarism*, *Facundo* contrasts civilization and barbarism as seen in early nineteenth-century Argentina.

63. Puri, *The Caribbean Postcolonial*, 76.

64. Within the first three decades of Spanish colonization, the native population of Hispaniola was reduced to eleven thousand. See Moya Pons, *Manual de historia dominicana*, and Candelario, *Black behind the Ears*.

65. Glissant, *Caribbean Discourse*, 66.

66. Sommer, *Foundational Fictions*.

67. Sommer, *Foundational Fictions*, 5.

68. De Utrera disputes the historical accuracy of Galván's novel (*Polémica de Enriquillo*, 1973), and Martínez Almánzar (*Enriquillo: Ídolo de barro*) brings attention to the inaccuracies of many of the "facts" Galván claims (such as the origins of Mencía and the extent of Enriquillo's relationship to Padre de Las Casas).

69. Friar Bartolomé de Las Casas was born in Seville in 1484 and went to the island of Hispaniola in 1502, right around the time when the indigenous population started to decrease due to disease and forced labor. After witnessing the assassination of Caonabo in 1513, Friar de Las Casas decided that the conquest of the Indians was inhumane and pronounced himself in favor of their rights. His book, *Brevísima relación de la destrucción de las Indias* (1552), narrates a series of violent acts and aggressions committed against the indigenous population. He advocated for protection of the indigenous peoples of the Americas while promoting African slavery.

70. Galván, *Enriquillo*, 289.

71. Vallejo, *Las madres de la patria y las bellas mentiras*, 141.

72. Deloria, *Playing Indian*.

73. Las Casas, *Brevísima relación de la destrucción de las Indias*.

74. Fischer, *Modernity Disavowed*, 177.

75. *Tradiciones* are short prose sketches in which a historical incident is related in an imaginative and literary style. An evocation of the South American past, the tradición may be set in the precolonial era, the age of conquest, the prerevolutionary era of romance and political intrigue, or the time of the struggle for self-determination in the nineteenth century. Stimulated by the Romanticists' search for national roots, the Peruvian writer Ricardo Palma's *Tradiciones peruanas* are considered the first published tradiciones.

76. Penson, *Las vírgenes de Galindo*, 198.

77. The Good Neighbor Policy, though associated with the beginning of the twentieth century in the 1904 Corollary by President Theodore Roosevelt, was actually based in the political work of Kentucky politician and two-time House Representative Henry Clay (1777–1852).

78. Though del Monte wrote his poem in 1860 while living in exile in Puerto Rico, he did not publish it in the Dominican Republic until 1885. The 1860 poem circulated in papers and letters as well as public readings. I quote the poem from the 1885 edition.

79. Del Monte, *Las vírgenes de Galindo*, 2.

80. Del Monte, *Las vírgenes de Galindo*, 1.

81. Del Monte, "Advertencia," ii.

82. *Caudillismo* refers to a postrevolutionary Latin American phenomenon through which charismatic militia leaders took hold of regions and governed people, sometimes against national orders.

83. Penson, *Las vírgenes de Galindo*, 245.

84. Mayes, *The Mulatto Republic*, 8.

85. Mayes, *The Mulatto Republic*, 8.

86. Penson, *Las vírgenes de Galindo*, 245.

87. Penson, *Las vírgenes de Galindo*, 225–27.

88. See Morgan, "Slavery and the Slave Trade" and "Some Could Suckle over Their Shoulders."

89. One example is Eugene O'Neill, *The Emperor Jones* (Cincinnati, OH: Stewart Kidd Company, 1921).

90. Other important titles include *The Goat without Horns* (1925), by Beale Davis; *Black Majesty* (1928), by John Vandercook; *The Magic Island* (1929), by William Seabrook; and the film *The White Zombie* (1932), directed by Victor Halperin.

91. Penson, *Las vírgenes de Galindo*, 227.

92. "Comprobante de protocolo José Troncoso," 1822, in Archivo de la Época Haitiana (1822–44), Legajo 2, Folder 7, AGN, Santo Domingo, DR.

93. "Proceso del crimen Galindo," in Sentencias Penales de la Época Haitiana (1822–31), AGN, Santo Domingo, DR.

94. Penson, "Notas del autor," 311.

95. Penson, *Las vírgenes de Galindo*, 258.

96. Del Monte, *Las vírgenes de Galindo*, 3.

97. "Proceso del crimen de Galindo," in Sentencias Penales de la Época Haitiana (1822–31), AGN, Santo Domingo, DR.

98. Del Monte, "Advertencia," i.

99. Del Monte, "Advertencia," ii.

100. Del Monte, "Advertencia," iii.

101. Penson, "Notas del autor," 309.

102. Penson, *Las vírgenes de Galindo*, 212.

103. Del Monte, *Las vírgenes de Galindo*, 45.

104. Penson, *Las vírgenes de Galindo*, 229.

105. *Facundo: O, civilización y barbarie* (Buenos Aires, 1845) by Argentine writer Domingo Faustino Sarmiento was a protest against the regime of Juan Manuel de Rosas (1835–1852). The book, an icon of Latin American literature, is a biography of caudillo Juan Facundo Quiroga, who is portrayed as an untamed and "barbaric" Argentine. The text proposes the need to civilize such leaders as the only way to achieve progress.

106. Balaguer, *La realidad dominicana*, 49.

107. In *Black behind the Ears*, Ginetta Candelario examines the role of the Plaza de la Cultura in Trujillo's national project, paying close attention to the Museo del Hombre as a monument to mestizaje.

108. See Vallejo, *Las madres de la patria*.

109. Vallejo, *Las madres de la patria*, 16.

110. See note 14.

111. Penson, *Las vírgenes de Galindo*, 221.

112. Penson, *Las vírgenes de Galindo*, 220.

113. Penson, *Las vírgenes de Galindo*, 220.

114. Penson, *Las vírgenes de Galindo*, 220.

115. Penson, "Notas del autor," 310.

116. Penson, "Notas del autor," 311.

117. Penson, *Las vírgenes de Galindo*, 207, 259, 310.

118. Freud, *The Standard Edition of the Complete Psychological Works of Sigmund Freud*.

119. Fischer, *Modernity Disavowed*, 178.

120. See Franco, *Plotting Women: Gender and Representation in Mexico* and *The Decline and Fall of the Lettered City*.

121. See Pratt, "Women, Literature, and National Brotherhood" and "Las mujeres y el imaginario nacional del siglo XIX."

122. Del Monte, *Las vírgenes de Galindo*, 12.

123. Anonymous poem "La madre africana," published in *El Porvenir*, June 22, 1873, Puerto Plata, DR. Parts of the poem are reproduced in Vallejo, *Las madres de la patria*, 192–93.

124. Pérez, "A Etnaí," in *Fantasías indígenas*.

125. Pérez, "A Etnaí."

126. Guidotti-Hernández, *Unspeakable Violence*, 2.

127. Penson, *Las vírgenes de Galindo*, 207.

128. Penson, *Las vírgenes de Galindo*, 259.

129. Max Henríquez Ureña was the brother of celebrated Dominican intellectual Pedro Henríquez Ureña. They had radically different political views.

130. Although there is a historical Lico Andújar listed as one of the conspirators, I have not found any evidence linking the historical character to the Galindo girls.

131. See García, *Compendio de la historia de Santo Domingo*, and Henríquez Ureña, *La Conspiración de los Alcarrizos*.

132. Henríquez Ureña, *La conspiración de los Alcarrizos*, 96.

133. See "Secretaría de Estado de Educación y Bellas Artes," Legajo 3, Folder 5, Archivo General de Trujillo, "Currículo de historia dominicana," in Colección Bernardo Vega, AGN, Santo Domingo, DR.

134. Hamlet Bodden recently adapted Penson's version into a play he also titled *Las vírgenes de Galindo* (2006). The production was sponsored by the Secretary of Arts (Secretaría de Bellas Artes).

Chapter 2: Of Bandits and Wenches

1. The term *cofradía*, for Afro-religious organizations founded by African slaves and free blacks as early as 1690, has the same religious connotation as the words "brotherhood" or "sisterhood," but it is gender-neutral and typically includes men and women. San Juan de la Maguana is one of the most important locations of cofradías.

2. "Letter from Dominga Alcántara to the Military Governor Harry Lee," Chief Naval Operations 1917–25, RG 38, Box 49, Folder 2 (226–50), Navy Department, Records of the United States Marines, Military Government of Santo Domingo (1916–24), National Archives, Washington, DC.

3. The word *batey* originally meant "community" and was used to name rural communities of mainly rayanos. Today "batey" refers mostly to neighborhoods or sugar barracks where the Haitian cane workers live. The account of Alcántara's preparations is from Adalberto Grullón's video *Fiesta de palos* (AAA Producciones, 2006).

4. Grullón, *Fiesta de palos*.

5. See note 10 for description of the guardias. In Afro-Dominican religiosity the word *atabal* (which in Spanish means drum) refers to the rhythm rather than the actual object. Documentos Guardia Nacional Dominicana (1920–22), Legajo 3, Folder 2, Archivo del Gobierno Militar de Santo Domingo (1916–24), AGN, Santo Domingo, DR.

6. Documentos Guardia Nacional Dominicana (1920–22), Legajo 3, Folder 2.

7. Documentos Guardia Nacional Dominicana (1920–22), Legajo 3, Folder 2.

8. Herrera, "When the Names of the Emperors Were Morgan and Rockefeller," 29–37, 46.

9. Herrera, "When the Names of the Emperors Were Morgan and Rockefeller," 47.

10. The GND was created during the US military regime. Guardias were trained by the marines and served under their command. During the last six years of the intervention, the GND was used to repress and torture people who were perceived as enemies of the nation (see Cassá, *Historia social y económica de la República Dominicana*). Eventually, after the occupation ended, the GND became a tool in service of the various Dominican dictatorships of the twentieth century (specifically Trujillo's and Balaguer's). To this date, the GND continues to be the main vehicle for exercising repression and censorship of Dominican people. The GND is often deployed during peaceful demonstrations to intimidate protesters. In May 2006, President Leonel Fernández ordered the GND to "exercise control over the population" (see Lozano, "Los legados de Leonel Fernández") after a national curfew prohibiting people from congregating after 11 p.m. on weekdays and 2 a.m. on weekends was declared by the executive power.

11. For raids, see "General Communications," June 27, 1922, Legajo 4, Folder 2, Archivo del Gobierno Militar de Santo Domingo (1916–24), AGN, Santo Domingo, DR. For imprisonment, see "Military Government of Santo Domingo, Executive Order N. 385," January 15, 1920, Signed Thomas Snowden, Rear Admiral, US Navy, "Leyes y Decretos," Archivo del Gobierno Militar de Santo Domingo (1916–24), AGN, Santo Domingo, DR.

12. See Puar, "Abu Ghraib: Arguing against Exceptionalism."

13. Renda, *Taking Haiti*, 44–45.

14. Renda, *Taking Haiti*, 44–45.

15. Renda, *Taking Haiti*, 44–45.

16. Unlike traditional Catholicism and other Afro-religious expressions such as Palo Monte and Candomblé, Dominican Afro-religious liturgy is often led by women who are in charge of organizing ceremonies and keeping alive the organization's memory. Therefore, cofradía queens often knew how to write. See Andújar, *Identidad cultural y religiosidad popular*, 104–5.

17. "Letter from Dominga Alcántara."

18. See map 2.1.

19. Wenceslao Ramírez, also known as Don Lao, was the most important caudillo in the area of San Juan. He was born in Azúa in 1843 and spent part of his youth in Bánica. In 1880 he became *jefe comunal*, a type of mayor selected by the community, in Bánica. In 1887 he obtained the same position in San Juan, a bigger, more prosperous city. Don Lao was good friends with dictator Ulises Heureaux (Lilís). Until his death in 1927, Ramírez remained the most influential caudillo in the region. See Martínez, *Palma Sola*, 415.

20. "Claim of Dominga Alcántara," Office of the Commandant, Chief Naval Operations 1917–25, RG 38, Box 49, Folder 2 (226–50), Navy Department, Records of the United States Marines, Military Government of Santo Domingo (1916–24), National Archives, Washington, DC.

21. Cabildos were Spanish colonial administrative councils.

22. Andújar, *Identidad cultural y religiosidad popular*, 104.

23. In 1920, 70 percent of the Dominican population was illiterate according to the Our World in Data literacy report, http://ourworldindata.org/data/education -knowledge/literacy/ (accessed May 14, 2013).

24. Document from June 20, 1922, General Communications, Director Department of South, PND, RG 38, Box 49, Folder 2 (226–50), AGN, Santo Domingo, DR.

25. Though San Juan is not on the border, its proximity to the border through both the southwest and the northwest Artibonito Valley has made it an extension of Las Matas and other border towns. Mateo lived in various towns in the surrounding border and crossed often to Haiti. See Document from June 20, 1922.

26. "Report on Contact with Dios Olivorio, submitted on July 8, 1922 by Lt. G. A. Williams," Chief Naval Operations 1917–25, RG 38, Box 50, Folder 8, Navy Department, Records of the United States Marines, Military Government of Santo Domingo (1916–24), National Archives, Washington, DC.

27. Document from June 20, 1922.

28. Dominican publications were subjected to the military government censorship laws, as shown by the significant number of publications that the government shut down. Executive Order 591 dictated that the military government had the power to forbid the publications of articles in magazines, newspapers, "pamphlets, periodicals, hand bills, publications which teach doctrines that create disturbances, lead to disorder or exhibit morals that are not of 'civil nations.'" A number of local newspapers, including *La Abeja* and *La Opinión*, had been shut down earlier that year by the regime. It is fair to conclude that the position of *El Cable*, as the only paper in the southwest that remained open during the intervention, was also the position of the military regime. See Military Government of Santo Domingo, "Executive Order 591 issued by Thomas Snowden" (Censorship Law), September 26, 1922, Chief Naval Operations 1917–25, RG 38, Box 49, Folder 2, Navy Department, Records of the United States Marines, Military Government of Santo Domingo (1916–24), National Archives, Washington, DC, and "Memorandum de Ley Ejecutiva," Legajo 1, Folder 21, Archivo del Gobierno Militar de Santo Domingo (1916–24), AGN, Santo Domingo, DR.

29. See "Executive Order 591" and "Executive Order 385," RG 45, Box 757, Navy Department, Records of the United States Marines, Military Government of Santo Domingo (1916–24), National Archives, Washington, DC.

30. See "Executive Order 591."

31. When conducting research on the eight-year occupation, I was overwhelmed by the number of documents that demonstrate the death toll of marines at the hands of the guerrillas. In addition, the constant imprisonment of intellectuals, writers, and artists—as well as the multiplicity of letters and editorials written against the regime—show that there was indeed a strong resistance. Bruce Calder's book *The Impact of the Intervention* was the first US historical account of the intervention that focused on the resistance, particularly that of gavilleros in the eastern part of the island. For examples of letters written by or on behalf of political prisoners, such as those by celebrated anti-American poet Fabio Fiallo (1866–1942), who was imprisoned during the occupation, see "General Correspondence," Box 50, Navy Department, Records of the

United States Marines, Military Government of Santo Domingo (1916–24), National Archives, Washington, DC.

32. Ureña Henríquez, *Los Yanquis en Santo Domingo*: *La verdad de los hechos*, n.p.

33. As discussed in chapter 1, Dominican intellectual production in the late nineteenth century was almost exclusively at the service of the dominant political project of national unity. This project, as examined throughout this book, was based on a contradictory rhetoric of civilization and progress through which Europeanness (whiteness) was celebrated as a sign of civility and as the true root of the national culture. In turn, African heritage was suppressed and deployed as foreign.

34. Adalberto Grullón, producer and director of the video *Fiesta de palos*, interview by the author, April 12, 2010.

35. Liborismo was banned during the Trujillo dictatorship (1930–61), though there is evidence that *liboristas* continued to congregate in secret. See Martínez, *Palma sola su geografía y mítica social*, 175, and Lundius and Lundahl, *Peasants and Religion*, 200 and 204.

36. I follow the 1908 date, as it is corroborated by oral tradition and several sources, including Garrido Puello's biography. But I should note that the date could be also earlier: 1899, during a hurricane that swept Hispaniola, or 1909, when Hurricane San Ciriaco also affected the island.

Lundahl and Lundius conducted interviews in the late 1970s and were able to meet some of the people who knew Olivorio Mateo. Though they do not give credit to testimony of the followers as historical truth, these findings are the most important for reconstructing Mateo's archive. Lundahl and Lundius, *Peasants and Religion*, 33.

37. Known as Hurricane II, the 1908 storm is the second documented storm of the twentieth century. Though its effects in the coast of Florida were minimal, the eye of the storm was fairly close to Hispaniola. Neumann, Jarvinen and Pike, *Tropical Cyclones of the North Atlantic Ocean*, 195.

38. See Garrido Puello, *Olivorio: Un ensayo histórico*, n.p. Emigdio Osvaldo Garrido Puello Badín (1893–1983) was one of the most important members of the San Juan City elite class. He was the descendant of the famous leader Carmito Ramírez, an important caudillo in San Juan Valley. He was a teacher as well as a writer, and he founded *El Cable*, the newspaper that was shut down in 1930 by Trujillo. Garrido Puello was very invested in the project of modernizing the nation and made it his life's mission to fight what he believed to be "Haitian" influence in Dominican culture (anything that resembled Afro-Dominican cultural traditions). His account of Olivorio and his people, although fairly informed, is also harsh, and exhibits his anti-Haitianism and class prejudice. His arguments are often biased as they render Liborismo as superstitious and barbaric.

39. Lundahl and Lundius, *Peasants and Religion*, 28.

40. Garrido Puello, *Olivorio*, 8.

41. Garrido Puello, *Olivorio*, 8.

42. In the Dominican Republic, particularly in the countryside, oral memory is linked to the seasons, the harvest, and the various natural disasters that have affected

the island. Because the practice of obtaining a birth certificate was not common until the 1940s, when Trujillo mandated it, many older peasants knew their age or the age of their family members by these nature markers. When I asked my grandfather how old he was, for instance, he responded: "Well, I was ten during San Zenón." San Zenón was a hurricane that hit the island in 1931; therefore I knew he was born in 1921. Liborismo is linked to La Gran Tormenta (The Great Storm), which took place in 1908; therefore it is easy to situate the beginning of the movement historically.

43. Hurricane San Zenón took place in 1931, destroying a vast portion of the island's infrastructure. Trujillo rose to power with the help of the United States and San Zenón, as he seized the opportunity to establish himself as a natural leader for a distressed and displaced population of farmers.

44. Cassá, "Problemas del culto olivorista," 6.

45. There is little data about this particular storm, though it could be deduced that if Mateo's family had decided to follow a funeral procession it is because the storm had taken other lives.

46. See Williams, "The Development of Literary Blackness in the Dominican Republic," 74; Prestol Castillo, "Paisajes y meditaciones de una frontera"; and Rueda, *La criatura terrestre.*

47. Baud, "Una frontera para cruzar."

48. Baud, "Una frontera para cruzar."

49. Military Government of Santo Domingo, "Report of contact with Dios Olivorio," submitted by Officer Colonel Bearss, May 23, 1922, Chief Naval Operations 1917–25, RG 38, Box 49, Navy Department, Records of the United States Marines, Military Government of Santo Domingo (1916–24), National Archives, Washington, DC, 1.

50. Garrido Puello, *Olivorio,* 19.

51. As in other US interventions of the time—in Haiti, Nicaragua, and the Philippines, to mention a few—the Dominican occupation provoked armed resistance. In the Dominican Republic, the guerrilla forces were concentrated in the eastern part of the island (opposite of the San Juan Valley). Although rarely mentioned in US narratives, the gavillero rebels of the east created many problems for the occupying forces and caused embarrassment for their leadership. Bruce Calder examines this particular history in *The Impact of the Intervention,* while Mary A. Renda, in *Taking Haiti,* looks at a similar situation in Haiti during the occupation of the western portion of the island (1914–35).

52. Lundius and Lundahl, *Peasants and Religion,* 667.

53. Lundius and Lundahl, *Peasants and Religion,* 667.

54. Starting in 2003, the Olivorio Festival has been celebrated in New York and Boston Dominican communities on June 14.

55. The Canudos Movement began at the end of the nineteenth century, led by Antônio Vicente Mendes Maciel AKA Antônio Conselheiro. See Da Cunha and Bernucci, *Os sertões: Campanha de Canudos.*

56. Lundius and Lundahl, *Peasants and Religion,* 28.

57. "Comarca from Maguana," from Grullón, *Fiesta de palos*, min. 23.

58. Grullón, interview by the author, June 13, 2006.

59. Felipe Umberto Acosta, interview by the author, San Juan de la Maguana, November 5, 2006.

60. Renda, *Taking Haiti*, 34.

61. "Memorandum from General Harry Lee to all Commanders," 1921, Legajo 1J, Folder 20, Archivo del Gobierno Militar de Santo Domingo (1916–24), AGN, Santo Domingo, DR; "The Brigade Attitude toward the Inhabitants and Its Places in the Occupation," memo issued to all officers by general Harry Lee on November 15, 1921, RG 38, Navy Department, Records of the United States Marines, Military Government of Santo Domingo (1916–24), National Archives, Washington, DC.

62. "Memorandum from General Harry Lee to all Commanders."

63. The memo also states that although no measures had been taken to punish the marines accused of such acts, he was concerned that if they continued in this way, attention from other Latin American countries would soon come, which would hurt marines personally as well as collectively as representatives of the United States Government. "Memo from Commander officer Knapp to all brigadiers #2816," October 26, 1918, RG 45: Naval Records 1911–1917 (WA-7), Box 757, Folder 6, Navy Department, Records of the United States Marines, Military Government of Santo Domingo (1916–24), National Archives, Washington, DC.

64. Wheeler, *The Complexion of Race*.

65. See Theodore Roosevelt, "Corollary to the Monroe Doctrine," in Annual Message to the United States Congress, 1904, House Records HR 58A-K2, Records of the U.S. House of Representatives, RG 233, Center for Legislative Archives, National Archives. For more on the effects of the Corollary, see Chomsky, *Hegemony or Survival*.

66. See Chomsky, *Hegemony or Survival*.

67. Wilson, "Remarks to the Associated Press in New York," 39.

68. Wilson, "Remarks to the Associated Press in New York," 39.

69. Renda, *Taking Haiti*, 13.

70. Renda, *Taking Haiti*, 64.

71. Renda, *Taking Haiti*, 64.

72. Renda, *Taking Haiti*, 64.

73. Blanco Fombona, *Crímenes del imperialismo norteamericano*, 97.

74. Calder, *The Impact of the Intervention*, 34.

75. The guerrillas, known as the aforementioned gavilleros, were fighting for the right to self-govern and understood the land and the environment. The marines, on the other hand, failed to understand their reasons and continued to attack guerrillas and regular peasants, causing larger outrage among the locals and therefore fueling the war. See Calder, *The Impact of the Intervention*, xxviii.

76. Blanco Fombona, *Crímenes del imperialismo norteamericano*, 34.

77. Blanco Fombona, *Crímenes del imperialismo norteamericano*, 34.

78. Report, Second Provisional Brigade, US Marine Corp, June 11, 1918, RG 45,

Box 756, Folder 6, Navy Department, Records of the United States Marines, Military Government of Santo Domingo (1916–24), National Archives, Washington, DC.

79. It is important to remember that Roosevelt's Manifest Destiny insisted on the need to help "impotent nations," particularly those in the neighboring Caribbean and Latin America, achieve "civility" and prosperity. Examples include the military interventions in Cuba and Puerto Rico in 1898 and in the early twentieth century.

80. Lundius and Lundahl, *Peasants and Religion*, 23.

81. See "Memo from the Second Provisional Brigade of the US Marine Corps regarding the preservation of order in the Dominican Republic," June 11, 1918, RG 45, Box 756, Folder 6, "Chief Naval Operations," Navy Department, Records of the United States Marines, Military Government of Santo Domingo (1916–24), National Archives, Washington, DC.

82. In studies of the occupations, the fact that the two nations are part of a larger Latin American intervention is acknowledged. However, a study that examines how the dual intervention of the island affected the Haitian-Dominican relationship does not yet exist.

83. The sanitation laws introduced in Haiti and the Dominican Republic were later implemented in places such as Nicaragua and Korea.

84. Castor, *La ocupación norteamericana de Haití y sus consecuencias*.

85. Castor, *La ocupación norteamericana de Haití y sus consecuencias*.

86. The poor treatment of the Haitian immigrant in the Dominican Republic is the single most studied topic related to Dominicans. There are over one million Haitians living in the Dominican Republic, many working in the sugar industry in slavery-like conditions. The topic has been depicted in the recent films *The Price of Sugar* (2007) and *Sugar Babies* (2007). However, the relationship between Haitian immigration to the DR and the US intervention is still understudied. In *Taking Haiti*, Renda mentions that the United States imposed a forced labor system (11) but explains neither what that entails, nor the relationship to the Dominican Republic.

87. See "Report on Dominican-Haitian Frontier," issued May 16, 1922, Office of the Military Governor, Legajo 4, Folder 37, Archivo del Gobierno Militar de Santo Domingo (1916–24), AGN, Santo Domingo, DR.

88. "Report on Dominican-Haitian Frontier."

89. "Report on Dominican-Haitian Frontier."

90. See 11th Endorsement, July 8, 1922, Report 14-186, March, Chief Naval Operations 1917–24, RG 38, Box 49, Navy Department, Records of the United States Marines, Military Government of Santo Domingo (1916–24), National Archives, Washington, DC.

91. When the Dominican Republic declared its independence from Haiti in 1844, the United States sent agent John Hogan to assess the nation's ability to govern itself in order to see if the United States could recognize its independence (a recognition it had denied Haiti for over twenty years after its independence from France). After spending a few months in the country, Hogan concluded that it had enough white

people, as well as lighter colored men, to be accepted as an independent nation. See Torres-Saillant, "The Tribulations of Blackness," 126.

92. Trouillot, *Silencing the Past*, 35.

93. This is evidenced in artistic movements such as Négritude and the Harlem Renaissance.

94. See Morgan, "Some Could Suckle over Their Shoulders," 123.

95. Carl Van Doren praised many of the literatures about Haiti as important in the construction of an American Empire. He was a professor of literature at Columbia University during the invasion. See Renda, *Taking Haiti*, introduction and chap. 7.

96. Encounter with Dios Olivorio, June 9, 1922, SS Robinson, RG 38, Box 49, Folder 2, Navy Department, Records of the United States Marines, Military Government of Santo Domingo (1916–24), National Archives, Washington, DC.

97. Garrido Puello, *Olivorio*, 13.

98. Garrido Puello, *Olivorio*, 9.

99. *El Cable*, June 1919.

100. "There are no letters to show that Olivorio was or is in any way connected or in communication with any of the former revolutionary leaders on the island." *El Cable*, April 1920.

101. Encounter with Dios Olivorio, June 9, 1922, SS Robinson, RG 38, Box 49, Folder 2, Navy Department, Records of the United States Marines, Military Government of Santo Domingo (1916–24), National Archives, Washington, DC.

102. Alexander, *Pedagogies of Crossing*, 4.

103. See chapters 1 and 3.

104. The reports highlight the use of Haitian rum and the "foreign element" of the Olivoristas, as well as the presumed suspicion of Olivorio's connection with Haitian rebels.

105. Alexander, *Pedagogies of Crossing*, 78.

106. Alexander, *Pedagogies of Crossing*, 78.

107. Alexander, *Pedagogies of Crossing*, 290.

108. Alexander, *Pedagogies of Crossing*, 290.

109. Alexander, *Pedagogies of Crossing*, 290.

110. See Sánchez-Carretero, "Santos y Misterios as Channels of Communication in the Diaspora."

111. The works of Junot Díaz, Julia Álvarez, Angie Cruz, and Loida Maritza Pérez also engage the role of the United States in twentieth-century Dominican historical conflicts, eventually linking them to the diaspora.

112. Rosario, *Song of the Water Saints*, 11.

113. Thompson, *An Eye for the Tropics*.

114. See Brennan, *What's Love Got to Do with It?*, 15–20.

115. Brennan, *What's Love Got to Do with It?*, 15.

116. Brennan, *What's Love Got to Do with It?*, 16.

117. I place *black* in parentheses to highlight the fact that the definition of what constituted blackness was mediated by the US military's racial perceptions.

118. "Memoradum regarding soldiers and local women," July 21, 1920, Legajo 2, Folder 31, Archivo del Gobierno Militar de Santo Domingo (1916–24), AGN, Santo Domingo, DR.

119. "Memoradum regarding soldiers and local women."

120. A memo issued on July 23, 1920, prohibits members of the military from marrying Dominican women. The reasoning behind it was that it was supposed these women were often prostitutes who allegedly bewitched the soldiers and tricked them into marrying them to escape government control. "Memorandum to the Military Governor," 1920, Legajo 1, Folder 31, Archivo del Gobierno Militar de Santo Domingo (1916–24), AGN, Santo Domingo, DR.

121. "Memorandum to the Military Governor."

122. See Blanco Fombona, *Crímenes del imperialismo norteamericano*.

123. I counted the number of women listed in all the record books 1916–24 as imprisoned for violating the sanitation law, and the total was 953. It is possible that some names were not recorded or that there were no records in the smaller provinces or towns. See Archivo del Gobierno Militar de Santo Domingo (1916–24), AGN, Santo Domingo, DR.

124. "Regarding the round out of prostitutes," memorandum from General Lee, May 1921, Legajo 2, Folder 5, Archivo del Gobierno Militar de Santo Domingo (1916–24), AGN, Santo Domingo, DR.

125. "Imprisonment of Luisa Salcedo," memorandum to the Director signed by Captain B. F. Weakland, La Vega, October 7, 1922, Legajo 1, Folder 7, Archivo del Gobierno Militar de Santo Domingo (1916–24), AGN, Santo Domingo, DR.

126. "Letter to the President Court of Appeal, signed by Judge J.R. Berrido," letter in support of Srta. Salcedo, accused of prostitution and venereal disease, La Vega, September 12, 1922, Legajo 1, Folder 7, Archivo del Gobierno Militar de Santo Domingo (1916–24), AGN, Santo Domingo, DR.

127. A series of petitions to the military governor asking for child support for children fathered by stationed marines can be found in the "Administration" files of the military government from 1917 to 1922. One in particular caught my attention. It is from April 12, 1919, signed by Altagracia Ortiz, a woman from San Luis, a town located just ten miles east of Santo Domingo, who says the father of her child, who was a marine, had died at the hands of the gavilleros and she could no longer support their child. She continues by saying that the marine had "taken me from my home and promised to marry me . . . but now I am alone in the world with this child and no help as my father will not take me dishonored." A memo denying Altagracia's request was issued one day after her letter was received. See Office of the Military Government, 32–27, Administración, 1917, RG 38, Box 757, Folder 17, Navy Department, Records of the United States Marines, Military Government of Santo Domingo (1916–24), National Archives, Washington, DC.

128. See Office of the Military Government, 32–27, Administración, 1917.

129. Blanco Fombona, *Crímenes del imperialismo norteamericano*.

130. "Letter to the president court of appeal, signed by Judge J.R. Berrido."

131. The Immigration Restriction League was the first American entity officially associated with eugenics. Founded in 1894 by three recent Harvard University graduates, the league sought to bar what it considered inferior races from entering America and diluting what it saw as superior American racial stock (upper-class northerners of Anglo-Saxon heritage).

132. For more on eugenics and compulsory sterilization, see Silver, "Eugenics and Compulsory Sterilization Laws," 862.

133. Mann Act, "Ch 395," Stat (1910): 825–27.

134. Warren and Bolduan, "War Activities of the United States Public Health Service," 1245.

135. Warren and Bolduan, "War Activities of the United States Public Health Service," 1245.

136. Rosario, *Song of the Water Saints*, 13–14.

137. Suárez, *The Tears of Hispaniola*, 11.

138. Catherina Vallejo's book *Las madres de la patria y las bellas mentiras* explores the construction of the Dominican racialized Madonna/whore depiction in literary representations from the mid-nineteenth century to the dawn of Trujillo's regime. Zeller, *Discursos y espacios femeninos en República Dominicana*, and Manley, "Poner Un Grano de Arena," explore how the ideology of nationalism in combination with the US-supported rhetoric resulted in numerous crimes against women during the Trujillo dictatorship. They also explore the ways women resisted and participated in the nation-building project.

139. See chapter 1.

140. The Monroe Doctrine, for example, was a policy of the United States introduced on December 2, 1823. It stated that further efforts by European nations to colonize land or interfere with states in North or South America would be viewed as acts of aggression, requiring US intervention.

141. See Cassá, *Historia social y económica de la República Dominicana*, 109–13, and Bosch, *Composición social dominicana*.

142. See Blanco Fombona, *En las garras del águila*.

143. During the Trujillo dictatorship, the right to assembly was tightly controlled. While organized religions such as Catholicism were somewhat respected, Afro-religious practices, particularly Liborismo, were prohibited. See "Memo del subsecretario de estado de la presidencia al señor secretario de interior y policía. Asunto: Supresión de prácticas liboristas," February 16, 1938, Bonetti Burgos, Archivo Particular del Generalísimo, Palacio Nacional, AGN, Santo Domingo, DR.

See Davis, "Revolutionary Quisqueya from Caonabo to Liborio" and "Papa Liborio: El Santo vivo de Maguana"; Grullón, *Fiesta de palos*.

144. After the assassination of Trujillo, the United States increased its involvement in Dominican affairs. It provided training for the creation of a police force, supported a coup of democratically elected president Juan Bosch, who was a Social-Democrat, and eventually launched another military intervention in 1965, which ended in confrontation with local guerrillas. After the 1965 war, the United States backed the

return of Joaquín Balaguer, Trujillo's right-hand man, who ruled for the following twelve years in what has become known as "The Terrible 12" in Dominican history because of the repression, disappearances, and brutal killings of civilians, particularly journalists and scholars. For more on "The Terrible 12," see Liberato, *Joaquín Balaguer, Memory, and Diaspora.*

145. Lundius and Lundahl, *Peasants and Religion*, 242.

146. Francisco Lizardo Lascocé wrote a novel about the event, *Palma Sola: La tragedia de un pueblo.* For more on the history of the Palma Sola Revival, see Martínez, *Palma Sola*, 60–65.

Chapter 3: Speaking in Silences

1. José Matos, local Afro-religious leader and santero, interview by author, Dajabón, March 19, 2006.

2. See introduction, note 7.

3. Richard Turits believes the number of victims to be about fifteen thousand. See Turits, *Foundations of Despotism*, 161. Other scholars mention figures as high as thirty thousand. See Fiehrer, "Political Violence in the Periphery," and Malek, "Dominican Republic's General Rafael Trujillo and the Haitian Massacre of 1937."

4. Turits, *Foundations of Despotism*, 161.

5. Despite overwhelming evidence collected by local and foreign scholars, as well as the testimony of survivors, the official position of the Dominican state continues to be ambivalent and vague. During the Trujillo dictatorship, the Massacre of 1937 was depicted as a conflict between peasants, though there is ample evidence that hundreds of Dominican troops had been deployed to the borderlands to carry out the massacre (see Turits, *Foundations of Despotism*, 163–67). Joaquín Balaguer, who served as one of the intellectual masterminds of the Trujillo regime, justifying the massacre, became president of the Dominican Republic for more than two decades after the US intervention in 1965. It was not until the twenty-first century that the trauma of the massacre was publicly confronted with Dominican state officials in a UN-mediated event that took place in New York in November 2000. To date, however, there are no monuments or public displays that memorialize the genocide. In addition, the massacre is not studied in any school curricula (public or private), thus the majority of the Dominican population still does not know that this event happened. In the diaspora, however, it is one of the most important topics addressed by Dominican, as well as foreign, scholars of the Dominican Republic.

6. Roorda, "Genocide Next Door," 302.

7. The Massacre of 1937 is one of the most studied events by US historians interested in the Dominican Republic. Derby, "Haitians, Magic, and Money"; Turits, *Foundations of Despotism*; and Roorda, "Genocide Next Door," study the massacre as a significant event in establishing the border between the two nations and locate it as a significant strategy of the Trujillo nationalist agenda. Although significant contributions to the study of Dominican and Haitian histories, these works contribute

to the imagining of Dominicans and Haitians as adversaries, shaping the intellectual dialogue regarding questions of Dominican ethnic and racial identity. Works that examine this horrible event in dialogue with the longer and more complex history of Haitian-Dominican relations are less common. Matibag's *Haitian-Dominican Counterpoint* attempts this task, insisting on the complexity of the rayano population and the long history of Haitian-Dominican solidarity. More recently Victoriano-Martínez's *Rayanos y Dominicanyorks* (2014) and Paulino's *Dividing Hispaniola* (2016) succeeded in analyzing the Massacre of 1937 as an ethnic rather than an immigrant attack on a borderland community.

8. *Bateyes* are sugar company towns where seasonal cane workers live. The inhumane conditions of the bateyes have attracted national and international attention for decades. Recently, the films *The Price of Sugar*, directed by Bill Haney (2007), and *The Sugar Babies*, directed by Amy Serrano (2007), shed light on the issue, raising awareness of the exploitation of Haitian workers and the slavelike conditions in which they are forced to work.

9. Danticat's participation in multiple roundtables, including a summit at the United Nations in New York that included delegates and political scientists from both nations, further solidified *The Farming of Bones* as historical truth.

10. Trouillot, *Silencing the Past*, 48.

11. See Paulino, *Dividing Hispaniola*, 60–63.

12. Turits, *Foundations of Despotism*, 159.

13. Turits, *Foundations of Despotism*, 159.

14. Matibag, *Haitian-Dominican Counterpoint*, 148.

15. Derby, "Haitians, Magic, and Money," 489.

16. Eugenio Matibag's *Haitian-Dominican Counterpoint* makes a compelling argument for the need to examine the existence of a multiethnic border community that traded and collaborated throughout the colonial period and during the early years of the republic. I further explore this topic in chapter 5.

17. Pedro Campo, interview by author, November 12, 1998, Mal Paso Market, Jimaní, DR.

18. Derby, "Haitians, Magic, and Money," 490.

19. Pedro Campo, interview by author, November 12, 1998.

20. Derby, "Haitians, Magic, and Money," 489.

21. Peña Batlle, *Historia de la cuestión fronteriza dominico-haitiana* and "Política de Trujillo." See also Balaguer, *La realidad dominicana*, and Incháustegui Cabral, *De literatura dominicana siglo veinte*.

22. Balaguer, *La realidad dominicana*, 45.

23. Chapter 1 of this work examines an array of nineteenth-century official documents and literary texts that show the emergence of this Hispanophile ideology and the beginning of an anti-Haitian discourse during the formative years of the republic. The works of such important late nineteenth-century intellectuals as Manuel de Jesús Galván, César Nicolás Penson, José Gabriel García, Francisco Bonó, and Juan Antonio Alix were extremely influential in drafting an idea of Dominican race that persisted in

claiming a cultural whiteness inherited from the colonial history. This ideology was complicated by the need to satisfy US imperial questioning of the legitimacy of the Dominican Republic and its ability to self-govern.

24. The official position of the regime during its first seven years was to create the appearance of tolerance and of a good relationship between the two states sharing the island. Trujillo made several trips to Haiti and delivered a series of speeches in which he spoke of the Haitian as the good neighbor and brother of the republic. The actions taken by the Trujillo government, however, were not as tolerant as its discourse and evidenced a clear desire to "whiten" the Dominican population. In 1931, for instance, Trujillo continued Horacio Vasquez's project of white colonization of the frontier by bringing European immigrants and light-skinned Dominicans to populate the border-land towns. In addition, a series of immigration laws regulating the influx of black laborers from Haiti and other Caribbean islands were drafted, although not successfully implemented, owing to pressure from the American-owned sugarcane corporations. For more information, please refer to Colección de Leyes, 1930–1935 and 1936–1940, AGN, Santo Domingo, DR.

25. Among the most important anti-Haitian nationalist texts that emerged after the Massacre of 1937 are Peña Batlle, *Historia de la cuestión fronteriza dominico-haitiana* and "Política de Trujillo," and Balaguer, *La realidad dominicana*.

26. Maldonado-Torres, *Against War*, xi.

27. Maldonado-Torres, *Against War*, xi.

28. See Austerlitz, *Merengue*.

29. Roorda, "Genocide Next Door," 304.

30. Turits, *Foundations of Despotism*, 144.

31. Following the publication of a *New York Times* article on November 6, 1937, a few weeks after the killings had stopped, the Dominican state was pressured to investigate and provide a public explanation of the events. US secretary of state Sumner Welles actively challenged Trujillo about the events. Ultimately, Cuban president Federico Ladero, Mexican president Lázaro Cárdenas, and Welles formed an international mediation committee. Trujillo agreed to pay Haiti monetary reparation (which was never paid in full) for the damages in the 1938 Haitian-Dominican Agreement signed in Washington, DC.

32. Balaguer, *Discursos*, 504.

33. Veloz-Maggiolo, "Tipología del tema haitiano en la literatura," 95.

34. Mateo, Mito y cultura en la era de Trujillo, 179.

35. Marrero Aristy, *Over*, 71, 82.

36. Marrero Aristy, *Over*, 112.

37. Letter from Commander White to Secretary of the Navy, November 1, 1917, 1–27, Box 5, William Shepherd Benson Papers (1855–1932), Library of Congress, Washington, DC.

38. Marrero Aristy, *Over*, 99.

39. Méndez's book *Narratives of Migration and Displacement in Dominican Literature* explores the various contradictions experienced by Dominican intellectuals at

the end of the nineteenth, beginning of the twentieth century. In *Nation and Citizen in the Dominican Republic, 1880–1916*, Martínez-Vergne locates those contra*dictions* within a larger Latin American intellectual anxiety about representation in the context of European ideologies of race that ultimately depicted the majority of Latin America's population as unfit for self-government.

40. In *Nation and Citizen*, Martínez-Vergne examines the role of the intellectual class in shaping the theoretical underpinnings of the socioeconomic system. In the case of Juan Bosch, his theory advanced into the political arena. He founded El Partido Revolucionario Dominicano (PRD) and ran for president after the fall of the regime. Along with Balaguer, Bosch became one of the most important and influential Dominican politicians of the twentieth century; he won the election in 1962, and the popular vote many times afterward.

41. Bosch, "Luis Pie," 53.

42. Bosch, "Luis Pie," 53.

43. Bosch, "Luis Pie," 57.

44. Dominican nationalization law states that children of illegal Haitian immigrants should not be recognized as Dominican citizens. After an active public awareness campaign launched in the context of UNICEF Rights of the Children, this law was revised to discriminate against all children of illegal immigrants in the Dominican Republic. According to a study by Batey Relief Alliance, there are over 500,000 children in the batey and rural areas without a birth certificate or access to public services such as health care and education.

45. "Carta de Juan Bosch sobre el tema haitiano," *Noticias*, February 10, 2010, http://www.cubadebate.cu/noticias/2010/02/21/revelan-carta-de-juan-bosch-de -1943-sobre-el-drama-haiti/.

46. Bosch, "Luis Pie," 60.

47. For example, Alejo Carpentier's *El reino de este mundo* and Langston Hughes's play *Popo and Fifina: Children of Haiti*.

48. Important intellectuals of the late nineteenth and early twentieth centuries — such as Alejo Carpentier, Booker T. Washington, W. E. B. Du Bois, and Arthur Schomburg — wrote extensively about Haiti, and specifically about the Haitian revolution, paying close attention to the links between spirituality and political freedom.

49. See Kazanjian, *The Colonizing Trick*.

50. Derrida, "The Violence of the Letter," 114.

51. See Valerio-Holguín, "Primitive Borders."

52. As I analyze Prestol Castillo's *El Masacre*, I find the text difficult to categorize as a novel or a testimony because of the stylistic changes within it and the author's involvement in the massacre.

53. Céspedes, *Antología del cuento dominicano*, 3.

54. Sommer, *El Masacre se pasa a pie*, 169.

55. For the ways he refers to the book, see Prestol Castillo, *El Masacre se pasa a pie*, 10.

56. Many contemporary Dominican critics find Prestol Castillo's text to be confus-

ing and, at best, not a good work of art. Pedro Conde and Diógenes Céspedes offer criticisms, ultimately categorizing the book as an overall failure. In a review presented at Livingston College in New Jersey, "El Masacre se pasa a pie: Guilt and Impotence Under Trujillo," Doris Sommer brings to light similar critiques of Prestol Castillo's narrative.

57. Prestol Castillo, *El Masacre se pasa a pie*, 63.

58. Prestol Castillo, *El Masacre se pasa a pie*, 7.

59. Prestol Castillo, *El Masacre se pasa a pie*, 84.

60. Turits, *Foundations of Despotism*, 89; Bhabha, *Nation and Narration*, 303.

61. See Brea, *Ensayo sobre la formación del estado capitalista en la República Dominicana y Haití*.

62. "Carta a Sumner Welles," Legajo 267, Folder 1, Archivo del Palacio Nacional (1940–50), AGN, Santo Domingo, DR.

63. Prestol Castillo devotes several pages of his autobiography to discussing his friendship with Pedro Henríquez Ureña, who offered him free passage to exile in Venezuela. The author, owing to fear and his inability to decide, ends up staying in the country. The autobiography does not specify what Prestol Castillo does after staying. However, public records available at the Dominican National Archives show that he occupied a variety of government positions, including that of general prosecutor for the province of Neyba; magistrate of Dajabón, San Cristóbal, and Santo Domingo; and state judge for the *tribunal de tierras* (land court). In all these positions, Prestol Castillo had to forcefully defend the state many times against peasant organizations or landowners.

64. After increasing international pressure, and in an effort to mask the genocide as a civilian conflict, an order was issued to prosecute peasants who had participated in the killings. Prestol Castillo was one of the various prosecutors in charge of conducting these proceedings. See Cuello, *Documentos del conflicto Dominico-Haitiano de 1937*.

65. This essay, published in Ciudad Trujillo by Editorial Cosmopolita in 1943, was never reprinted. The author does not mention this previous text in his novel or in any of his later publications about the Dominican Frontier compiled under the title "La Tabla Gesta y Cantares del Valle de Neyba" (Santo Domingo, 1950). While conducting research in the Dominican National Archives, I stumbled on the title of this essay through a newspaper article published in La Nación. Thinking that it could have been an earlier version of *El Masacre se pasa a pie*, I undertook the task of finding the text. After a year of research, and with the support of historian Raymundo González, I was able to find a copy of this essay in the personal library of a Dominican historian. The mystery and silence surrounding this particular publication is as fascinating as the text itself, for it contradicts the very public life the author lived.

66. Prestol Castillo, "Paisajes," 23

67. Prestol Castillo, *El Masacre se pasa a pie*, 62.

68. Prestol Castillo, "Paisajes," 30–32.

69. Prestol Castillo, "Paisajes," 41.

70. Prestol Castillo, "Paisajes," 11.

71. Prestol Castillo, "Paisajes," 12.

72. Gil, "'El Masacre se pasa a pie' de Freddy Prestol Castillo," 43.

73. Tamara Alonzo, bruja santera from Cristo Rey, interview by the author, October 6, 2006.

74. Tamara Alonzo, bruja santera from Cristo Rey, interview by the author, November 10, 2006.

75. Alexis was well known for his activities in the Partie Démocratique Populaire de la Jeunesse Haïtienne (to which other important Haitian intellectuals, such as René Depestre, belonged). He was a friend and collaborator of Marie Vieux Chauvet and Jacques Roumain, with whom he shared the ideals of social responsibility of literature.

76. The term "proletarian" refers to Haitian social-realist literature of the 1940s and 1950s that depict peasants' reality in confronting poverty and hunger.

77. Alexis, *General Sun, My Brother*, 290.

78. Dayan, *Haiti, History and the Gods*, 46. On the use of the body, see Suárez, *Tears of Hispaniola*, chap. 2.

79. Alexis, *General Sun, My Brother*, 16–17.

80. Martínez-San Miguel, *Caribe Two Ways*.

81. See Pratt, *Imperial Eyes*.

82. Matibag, *Haitian-Dominican Counterpoint*, 3.

83. Alexis, *General Sun, My Brother*, 47.

84. Alexis, *General Sun, My Brother*, 149.

85. Shortly after the novel was published, an interdisciplinary forum was held in the UN Building in New York City (November 1999). Danticat served as a mediator. The speakers included Dominican and Haitian politicians, community leaders, and political scientists. In addition, a series of debates regarding the events in light of the novel have emerged in the three geographical spaces, the most celebrated being the famous discussion between Danticat and Dominican historian Bernardo Vega, which has been published widely in the Internet. Vega questioned the accuracy of Danticat's narrative, while the latter defended her narrative space as a place from which the memory of the dead and the survivors could be articulated. See "Bernardo Vega y Edwidge Danticat discuten la matanza del 1937," *Periódico Hoy*, July 5, 2004, Archivo de Prensa, AGN, Santo Domingo, DR.

86. Danticat, *The Farming of Bones*, 224.

87. Shea, "The Hunger to Tell," 12, 22.

88. Suárez, *The Tears of Hispaniola*, 30.

89. Suárez, *The Tears of Hispaniola*, 30.

90. Suárez, *The Tears of Hispaniola*, 26.

91. Danticat, *The Farming of Bones*, 69.

92. San Miguel, *La isla imaginada*.

93. See "Bernardo Vega y Edwidge Danticat discuten la matanza del 1937."

Chapter 4: *Rayano* Consciousness

1. For more on the damage and casualty losses of the earthquake, see Bilham, "Lessons from the Haiti Earthquake," 878.

2. It is estimated that before international assistance arrived, more than nine thousand Haitians were cared for in Dominican hospitals. In addition, hundreds of Dominican medical personnel went to Haiti within hours of the quake, offering first aid and helping to rescue victims prior to the arrival of international aid. For more on the Dominican response to the Haitian Earthquake, see Margesson and Taft-Morales, "Haiti Earthquake," and Auerbach et al., "Civil-Military Collaboration in the Initial Medical Response to the Earthquake in Haiti."

3. Viviano de León, "Madre dominicana amamanta niños de Haití lesionados," *Listín Diario*, January 17, 2010, http://www.listin.com.do/la-republica/2010/1/17/128354/Madre-dominicana-amamanta-ninos-de-Haiti-lesionados.

4. See Freddy Vargas, http://vimeo.com/35493047 (accessed May 1, 2012).

5. *El seno de la esperanza* (Milk of Hope), directed by Freddy Vargas (V Films, 2012).

6. *Bateyes* are the impoverished barrack towns where sugarcane workers live. See chapter 3, note 8.

7. Grosz, *Volatile Bodies*, 141–42.

8. Sonia Marmolejos, interview by *Teleantillas*, https://www.youtube.com/watch?v=hyZIwts2_jI (accessed February 2, 2012).

9. Altagracia García, director of Colectivo Mujer y Salud, interview by author, May 13, 2014, Loma de Cabrera, DR.

10. Clinton was charged with managing the relief funds, while Fernández was to serve as liaison, offering "superior" Dominican state infrastructure for the disbursement of funds and the coordination of international relief. Only two years after the quake, however, while Haitian refugees continued to live in tents and slums, scandal surrounded Clinton and Fernández, as both ex-heads of state were accused of mismanaging, stealing, or otherwise profiting from the funds meant to relieve the victims of the quake.

11. Taylor, *The Archive and the Repertoire*, 2.

12. Torres-Saillant, "La condición rayana," 222.

13. In 1920, nearly 20 percent of the population of Monte Cristi was ethnic Haitian, and by 1930, over 40 percent of all Dominican ethnic Haitians lived in Monte Cristi.

14. Rueda, prologue to "Cantos de la frontera," in *La criatura terrestre*, 25.

15. Rueda, *La criatura terrestre*, 32–33.

16. Moreno, "Bordes líquidos, fronteras y espejismos."

17. Glissant, "Caribbean Discourse," 139.

18. Rueda, prologue to "Cantos de la frontera," in *La criatura terrestre*, 3.

19. Silié, "Aspectos y variables de las relaciones entre República Dominicana y Haití."

20. San Miguel, *La isla imaginada*, 23.

21. Torres-Saillant, "La condición rayana," 222.

22. Silié, "Aspectos y variables." See also Torre-Saillant, "La condición rayana."

23. Rueda, prologue to "Cantos de la Frontera," in *La criatura terrestre*, xi.

24. See chapter 1.

25. Rueda, *La criatura terrestre*, 27.

26. Rueda, *La criatura terrestre*, 28.

27. Rueda, *La criatura terrestre*, 30.

28. Bhabha, *The Location of Culture*, 4.

29. Rueda, *La criatura terrestre*, 29.

30. Rueda, *La criatura terrestre*, 29.

31. At age eighteen, Rueda left for Chile to study music on a government fellowship. He lived there from 1939 to 1951, when he came back to the island as a celebrated musician and poet. In Chile, Rueda was a pupil of Vicente Huidobro and a good friend of Enrique Lihn. He was influenced by Pablo Neruda and by Nicanor Parra's *anti-poesía*.

32. Rueda, "Canción del rayano," in *La criatura terrestre*, 30.

33. Rueda, "Canción del rayano," in *La criatura terrestre*, 30.

34. Latin American art and literature of the first half of the twentieth century was strongly marked by social realism, which, in the case of Latin America, was intertwined with a concern about US involvement in Latin American politics.

35. Incháustegui Cabral, *De literatura dominicana siglo veinte*, 222.

36. See Alcántara Almánzar, *Estudios de poesía dominicana* and *Los escritores dominicanos y la cultura*.

37. Rueda and Alcántara Almánzar, *Dos siglos de literatura dominicana*, 243.

38. The exact year in which the poem was written is unknown. Rueda mentions in his prologue to *La criatura terrestre* that "the poems in this collection were written a long while ago." Sandra Borrel Garrido and Maril Núñez Yangüela mention "Cantos de la frontera" as one of Rueda's first poems and locate the writing circa 1945. See *Pluralismo*.

39. Rueda, *La criatura terrestre*, 40.

40. Rueda, *La criatura terrestre*, 40.

41. Derby, "Haitians, Magic, and Money," 490.

42. Turits, *Foundations of Despotism*, 145, 147–49.

43. Turits, *Foundations of Despotism*, 147.

44. I specify that the attack was on Haitians and rayanos because the goal of the Massacre of 1937 was to define the frontier. Therefore, contrary to popular ideas about the massacre, there were no killings in the major cities or in the sugarcane barracks. The massacre happened in the borderlands.

45. Díaz, "Apocalypse."

46. David "Karmadavis" Pérez, interview by author, July 3, 2013.

47. Grosz, *Volatile Bodies*, 117.

48. Valdez, "Language in the Dominican Republic," 182–83.

49. Celada and Lagares, "República Dominicana/Haití," 167.

50. Maldonado-Torres, *Against War*, 8.

51. David Pérez, interview by author, July 3, 2013.

52. Pérez, interview by author.

53. Fumagalli, "'Isla Abierta' or 'Isla Cerrada'?," 421.

54. Minich, *Accessible Citizenships*, 3.

55. Minich, *Accessible Citizenships*, 7.

56. McRuer, *Crip Theory*, 30.

57. See Rodríguez, *Las nuevas relaciones dominico-haitianas*.

58. Rodríguez, *Las nuevas relaciones dominico-haitianas*.

59. See *El seno de la esperanza* (Milk of Hope), dir. Vargas.

60. Díaz, "Apocalypse," 7.

61. Wucker, *Why the Cocks Fight*.

62. The song was written and performed by Hernández. Engel Leonardo directed the music video.

63. *Ceiba pentandra* is a large tropical tree with an umbrella-shaped crown that provides a home for countless species of animals. The Taínos, as well as the Maya, believed that a great ceiba tree stood at the center of the earth, connecting the terrestrial world to the spirit world above. The long thick vines hanging down from its spreading limbs provided a connection to the heavens for the souls that ascended them. Because of this belief, ceiba trees are regularly spared when forests are cut; it is common to see lone, isolated ceiba trees in the Haitian landscape.

64. The use of white pants is symbolic of Afro-Dominican religious cleansing rituals, or *despojos*, where the subject seeking the cleansing must wear white. White is the canvas onto which light can reflect, allowing the spirit to enter the bodies of the subjects and cleanse them of all ailments.

65. A red rooster symbolized the Partido Reformista, Joaquín Balaguer's populist party. Similarly, a rooster was the symbol for the Lavalas, the left-wing populist party founded by Jean-Bertrand Aristide in Haiti.

66. Wucker's sociopolitical analysis of Haiti and the Dominican Republic is grounded on the author's experiences as a Texan and from her understanding of the US-Mexican border: "I began to realize that the reactions of Dominicans to Haitians closely resembled the way Texans spoke about Mexicans in that illegal immigration, jobs, and land were the real issues behind the racist slurs" (*Why the Cocks Fight*, ix). Wucker's insights are incredibly suggestive of the need for a transnational dialogue on questions of border identities and relations, yet I find her comparison of the US-Mexican border to the DR-Haitian border conflicts to be rather simplistic, lacking historical grounding. A comparative border/migration analysis necessitates a more clear distinction on the complexities of US-Mexico relations as they are linked to imperialism, economic, and US-racial formation in contrast with Haitian-Dominican economic, social, and political history. A more fruitful comparison would perhaps begin with the analysis of US involvement in the demarcation and sustaining of the division between both nations, at geographical and political as well as symbolic levels. As demonstrated in this study, the US imaginary, as well as the country's imperial

expansion over the Caribbean, was pivotal in sustaining anti-Haitianism on the island. Furthermore, as seen in chapters 2 and 3, US notions of border control and US anxiety over national bordering were transplanted to the island during the interventions of Haiti (1914) and the DR (1916), leading to the creation of border patrols, bracero programs (Haitians to the DR), and immigration control.

67. Turits, "A World Destroyed, a Nation Imposed," 595.

68. Alexander, *Pedagogies of Crossing*, 14.

69. This process is examined in chapter 1, particularly through the work of Penson and del Monte.

70. Rita Indiana Hernández, "Da pa lo do."

71. Hernández, "Da pa lo do."

72. Hernández, "Da pa lo do."

73. Hernández, "Da pa lo do."

74. Hernández, "Da pa lo do."

75. These US policies are explored in chapter 2.

76. Hernández, "Da pa lo do."

77. Dubois, *Haiti*, 6.

78. Ryan Smith, "Pat Robertson: Haiti 'Cursed' after 'Pact with the Devil,'" CBS News, January 13, 2010, http://www.cbsnews.com/8301-504083_162-12017-504083 .html.

79. David Brooks, "The Underlying Tragedy," *New York Times*, January 14, 2010, http://www.nytimes.com/2010/01/15/opinion/15brooks.html.

80. See chapter 2.

81. See chapters 1 and 2.

82. Alexander, *Pedagogies of Crossing*, 15.

83. Though I come from an immigrant working-class background, I have a PhD and immense privilege, setting me apart from the immigrant communities to which I still subscribe. Though I am constantly reminded of my origins in academic circles, privilege is something I insist on acknowledging.

84. See Howard, *Coloring the Nation*; Torres-Saillant, "The Tribulations of Blackness"; and Candelario, *Black behind the Ears*.

85. Gates, *Black in Latin America*. The expression "Black denial," often used to describe the complex Dominican racial identification process, was popularized in a *Miami Herald* article published in 2007. See Frances Robles, "Black Denial," *Miami Herald*, June 13, 2007, http://www.miamiherald.com/multimedia/news/afrolatin/ part2/.

86. While standing in El Conde Street in Santo Domingo, Gates says to the camera, "In the US all these people would be black." Gates, *Black in Latin America*, Episode 1.

87. See Roth, "A Single Shade of 'Negro,'" 93. In a recent article that appeared in the *New York Times*, Harvard professor Jennifer L. Hochschild argued similarly, "The court, or some clever clerk, doesn't really want to use the word white in part because roughly half of Hispanics consider themselves white. . . . White turns out to be a much

more ambiguous term now than we used to think it was." Sheila Dewan, "Has 'Caucasian' Lost Its Meaning?," *New York Times*, July 6, 2013, http://www.nytimes.com/2013/07/07/sunday-review/has-caucasian-lost-its-meaning.html?smid=fb-share_r=0.

88. Although the (diasporic) coverage of issues related to Dominicans is much more common in US and Puerto Rican media, there has been a significant growth in interests regarding issues of dominicanidad in Europe, especially in Spain and Italy, where new diasporic Dominican communities are emerging. One important example of this growth can be located in the 1996 victory of Denny Méndez in the Miss Italy pageant. The coronation of this Dominican immigrant caused a major controversy and scandal after two of the judges argued that a black woman could not represent Italian beauty. See "First Black Miss Italy Picked amidst Two Judges' Disapproval," and de Giorgi, *Denny Méndez*.

89. Frances Robles, "Black Denial," *Miami Herald*, June 13, 2007.

90. Frances Robles, the author of "Black Denial," conducted a series of interviews in Dominican hair salons and visited various Dominican scholars from the island as well as the diaspora. Ramona Hernández, director of the Dominican Studies Institute in New York, and Ginetta Candelario, professor of Women's Studies at Smith College, were quoted in the article asserting the author's thesis regarding Dominicans' "black denial" as evidenced in hair-straightening practices. Both scholars, however, insisted that they had been misquoted and that they disagreed with the simplicity of Robles's argument. They wrote letters to the editor that were never published by the *Herald* but which have appeared on various blogs. Ramona Hernández's letter stated: "The portrayal of the views attributed to me in your article of June 13, 'Black Denial,' is utterly false, and absolutely opposed not only to what I believe, but also to what I have dedicated my professional life to changing." See Ramona Hernández, "Open Letter to the Editor," *Dominican Republic News and Reports*, New York, June 2007.

91. Taína Mirabal is a Latina film producer from Los Angeles. Her first film, *Father of Racism* (2007), examines the life of Juan Pablo Duarte, the founder of the Dominican Republic. Mirabal's film alleges that Duarte was a white supremacist whose independence movement was actually a racial separation movement and whose secret society—La Trinitaria—was a link to the KKK. The allegations made in Mirabal's film set off a series of controversies that were highlighted in many newspapers and blogs through the fall of 2007. See *El Diario La Prensa*, August 31, 2007, and *New York Times*, September 2, 2007.

92. Miguel Cruz Tejeda, "Taína Mirabal, una antiduartiana," *Diario Libre*, September 11, 2007, http://www.diariolibre.com/noticias/tana-mirabal-una-anti-duartiana-radical-que-afirma-la-historia-ha-sido-distorsionada-FNDL149590.

93. Rita Indiana Hernández, interview by author, September 20, 2013.

94. Hernández, interview by author.

95. I borrow the term from Kazanjian, *The Colonizing Trick*.

96. Hoffnung-Garskof, *A Tale of Two Cities*, 201, 205.

97. Hoffnung-Garskof, *A Tale of Two Cities*, 205.

98. Hernández, "Da Pa lo do."

99. Muñoz, *Disidentifications.*

100. Combs-Gonzalez, "El Drag Guadalupista."

101. Hernández, *Papi.*

102. Hernández, "Da pa lo do."

103. Marmolejos, *Teleantillas*, Noticias, March 21, 2010, feed://rs.resalliance.org/category/ideas/vulnerability/feed/.

104. Marmolejos, *Teleantillas.*

Chapter 5: Writing from El Nié

1. Invited guest lecture at FLACSO, April 22, 2006.

2. Torres-Saillant, *El retorno de las yolas.*

3. Martínez-San Miguel, *Caribe Two Ways.*

4. For more on the term, see Hoffnung-Garskof, *A Tale of Two Cities.*

5. Since the 1980s there has been a growth in Dominican migration to Europe, particularly to Spain, Italy, Switzerland, and Holland. In addition, there has been a long-established community of Dominicans in Puerto Rico. The use of the term *dominicanos ausentes* allows for a comparative examination of all these different immigrant communities.

6. Torres-Saillant, *El retorno de las yolas*, 18.

7. "El Nié" means "ni es una cosa, ni es la otra" or "it is neither one thing nor the other." It is common slang used in Dominican popular culture. Josefina Báez appropriates the term in her performance-text *Levente no.* to signify a space of in-betweenness for Domincanyorks who live neither "here" nor "there." See the introduction.

8. Anzaldúa, *Borderlands/La Frontera*, 6.

9. See Rama, *La ciudad letrada.*

10. San Miguel, *La isla imaginada*, 28.

11. Kury, *Juan Bosch*, 31.

12. The Confederación Antillana was an idea introduced by Puerto Rican thinker Ramón Emeterio Betances that promoted the need for natives of the Spanish Greater Antilles to unite into a regional entity that would preserve the sovereignty and well-being of Cuba, the Dominican Republic, and Puerto Rico.

13. Kury, *Juan Bosch*, 35.

14. Kury, *Juan Bosch*, 47.

15. According to Kury, Bosch was asked by Henríquez to organize the Dominican exiles into a cohesive force that would ideologically combat the regime (*Juan Bosch*, 45). But because in the early 1940s the Dominican diaspora was small and had not yet concentrated in one geographical area, this was an extraordinarily difficult task for Bosch, who had to travel constantly between New York, San Juan, and Caracas, among other places, to meet with the exiles who resided there. The fact that he was a known writer, who was often published in the local papers of these cities, allowed him to gain the trust and solidarity of many exiles and of the local Latin American leaders.

16. Anderson, *Imagined Communities.*

17. Kury, *Juan Bosch*, 105.

18. Quotation is from Piña-Contreras, *En primera persona*, 36.

19. Morrison and Bermúdez, "Encuentro con Juan Bosch," 62.

20. Bosch's short stories appeared in two collections published abroad, which he titled *Cuentos escritos en el exilio* and *Más cuentos escritos en el exilio* upon his return to the Dominican Republic in 1962.

21. Morrison and Bermúdez, "Encuentro con Juan Bosch," 44.

22. Torres-Saillant, *El retorno de las yolas*, 114.

23. For example: Díaz, *The Brief Wondrous Life of Oscar Wao* (2007); Alvarez, *In the Time of the Butterflies* (1994); Rosario, *Song of the Water Saints* (2002); Cruz, *Let It Rain Coffee* (2006).

24. Torres-Saillant, *El retorno de las yolas*, 13.

25. On April 28, 1965, the United States intervened in the civil war and dispatched forty-two thousand troops to the island. President Lyndon Johnson justified the invasion based on his belief that the PRD was filled with communists. See Gliejeses, *The Dominican Crisis*.

26. Piña-Contreras, *En primera persona*, 187.

27. Hoffnung-Garskof, *A Tale of Two Cities*, 74–75.

28. I examine Vergés's novel and its relationship to Bosch's exile and political trajectory in "*Más que cenizas.*"

29. Madrid, *Music in Mexico*, 39.

30. The UCN emerged in 1962 as a patriotic movement whose sole purpose was to demand the expatriation of Trujillo's family and the recovery of the national treasury, which then lay in the hands of the Trujillos. The movement represented the petit bourgeoisie values of the time. In 1962 the UCN became an organized political party and ran against Bosch.

31. Vergés, *Sólo cenizas hallarás*, 43.

32. Vergés, *Sólo cenizas hallarás*, 108.

33. Vergés, *Sólo cenizas hallarás*, 108.

34. Sommer, *Foundational Fictions*.

35. Lipsitz, *Footsteps in the Dark*, xvi

36. Rivas, "Cenizas."

37. Rivas, "Cenizas."

38. Vergés, *Sólo cenizas hallarás*, 260.

39. Vergés, *Sólo cenizas hallarás*, 15.

40. Martínez-San Miguel, *Caribe Two Ways*, 323.

41. The performance-text, *Dominicanish*, was published in 2000, while the performance itself was first presented in 1999 in the Dance Theater Workshop in New York City.

42. I use the term "American Dream" to refer to the American narrative of success that promotes the possibility of progress and financial mobility of the individual, no matter what his/her racial, ethnic, or economic background may be.

43. Báez, *Dominicanish*, 43.

44. Candelario, *Black behind the Ears*.

45. "Belly of the beast" is a popular phrase used by Cuban independence leader José Martí to refer to his own contra*diction* of living in New York while drafting an anti-imperialist agenda.

46. For a detailed account of the process and negotiations between Puerto Rico and the United States that led to the final decision of 1917 that declared all Puerto Ricans US citizens, see Erman, *Puerto Rico and the Promise of United States Citizenship*.

47. For more on the Zoot Suit Riots, see Griswold del Castillo, "Zoot Suit Riots Revisited."

48. Lowe, *Immigrant Acts*, 37.

49. See Dávila, *Latinos Inc.*

50. Báez, *Dominicanish* (v H s, min. 16). This recording is from the first public performance of *Dominicanish* in Dance Theater Workshop in New York, September, 1999.

51. The construction of the "Indian" myth is explored in depth in chapter 1.

52. Hernández and Torres-Saillant, *The Dominican Americans*, 131.

53. Báez, "Dialogue and Reading."

54. Báez, *Dominicanish*, 12.

55. I borrow W. E. B. Du Bois's term "double-consciousness" as employed by Paul Gilroy in his book *The Black Atlantic* to describe the tensions between race and nationality in the modern Afro-Diasporic experience. Báez's experience as a black-Dominicanyork deals with these tensions, which to her, as I prove, become a way of transcending the limits of identification, location, and rigid cultural structures.

56. Báez, *Dominicanish*, 26.

57. Lipsitz, *Footsteps in the Dark*, xi.

58. Torres-Saillant, *Introduction to Dominican Blackness*, 25.

59. Torres-Saillant, *Introduction to Dominican Blackness*, 25.

60. Moya Pons, "Dominican National Identity and Return Migration," 33.

61. Torres-Saillant, "The Tribulations of Blackness," 5.

62. Torres-Saillant, "The Tribulations of Blackness," 26–27.

63. Josefina Báez, interview by author, December 27, 2012.

64. Torres-Saillant, *El retorno de las Yolas*, 22.

65. Báez, *Dominicanish*, 48.

66. Báez, *Comrade Bliss Ain't Playin'*, 79.

67. Báez, *Comrade, Bliss Ain't Playin'*, 5.

68. Báez, *Dominicanish*, 19. Báez juxtaposes verses from the Dominican National anthem and then states, "Thank God that in 107 we dance to Pacheco." Johnny Pacheco is one of the most important Dominican musicians of the twentieth century.

69. Báez, *Dominicanish*, 19.

70. De Certeau, *The Practice of Everyday Life*, 24.

71. Báez, *Dominicanish* (v H s, min. 32).

72. See Butler, *Bodies That Matter*.

73. See Butler, *Bodies That Matter*.

74. Josefina Báez, interview by author, December 28, 2012.

75. Yolanda Martínez-San Miguel examines Cuban, Dominican, and Puerto Rican migration from 1965 to 1995 by looking at particular urban spaces such as San Juan and New York. Her book *Caribe Two Ways* examines the impact of migration in the definition of national entities at the end of the twentieth century through art, literature, and performance.

76. Báez, *Levente no.*, preface, np.

77. Puri, *The Caribbean Postcolonial*, 45.

78. Here I borrow the term from Phil Deloria's book *Playing Indian*, in which the author brilliantly argues how the US independence movement was grounded on claims of Indianness. Deloria argues that this assertion helped "define custom and imagine themselves [colonists] as a legitimate part of the continent's ancient history" (25). For Dominicans, "playing Indian" allowed them to claim authenticity, obtaining legitimacy as a nation independent of Haiti (although within the same insular territory) and gaining US support.

79. Báez, *Dominicanish*, 37.

80. Báez, *Dramaturgia Ay Ombe I*, n.p.

81. Ngai, *Impossible Subjects*.

82. Báez, *Dominicanish* (VHS, min. 12).

83. Josefina Báez, interview by author, June 22, 2012.

84. Méndez, *Narratives of Migration*, 150.

85. Deleuze and Guattari, *Kafka*, 12.

86. Anzaldúa, *Borderlands/La Frontera*, 77.

87. Báez, *Dominicanish*, 22.

88. Báez, *Levente no.*, n.p.

89. Willett, *Brecht on Theatre*, 91.

90. Báez, *Dominicanish* (VHS, min. 3).

91. Willett, *Brecht on Theatre*, 97.

92. Báez, *Dominicanish* (VHS, min. 40).

Postscript

Epigraphs: Testimony of María Pierre, *Noticias Sims*, Santo Domingo, November 12, 2013. Speech given by Elizabeth Garibay in front of the Atlanta City Hall during protest against Georgia HB87 legislation, November 9, 2011.

1. "Sentencia 168-13," Expediente número TC-05-2012-0077, October 2013, Tribunal de Sentencia de la República Dominicana, Santo Domingo, DR.

2. "Sentencia 168-13."

3. I use quotations to indicate that these myths, as I argue in the previous chapter, refer not only to immigrants from Haiti but also to ethnic Haitians and mixed people.

4. Testimonio of Sonia Pierre, November 2, 2007, https://www.frontlinedefenders .org/node/2018 (accessed June 1, 2015).

5. Testimonio of Sonia Pierre.

6. There are multiple examples of important cross-border collaborations that have led to small- and large-scale revolts. The Restoration War of 1865 is the most important historical example. However, there are other examples of intra-ethnic collaboration in the twentieth and twentieth-first centuries, particularly among the working class and farmers.

7. *Fronterizas* (2014), directed by Loré Durán, was a finalist in the Sundance Institute Short Film Challenge 2014. The short film documents the Border Network of Women Artisans formed by ninety women from seven frontier communities between Haiti and DR. They recycle and take advantage of the resources around them, seeking a better future for their families and their communities. The project has created a better relationship between the communities and, as some of the women testify, actively challenged border policies.

8. *El País*, November 11, 2013.

9. Rivero, "Junot Díaz and Edwidge Danticat Jointly Speak Out against Dominican Republic Refugee Crisis."

10. Rivero, "Junot Díaz and Edwidge Danticat Jointly Speak Out against Dominican Republic Refugee Crisis."

11. Latino Rebels, "Dominican Govt Official's Email to Junot Díaz."

12. Latino Rebels, "Dominican Govt Official's Email to Junot Díaz."

13. Anzaldúa, "How to Tame a Wild Tongue," in *Borderlands/La Frontera*, 55.

14. On October 14, 2010, the University of Georgia Board of Regents voted 14 to 2 "to prohibit public universities from enrolling students without papers in any school that has rejected other qualified applicants for the past 2 years because of lack of space." The policy, which keeps academically qualified students from attending the top-five public research universities of this state, was based on the belief that undocumented students were taking the seats of citizens in the public university system. However, a study conducted by the very Board of Regents enacting this policy found that undocumented students compose less than 0.2 percent of all public university students; most of these students are enrolled in technical and community colleges. Board of Regents University System of Georgia, 2010, Policy 413, http://www.usg.edu/news/release/regents_adopt_new_policies_on_undocumented_students (accessed June 1, 2014).

15. Guidotti-Hernández, "Old Tactics, New South."

16. Ida B. Wells-Barnet Distinguished Lecture, Spelman College, Atlanta, September 17, 2012.

17. Raziye Akkoc, Jessica Winch, and Nick Squires, "Mediterranean Migrant Death Toll '30 Times Higher than Last Year': As It Happened," *Telegraph*, April 21, 2015, http://www.telegraph.co.uk/news/worldnews/europe/italy/11548995/Mediterranean-migrant-crisis-hits-Italy-as-EU-ministers-meet-live.html.

18. Tomlinson and Lipsitz, "American Studies as Accompaniment."

BIBLIOGRAPHY

Archival Collections

Archivo General de la Nación Dominicana (AGN), Santo Domingo
    Archivo de la Época Haitiana (1822–44): Legajos 1–4: Record books, court proceedings, and miscellaneous sales and statistical information of the Hispaniola unification period.
    Archivo del Gobierno Militar de Santo Domingo (1916–24): A document collection that includes all available papers of the military government, especially of the ministries of health and immigration and the GND.
    Archivo del Palacio Nacional (1940–50): A vast collection that includes all administrative and military memos addressed to or by Trujillo between 1940 and 1950.
    Archivo de Prensa: A periodical collection containing every existing newspaper published in the territory of the Dominican Republic since the beginning of the republic in 1844.
    Archivo General de la República: The umbrella archive under which all collections concerning the various branches of Dominican government are housed.
    Archivo Particular del Generalísimo, Palacio Nacional: A collection of papers and memos including daily intelligence reports, private correspondence, requests by diplomatic personnel, and notes regarding Trujillo's persecution of the Afro-religious and other dissidents. This collection is now part of the larger Archivo del Palacio Nacional.
    Colección Bernardo Vega: Contains documents and information pertaining to the US military occupation (1916–24), the presidency of Horacio Vázquez (1924–30), the Trujillo dictatorship (1930–61), and various political and military processes affecting the Dominican state (1961–80).
    Colección José Gabriel García (1738–1968): A series of letters and documents collected by historian José Gabriel García (1834–1910), including the diary of Rosa Duarte, documents related to García's various government positions, and letters by important world leaders written to García.
    Colección Leyes, Decretos y Resoluciones (1844–1961): A collection of decrees and resolutions passed by the various governments of the republic; of particular importance are the ordinances related to immigration and border demarcation.

Documentos de la República (1844–60): A series of documents related to the First Dominican Republic prior to the annexation to Spain; of particular importance is the original 1844 constitution and Juan Pablo Duarte's writings, which have also been published as Rosa Duarte's journal.

Secretaría de Estado de Interior y Policía (1844–1993): A series of bureaucratic documents pertaining to the functioning and organization of the police; of particular importance are documents related to the Trujillo dictatorship.

Sentencias Penales de la Época Haitiana (1822–31): A valuable collection of court cases, proceedings, sentencing, and records organized by Ramón Lugo Lovatón in 1944; it includes the proceedings against the rebels conspiring for independence in 1823 in Alcarrizos and the sentencing of Galindo murderers in 1822.

Library of Congress, Washington, DC

William Shepherd Benson Papers (1855–1932): Correspondence, memoranda, dispatches, speeches, reports, naval appointments, family papers, printed matter, maps, photographs, and other papers relating primarily to Benson's service as US chief of naval operations during World War I.

National Archives, Washington, DC

Navy Department. Records of the United States Marines. Military Government of Santo Domingo (1916–24): Papers that outline the operations conducted by the military government during the eight-year military intervention on the Dominican Republic (1917–24).

Other Sources

Alcántara Almánzar, José. *Estudios de poesía dominicana*. Santo Domingo: Editora Alfa y Omega, 1979.

———. *Los escritores dominicanos y la cultura*. Vol. 21. Santo Domingo: Instituto Tecnológico de Santo Domingo, 1990.

Alexander, M. Jacqui. *Pedagogies of Crossing: Meditations on Feminism, Sexual Politics, Memory, and the Sacred*. Durham: Duke University Press, 2005.

Alexis, Jacques Stéphen. *General Sun, My Brother* [*Compère Général Soleil*]. Charlottesville: University of Virginia Press, 1999.

Althusser, Louis. "Ideology and Ideological State Apparatuses (Notes towards an Investigation)." In *The Anthropology of the State: A Reader*, edited by Aradhana Sharma and Akhil Gupta, 86–111. Hoboken: Wiley-Blackwell, 2006.

Álvarez, Julia. *In the Time of the Butterflies*. Chapel Hill, NC: Algonquin Books, 1994.

Anderson, Benedict. *Imagined Communities: Reflections on the Origin and Spread of Nationalism*. New York: Verso, 1983.

Andújar, Carlos. *Identidad cultural y religiosidad popular*. Santo Domingo: Ediciones Calíope, [1999] 2004.

Anzaldúa, Gloria. *Borderlands/La Frontera: The New Mestiza*. Minneapolis: Aunt Lute Books, [1987] 2007.

Anzaldúa, Gloria, and Cherríe Moraga. *This Bridge Called My Back: Writings by Radical Women of Color*. New York: Kitchen Table/Women of Color Press, 1983.

Arroyo, Jossianna. *Writing Secrecy in Caribbean Freemasonry*. New York: Palgrave Macmillan, 2013.

Auerbach, Paul S., Robert L. Norris, Anil S. Menon, Ian P. Brown, Solomon Kuah, Jennifer Schwieger, Jeffrey Kinyon, Trina N. Helderman, and Lynn Lawry. "Civil-Military Collaboration in the Initial Medical Response to the Earthquake in Haiti." *New England Journal of Medicine* 362, no. 10 (2010): e32(1–4). http://www.nejm.org/doi/pdf/10.1056/NEJMp1001555.

Austerlitz, Paul. *Merengue: Dominican Music and Dominican Identity*. Philadelphia: Temple University Press, 1997.

Azuela, Mariano. *Los de abajo*. Mexico: Fondo de Cultura Económica, [1914] 1946.

Báez, Josefina. *Comrade, Bliss Ain't Playin'*. New York: Josefina Báez, 2007.

———. "Dialogue and Reading." Lecture presented at Miller Learning Center, University of Georgia, Athens, February 29, 2012.

———. *Dominicanish: A Performance Text*. New York: Josefina Báez, 2000.

———. *Dominicanish*. Performance. VHS. New York: I Ombe Theater, 1999.

———. *Dramaturgia Ay Ombe I*. New York: I.Om.Be Press, 2014.

———. *Levente no. Yolayorkdominicanyork*. New York: I.Om.Be Press, 2011.

Balaguer, Joaquín. *Discursos: Temas históricos y literarios*. Santo Domingo: Sirvensae, 1977.

———. *La realidad dominicana: Semblanza de un país y de un régimen*. Buenos Aires: Imprenta Ferrari, 1947.

Balibar, Etienne, and Immanuel Wallerstein. *Race, Nation, Class: Ambiguous Identities*. London: Verso, 1991.

Baud, Michiel. "Una frontera para cruzar: La sociedad rural a través de la frontera dominico-haitiana (1870–1930)." *Estudios Sociales* 26, no. 94 (1993): 5–29.

Bhabha, Homi. *The Location of Culture*. New York: Routledge, 2004.

———. *Nation and Narration*. New York: Routledge, 1990.

Bilham, Roger. "Lessons from the Haiti Earthquake." *Nature* 463, no. 7283 (2010): 878–89.

Blanco Fombona, Horacio. *Crímenes del imperialismo norteamericano*. Mexico City: Ediciones Churubusco, 1927.

———. *En las garras del águila: Crímenes de los yanquis en Santo Domingo*. Santo Domingo: Antigua imprenta de Murguía, 1921.

Bonó, Pedro Francisco. "Apuntes para los cuatro ministerios de la República." In *Papeles de Pedro Francisco Bonó*, edited by Emilo Rodríguez. Barcelona: Gráficas, [1856] 1980.

Borrel Garrido, Sandra, and Maril Núñez Yangüela. *Pluralismo: Manuel Rueda*. Santo Domingo: Taller Isabel La Católica, 1988.

Bosch, Juan. *Composición social dominicana: Historia e interpretación*. Santo Domingo: Editora Tele-3, 1971.

———. *Cuentos escritos en el exilio*. Santo Domingo: Alfa y Omega, 1962.

———. "Luis Pie." In *Obras completas. Tomo II: Narrativa*. Santo Domingo: Fundación Bosch, 2003.

———. *Más cuentos escritos en el exilo*. Santo Domingo: Editorial Librería Dominicana, 1964.

Brantley, Daniel. "Black Diplomacy and Frederick Douglass' Caribbean Experiences, 1871 and 1889–1891: The Untold History." *Phylon* 45, no. 3 (1984): 197–209.

Brea, Ramonina. *Ensayo sobre la formación del estado capitalista en la República Dominicana y Haití*. Santo Domingo: Editora Taller, 1983.

Brennan, Denise. *What's Love Got to Do with It? Transnational Desires and Sex Tourism in the Dominican Republic*. Durham: Duke University Press, 2004.

Butler, Judith. *Bodies That Matter: On the Discursive Limits of "Sex."* New York: Routledge, 1993.

Cabral, Manuel del. *Compadre Mon*. Buenos Aires: Los Editores del Autor, 1942.

Calder, Bruce. *The Impact of the Intervention: The Dominican Republic during the U.S. Occupation of 1916–1924*. Austin: Texas University Press, 1984.

Candelario, Ginetta. *Black behind the Ears: Dominican Racial Identity from Museums to Beauty Shops*. Durham: Duke University Press, 2007.

Carpentier, Alejo. *El reino de este mundo*. México: Siglo XXI, [1949] 1994.

Cassá, Roberto. *Historia social y económica de la República Dominicana*. Santo Domingo: Alfa y Omega, 2004.

———. "Problemas del culto olivorista." In *La ruta hacia Liborio: Mesianismo en el sur profundo dominicano*, edited by Martha Ellen Davis, 3–44. Santo Domingo: Secretario de Estado de Cultura and UNESCO, Editorial Manatí, 2004.

Castillo, Marino Vinicio (Vincho). "Discurso: Danilo, Quirino, Obama, inmigración y seguridad nacional." *Diario Horizonte*, February 2, 2014. www.diario horizonte.com/noticia/vincho-danilo-obama-immigración.

Castor, Suzy. *La ocupación norteamericana de Haití y sus consecuencias (1915–1934)*. Mexico: Siglo veintiuno editores, 1971.

Celada, Maite, and Xoán Lagares. "República Dominicana/Haití: Fronteras lingüísticas y políticas en el territorio de la Hispaniola." *Abehache* 2, no. 2 (2012): 167–73.

Céspedes, Diógenes, ed. *Antología del cuento dominicano*. Santo Domingo: Editora Manatí, 2000.

Chomsky, Noam. *Hegemony or Survival: America's Quest for Global Dominance*. New York: Henry Holt, 2003.

Combs-Gonzalez, Rachel. "El Drag Guadalupista: Confronting Hegemony in Chicana Feminist and Queer Performance." *Journal of American Studies of Turkey* 42 (spring 2015): 81–106.

Coronado, Raúl. *A World Not to Come: A History of Latino Writing and Print Culture*. Cambridge, MA: Harvard University Press, 2013.

Cruz, Angie. *Let It Rain Coffee*. New York: Simon and Schuster, 2005.

———. *Soledad*. New York: Simon and Schuster, 2001.

Cuello, Israel. *Documentos del conflicto domínico-haitiano de 1937*. Santo Domingo: Taller, 1985.

Da Cunha, Euclides, and Leopoldo M. Bernucci. *Os sertões: Campanha de Canudos*. Vol. 1. São Paulo: Ateliê Editorial, 2002.

Danticat, Edwidge. *The Farming of Bones*. New York: Penguin Books, 1998.

Dávila, Arlene. *Latinos Inc.: The Marketing and Making of a People*. Berkeley: University of California Press, 2000.

Davis, Martha Ellen. "Papa Liborio: El Santo vivo de Maguana." Presentation, Society for Ethnomusicology, Miami, FL, October 2003.

———. "Revolutionary Quisqueya from Caonabo to Liborio." Presentation notes, annual meeting of the Latin American Studies Association, Las Vegas, NV, October 2004.

Dayan, Joan. *Haiti, History, and the Gods*. Berkeley: University of California Press, 1998.

de Certeau, Michel. *The Practice of Everyday Life*. Translated by Steven Rendall. Berkeley: University of California Press, 1984.

de Giorgi, Omar. *Denny Méndez*. Maldonado, Uruguay: Arroyo Salado Editorial, 2003.

Deleuze, Gilles, and Félix Guattari. *Kafka: Toward a Minor Literature*. Minneapolis: University of Minnesota Press, 1986.

del Monte, Félix María. "Canción dominicana." *Antología de la poesía dominicana, 1844–1944*, edited by Vicente Llorens. Santo Domingo: Sociedad Dominicana de Bibliófilos, 1984.

———. *Las vírgenes de Galindo o la invasión de los haitianos sobre la parte española de Santo Domingo*. Santo Domingo: Imprenta García Hermanos, 1885.

Deloria, Phil. *Playing Indian*. New Haven: Yale Historical Publications, 1998.

Derby, Lauren. "Haitians, Magic, and Money: Raza and Society in the Haitian-Dominican Borderlands, 1900 to 1937." *Comparative Studies in Society and History* 36, no. 3 (1994): 488–526.

Derridá, Jacques. "The Violence of the Letter: From Lévi Strauss to Rousseau." In *Of Grammatology*. Translated by G. Spivak. Baltimore: Johns Hopkins University Press, 1976.

Díaz, Junot. "Apocalypse: What Disasters Reveal." *Boston Review*, May 1, 2011. http://www.bostonreview.net/junot-diaz-apocalypse-haiti-earthquake.

———. *The Brief Wondrous Life of Oscar Wao*. New York: Riverhead Books, 2007.

Douglass, Frederick. *Life and Times of Frederick Douglass* [1892]. New York: Collier Books, 1962.

Duany, Jorge. *Quisqueya on the Hudson: The Transnational Identity of Dominicans in Washington Heights*. Dominican Research Monograph No. 1. 2nd ed. New York: Dominican Studies Institute, City University of New York, [1994] 2008.

Duarte, Juan Pablo. "Unidad de las razas." 1839.

Duarte, Rosa. *Apuntes: Archivo y versos de Juan Pablo Duarte*. Santo Domingo: Editora del Caribe, 1970.

Dubois, Laurent. *Haiti: The Aftershocks of History*. New York: Macmillan, 2012.

Durán, Loré. *Fronterizas*. Film. 2014.

Erman, Sam. *Puerto Rico and the Promise of United States Citizenship: Struggles around Status in a New Empire, 1898–1917*. PhD diss., University of Michigan, Ann Arbor, 2010.

Fiehrer, Thomas. "Political Violence in the Periphery: The Haitian Massacre of 1937." *Race and Class* 32, no. 2 (1990): 1–20.

"First Black Miss Italy Picked amidst Two Judges' Disapproval." *Jet Magazine*, September 23, 1996.

Fischer, Sibylle. *Modernity Disavowed: Haiti and the Cultures of Slavery in the Age of Revolution*. Durham: Duke University Press, 2004.

Fordham, Monroe. "Nineteenth Century Black Thought in the United States: Some Influence of the Santo Domingo Revolution." *Journal of Black Studies* 6 (1975): 115–26.

Foucault, Michel. "Nietzsche, Genealogy, History." In *Language, Counter-Memory, Practices*. Edited by Donald F. Bouchard, translated by D. F. Bouchard and S. Simon, 64–139. Ithaca: Cornell University Press, 1977.

Franco, Franklin. *Historia de las ideas políticas en la República Dominicana*. Santo Domingo: Editora Nacional, 1989.

Franco, Jean. *The Decline and Fall of the Lettered City: Latin America in the Cold War*. Cambridge, MA: Harvard University Press, 2002.

———. *Plotting Women: Gender and Representation in Mexico*. New York: Columbia University Press, 1989.

Freud, Sigmund. *The Standard Edition of the Complete Psychological Works of Sigmund Freud*. Edited by James Strachey. New York: W. W. Norton, 1964.

Fumagalli, María Cristina. "'Isla Abierta' or 'Isla Cerrada'? Karmadavis's Pre- and Post-earthquake Hispaniola." *Bulletin of Latin American Research* 32, no. 4 (2013): 421–37.

Gallagher, John Paul. "Dulce Despojo." Photograph. Santo Domingo, 2006.

Galván, Manuel de Jesús. *Enriquillo*. 1879.

García, José Gabriel. *Compendio de la historia de Santo Domingo*. Santo Domingo: Imprenta de García Hermanos, 1894.

García-Peña, Lorgia. "*Más que cenizas*: An Analysis of Juan Bosch's Dissident Narration of *Dominicanidad* (Ausente)." In *Hispanic Caribbean Literature of Migration: Narratives of Displacement*, edited by Vanessa Pérez Rosario, 39–56. New York: Palgrave, 2010.

———. "Translating Blackness: Dominicans Negotiating Race and Belonging." *Black Scholar* 45, no. 2 (2015): 10–20.

Garrido Puello, Emigdio. *Olivorio: Un ensayo histórico*. Santo Domingo, 1963.

Gates, Henry Louis, Jr. *Black in Latin America: Haiti and The Dominican Republic: An Island Divided*. DVD. Arlington, VA: Public Broadcasting System, 2011.

Gil, Lydia M. "'El Masacre se pasa a pie' de Freddy Prestol Castillo ¿Denuncia o defensa de la actitud dominicana ante El Corte?" *Afro Hispanic Review* 16 (1997): 38–44.

Gilroy, Paul. *The Black Atlantic: Modernity and Double Consciousness*. Cambridge, MA: Harvard University Press, 1993.

Gliejeses, Piero. *The Dominican Crisis: The 1965 Constitutional Revolt and American Intervention*. Baltimore: Johns Hopkins University Press, 1978.

Glissant, Édouard. *Caribbean Discourse: Selected Essays*. Translated by J. Michael Dash. Charlottesville: University of Virginia Press, 1989.

González, Raymundo. *Bonó: Un intelectual de los pobres*. Santo Domingo: Centro de Estudios Sociales Padre Juan Montalvo, S.J., 1964.

Griswold del Castillo, Richard. "'Zoot Suit Riots' Revisited: Mexican and Latin American Perspectives." *Mexican Studies/Estudios Mexicanos* 16, no. 2 (summer 2000): 367–91.

Grosz, Elizabeth. *Volatile Bodies: Toward a Corporeal Feminism*. Indianapolis: Indiana University Press, 1994.

Grullón, Adalberto, dir. *Fiesta de palos: El ritmo de la resistencia*. DVD. Santo Domingo: AAA Producciones, 2006.

Guerra Sánchez, Antonio José Ignacio. "Toponia y Genealogía: Galindo o Barrio Mejoramiento Social." *Areíto*, March 17, 2007, 11–15.

Guidotti-Hernández, Nicole. "Old Tactics, New South." Ms. Magazine Blog, November 16, 2011. http://msmagazine.com/blog/blog/2011/11/16/old-tactics-new-south/.

———. *Unspeakable Violence: Remapping U.S. and Mexican National Imaginaries*. Durham: Duke University Press, 2011.

Henríquez Ureña, Max. *La conspiración de los Alcarrizos*. Lisbon: Sociedade Industrial de Tipografía, 1941.

———. *Los Yanquis en Santo Domingo*. Santo Domingo: Sociedad dominicana de bibliófilos, 1977.

Hernández, Ramona, and Silvio Torres-Saillant. *The Dominican Americans*. Westport, CT: Greenwood, 1998.

Hernández, Rita. "Da pa lo do." *El Juidero*. Premium Latin Music, Inc., 2010.

———. *Papi*. San Juan: Ediciones Vértigo, 2005.

Herrera, Rémy. "When the Names of the Emperors Were Morgan and Rockefeller . . . Prerevolutionary Cuba's Dependency with Regard to U.S. High Finance." *International Journal of Political Economy* 34, no. 4 (winter 2004–5): 24–48.

Hoffnung-Garskof, Jesse. *A Tale of Two Cities: Santo Domingo and New York after 1950*. Princeton: Princeton University Press, 2007.

Howard, David John. *Coloring the Nation: Race and Ethnicity in the Dominican Republic*. Boulder: L. Rienner, 2001.

Hughes, Langston, and Arna Bontemps. *Popo and Fifina: Children of Haiti*. Oxford: Oxford University Press, 1932.

Incháustegui Cabral, Héctor. *De literatura dominicana siglo veinte*. Vol. 6. Santiago, Dominican Republic: Universidad Católica Madre y Maestra, 1968.

Kazanjian, David. *The Colonizing Trick: National Culture and Imperial Citizenship in Early America*. Minneapolis: University of Minnesota Press, 2003.

Kury, Farid. *Juan Bosch: Entre el exilio y el golpe de estado*. Santo Domingo: Editora Búho, 2000.

Las Casas, Bartolomé de. *Brevísima relación de la destruición de las Indias, colegida por el obispo don fray Bartolomé de Las Casas o Casaus, de la orden de Santo Domingo*. 1552.

Latino Rebels. "Dominican Govt Official's Email to Junot Díaz: You're a 'Fake and Overrated Pseudo Intellectual' Who Needs to Speak Spanish Better." *Latino Rebels*, December 3, 2013. http://www.latinorebels.com/2013/12/03/dominican -govt-officials-email-to-junot-diaz-youre-a-fake-and-overrated-pseudo-intellect ual-who-needs-to-speak-spanish-better/.

Lazo, Rodrigo. *Writing to Cuba: Filibustering and Cuban Exiles in the United States*. Chapel Hill: University of North Carolina Press, 2005.

Liberato, Ana S. Q. *Joaquín Balaguer, Memory, and Diaspora: The Lasting Political Legacies of an American Protégé*. Lanham, MD: Lexington Books, 2013.

Lipsitz, George. *Footsteps in the Dark: The Hidden Histories of Popular Music*. Minneapolis: University of Minnesota Press, 2007.

Lizardo Lascocé, Luis Francisco. *Palma sola: La tragedia de un pueblo*. Santo Domingo: Editora Manatí, 2001.

Lloréns, Vicente. *Antología de la poesía dominicana, 1844–1944*. Vol 52. Santo Domingo: Sociedad Dominicana de Bibliófilos, 1984.

Lowe, Lisa. *Immigrant Acts: On Asian American Cultural Politics*. Durham: Duke University Press, 1996.

Lozano, Wilfredo. "Los legados de Leonel Fernández." *Acento*, July 19, 2012. http:// acento.com.do/2012/opinion/205184-los-legados-de-leonel-fernandez/.

Lundius, Jan, and Mats Lundahl. *Peasants and Religion: A Socieconomic Study of Dios Olivorio and the Palma Sola Movement in the Dominican Republic*. New York: Routledge, 2000.

Madrid, Alejandro L. *Music in Mexico: Experiencing Music, Expressing Culture*. Oxford: Oxford University Press, 2013.

Maldonado-Torres, Nelson. *Against War: Views from the Underside of Modernity*. Durham: Duke University Press, 2008.

Malek, R. Michael. "Dominican Republic's General Rafael Trujillo and the Haitian Massacre of 1937: A Case of Subversion in Inter-Caribbean Relations." *SECOLAS Annals: Journal of the Southeastern Conference on Latin American Studies* (1980): 137–55.

Manley, Elizabeth. "Poner Un Grano de Arena: Gender and Women's Political Par-

ticipation under Authoritarian Rule in the Dominican Republic, 1928–1978."
PhD diss., Tulane University, 2008.

Margesson, Rhoda, and Maureen Taft-Morales. "Haiti Earthquake: Crisis and Response." Congressional Research Service, Library of Congress, Washington, DC, 2010.

Marrero Aristy, Ramón. *Over*. Ciudad Trujillo: Imprenta La Opinión, 1939.

Martínez, Lusitania. *Palma Sola: Su geografía y mítica social*. Santo Domingo: Ediciones CEDEE, 1991.

Martínez Almánzar, Juan Francisco. *Enriquillo: Ídolo de barro*. Santo Domingo: Editorial Fuente, 1986.

Martínez-San Miguel, Yolanda. *Caribe Two Ways: Cultura de la migración en el Caribe insular hispánico*. San Juan: Ediciones Callejón, 2003.

———. *Coloniality of Diasporas: Rethinking Intra-Colonial Migrations in a Pan-Caribbean Context*. New York: Palgrave Macmillan, 2014.

Martínez-Vergne, Teresita. *Nation and Citizen in the Dominican Republic, 1880–1916*. Chapel Hill: University of North Carolina Press, 2005.

Mateo, Andrés L. *Mito y cultura en la era de Trujillo*. Santo Domingo: Editora Manatí, 2005.

Matibag, Eugenio. *Haitian-Dominican Counterpoint: Nation, State, and Race on Hispaniola*. London: Palgrave Macmillan, 2003.

Mayes, April. *The Mulatto Republic: Class, Race, and Dominican National Identity*. Gainesville: University Press of Florida, 2014.

McRuer, Robert. *Crip Theory: Cultural Signs of Queerness and Disability*. New York: New York University Press, 2006.

Méndez, Danny. *Narratives of Migration and Displacement in Dominican Literature*. New York: Routledge, 2012.

Mignolo, Walter. *Local Histories/Global Designs: Coloniality, Subaltern Knowledges, and Border Thinking*. Princeton: Princeton University Press, 2000.

Minich, Julie Avril. *Accessible Citizenships: Disability, Nation, and the Cultural Politics of Greater Mexico*. Philadelphia: Temple University Press, 2014.

Moreno, Marisel. "Bordes Líquidos, fronteras y espejismos: El dominicano y la migración intra-caribeña en 'Boat People' de Mayra Santos Febres." *Revista de Estudios Hispánicos* 34, no. 2 (2007): 17–34.

Morgan, Jennifer. "Slavery and the Slave Trade, 1600–1760." In *A Companion to American Women's History*, edited by Nancy Hewitt, 20–34. Malden, MA: Blackwell, 2002.

———. "Some Could Suckle over Their Shoulders: Male Travelers, Female Bodies, and the Gendering of Racial Ideology." *William and Mary Quarterly* 54 (1997): 167–92.

Morrison, Mateo, and Jóvine Bermúdez. "Encuentro con Juan Bosch." *La Noticia*, Santo Domingo, August 10, 1965, 2–5.

Moya Pons, Frank. "Dominican National Identity and Return Migration." In *Migra-*

tion and Caribbean Cultural Identity: Selected Papers from Conference Cele-
brating the 50th Anniversary of the Center, 25–33. Gainesville: Center for Latin
American Studies, University of Florida, 1982.

———. *The Dominican Republic: A National History.* Princeton: Markus Wiener,
1998.

———. *El pasado dominicano.* Santo Domingo: Fundación J. A. Carlo Álvarez,
1986.

———. "Las tres fronteras: Introducción a la frontera dominico-haitiana." In *La
cuestión haitiana en Santo Domingo: Migración internacional, desarrollo y relaciones inter-estatales entre Haití y República Dominicana*, edited by Wilfredo
Lozano. Santo Domingo: FLACSO, 1992.

———. *Manual de historia de la República Dominicana.* Santo Domingo: Caribbean Publishers, 2000.

Muñoz, José Esteban. *Disidentifications: Queers of Color and the Performance of Politics.* Minneapolis: University of Minnesota Press, 1999.

Neumann, Charles J., Brian R. Jarvinen, and Arthur C. Pike. *Tropical Cyclones of
the North Atlantic Ocean, 1871–1986.* Asheville, NC: National Climactic Data
Center, 1988.

Ngai, Mae. *Impossible Subjects: Illegal Aliens and the Making of Modern America.*
Princeton: Princeton University Press, 2005.

O'Neill, Eugene. *The Emperor Jones.* Cincinnati: Stewart Kidd Company, 1921.

Ortíz, Ricardo L. *Cultural Erotics in Cuban America.* Minneapolis: University of
Minnesota Press, 2007.

Palma, Ricardo. *Tradiciones peruanas.* Lima: Montaner y Simón, 1893.

Paulino, Edward. *Dividing Hispaniola. The Dominican Republic's Border Campaign
against Haiti, 1930–61.* Pittsburgh: University of Pittsburgh Press, 2016.

Peña Batlle, Manuel Arturo. *Constitución Política y reformas constitucionales, 1844–
1942.* Santiago: Editorial El Diario, 1944.

———. *Historia de la cuestión fronteriza dominico-haitiana.* Santo Domingo:
Sociedad Dominicana de Bibliófilos, 1946.

———. "Política de Trujillo." Ciudad Trujillo: Impresora Dominicana, 1954.

Penson, César Nicolás. *Las vírgenes de Galindo.* Tradición. 1891.

Pérez, José Joaquín. "Etnaí." In *Fantasías indígenas y otros poemas.* Santo Domigo:
Editora Corripio, [1883] 1989.

Pérez Firmat, Gustavo. *Life on the Hyphen: The Cuban-American Way.* Austin: University of Texas Press, 1994.

Piña-Contreras, Guillermo. *En primera persona: Entrevistas con Juan Bosch.* Santo
Domingo: Editoras Feriadelibro, 2000.

Pratt, Mary Louise. *Imperial Eyes: Travel Writing and Transculturation.* New York:
Routledge, 1992.

———. "Las mujeres y el imaginario nacional del siglo XIX." *Revista de Crítica
Latinoamericana* 19, no. 38 (1993): 51–62.

———. "Women, Literature, and National Brotherhood." *Nineteenth-Century Contexts* 18, no. 1 (1994): 27–47.

Prestol Castillo, Freddy. *El masacre se pasa a pie.* Santo Domingo: Taller, 1973.

———. "Paisajes y meditaciones de una frontera." Essay. Ciudad Trujillo: Editora Cosmopolita, 1943.

Puar, Jasbir K. "Abu Ghraib: Arguing against Exceptionalism." *Feminist Studies* 30, no. 2 (2004): 522–34.

Puri, Shalini. *The Caribbean Postcolonial: Social Equality, Post/nationalism and Cultural Hybridity.* New York: Palgrave Macmillan, 2004.

Quintero Rivera, Ángel G. *Cuerpo y cultura: Las músicas mulatas y la subversión del baile.* Vol. 24. Madrid: Iberoamericana Editorial, 2009.

Rama, Ángel. *La ciudad letrada.* Hanover, NH: Ediciones del Norte, 1984.

Renda, Mary A. *Taking Haiti: Military Occupation and the Culture of U.S. Imperialism 1915–1940.* Chapel Hill: University of North Carolina Press, 2001.

Rivas, Wello. "Cenizas" bolero. Mexico, 1952.

Rivero, Daniel. "Junot Díaz and Edwidge Danticat Jointly Speak Out against Dominican Republic Refugee Crisis." *Fusion,* June 25, 2015. http://fusion.net /story/156597/junot-diaz-and-edwidge-danticat-jointly-call-for-travel-boycott -of-the-dominican-republic/.

Rodríguez, Manuel. *Las nuevas relaciones domínico-haitianas.* Santo Domingo: Centro de Información Gubernamental, 2011.

Rodríguez Demorizi, Emilio. *Pintura y escultura en Santo Domingo.* Santo Domingo: Colección Pensamiento Dominicano, Postigo E Hijos Editores, 1972.

Roorda, Eric Paul. "Genocide Next Door: The Good Neighbor Policy, the Trujillo Regime, and the Haitian Massacre of 1937." *Diplomatic History* 20, no. 3 (1996): 301–19.

Rosario, Nelly. *Song of the Water Saints.* New York: Pantheon, 2002.

Roth, Wendy D. "A Single Shade of 'Negro': Henry Louis Gates' Depictions of Blackness in the Dominican Republic." *Latin American and Caribbean Ethnic Studies* 8, no. 1 (2013): 92–96.

Rueda, Manuel. *La criatura terrestre.* Santo Domingo: Editora del Caribe, 1963.

Rueda, Manuel, and José Alcántara Almánzar. *Dos siglos de literatura dominicana: XIX–XX.* Vol. 10. Santo Domingo: Comsión Oficial del Sesquincetenario de la independenica nacional, 1996.

Sagás, Ernesto. *Race and Politics in the Dominican Republic.* Gainesville: University Press of Florida, 2000.

Saldívar, José David. *Trans-Americanity: Subaltern Modernities, Global Coloniality, and the Cultures of Greater Mexico.* Durham: Duke University Press, 2012.

Sanchez, George J. *Becoming Mexican American: Ethnicity, Culture and Identity in Chicano Los Angeles, 1900–1945.* New York: Oxford University Press, 1993.

Sánchez, Luis Rafael. *La guagua aérea.* San Juan: Editorial Cultural, 1994.

Sánchez-Carretero, Cristina. "Santos y Misterios as Channels of Communication in the Diaspora: Afro-Dominican Religious Practices Abroad." *Journal of American Folklore* 11, no. 469 (summer 2005): 308–26.

Sánchez Valverde, Antonio. *Ensayos*. Vol. 5 of *Biblioteca de Clásicos Dominicanos*. Santo Domingo: Ediciones de la Fundación Corripio, 1988.

San Miguel, Pedro Luís. *La isla imaginada: Historia, identidad y utopía en La Española*. San Juan: Isla Negra, 1997.

Sarmiento, Domingo Faustino. *Facundo: O, civilización y barbarie*. Buenos Aires, 1845.

Shea, Renée. "The Hunger to Tell: Edwidge Danticat and the Farming of Bones." *MaComère* 2 (1999): 12–22.

Silié Valdez, Rubén Arturo. "Aspectos y variables de las relaciones entre República Dominicana y Haití." *Futuros: Revista Trimestral Latinoamericana y Caribeña de Desarrollo Sustentable* 3, no. 9 (2005): 3–20.

Silver, Michael. "Eugenics and Compulsory Sterilization Laws: Providing Redress for the Victims of a Shameful Era in United States History." *George Washington Law Review* 72 (2003): 862.

Sommer, Doris. *El masacre se pasa a pie: Guilt and Impotence under Trujillo*. Piscataway, NJ: Livingston College, 1979.

———. *Foundational Fictions: The National Romances of Latin America*. Berkeley: University of California Press, 1993.

Stinchcomb, Dawn F. *The Development of Literary Blackness in the Dominican Republic*. Gainesville: University Press of Florida, 2004.

Suárez, Lucía. *The Tears of Hispaniola: Haitian and Dominican Diaspora Memory*. Gainesville: University Press of Florida, 2006.

Taylor, Diana. *The Archive and the Repertoire: Performing Cultural Memory in the Americas*. Durham: Duke University Press, 2003.

Thompson, Krista. *An Eye for the Tropics: Tourism, Photography, and Framing of the Caribbean Picturesque*. Durham: Duke University Press, 2006.

Tomlinson, Barbara, and George Lipsitz. "American Studies as Accompaniment." *American Quarterly* 65, no. 1 (2013): 1–30.

Torres-Saillant, Silvio. *El retorno de las yolas: Ensayos sobre diáspora, democracia y dominicanidad*. Santo Domingo: Trinitaria, 1999.

———. *Introduction to Dominican Blackness*. New York: CUNY Dominican Studies Institute, City College of New York, 1999.

———. "La condición rayana: La promesa ciudadana en el lugar del 'Quicio.'" In *La frontera: Prioridad en la agenda nacional del siglo XXI*, 220–228. Santo Domingo: Secretaria de Estado de las Fuerzas Armadas, 2003.

———. "The Tribulations of Blackness: Stages in Dominican Racial Identity." *Latin American Perspectives* 25, no. 3 (May 1998): 126–46.

Treudley, Mary. "The United States and Santo Domingo, 1789–1866." *Journal of Race Development* 7 (July 1916): 83–145.

Trouillot, Michel-Rolph. *Silencing the Past: Power and the Production of History*. Boston: Beacon, 1995.

Turits, Richard Lee. *Foundations of Despotism: Peasants, the Trujillo Regime, and Modernity in Dominican History*. Stanford: Stanford University Press, 2003.

———. "A World Destroyed, a Nation Imposed: The 1937 Haitian Massacre in the Dominican Republic." *Hispanic American Historical Review* 82, no. 3 (August 2002): 589–635.

Ureña, Salomé. *Poesías de Salomé Ureña de Henríquez*. Santo Domingo: García Hermanos, 1880.

Utrera, Cripriano de, and Emilio Demorizi. *Polémica de Enriquillo*. Santo Domingo: Editora del Caribe, 1973.

Valdez, Juan R. "Language in the Dominican Republic: Between Hispanism and Panamericanism." In *A Political History of Spanish: The Making of a Language*, edited by José del Valle, 182–96. Cambridge: Cambridge University Press, 2013.

Valerio-Holguín, Fernando. "Primitive Borders: Cultural Identity and Ethnic Cleansing in the Dominican Republic." In *Primitivism and Identity in America: Essays on Art, Literature, and Culture*, edited by José Eduardo González, 75–88. Tucson: University of Arizona Press, 2000.

Vallejo, Catharina. *Las madres de la patria y las bellas mentiras: Imágenes de la mujer en el discurso literario nacional de la República Dominicana, 1844–1899*. Miami: Universal, 1999.

Vargas, Freddy, dir. *El seno de la esperanza* [Milk of Hope]. V Films, 2012.

Veloz-Maggiolo, Marcio. "Tipología del tema haitiano en la literatura." In *Sobre cultura dominicana . . . y otras culturas*, 93–144. Santo Domingo: Alfa y Omega, 1977.

Vergés, Pedro. *Sólo cenizas hallarás (bolero)*. Barcelona: Destino, 1980.

Victoriano-Martínez, Ramón Antonio. *Rayanos y Dominicanyorks: La dominicanidad del siglo XXI*. Pittsburg: Instituto Internacional de Literatura Iberoamericana, 2014.

Warren, Benjamin S., and Charles F. Bolduan. "War Activities of the United States Public Health Service." *Public Health Reports* 134, no. 23 (June 6, 1919): 1245–48.

Welles, Sumner. *Naboth's Vineyard: The Dominican Republic (1844–1924)*. Mamaroneck, NY: Paul P. Appel, [1928] 1966.

Wheeler, Roxann. *The Complexion of Race: Categories of Difference in Eighteenth-Century British Culture*. Philadelphia: University of Pennsylvania Press, 2000.

Willet, John, ed. and trans. *Brecht on Theatre*. New York: Hill and Wang, 1964.

Williams, Claudette. "The Development of Literary Blackness in the Dominican Republic." *Caribbean Quarterly* 52, no. 1 (2006): 74.

Wilson, Woodrow. "Remarks to the Associated Press in New York." April 20, 1915. In *The Papers of Woodrow Wilson*, vol. 33, edited by Arthur S. Link. Princeton: Princeton University Press, 1980.

Wucker, Michelle. *Why the Cocks Fight: Dominicans, Haitians, and the Struggle for Hispaniola*. New York: Hill and Wang, 2000.

Zeller, Neici M. *Discursos y espacios femeninos en República Dominicana, 1880–1961*. Santo Domingo: Editorial Gráfica, 2012.

INDEX

Abu Ghraib, 60–61
Accessible Citizenship (Minich), 152
advertisement industry, absence of Dominicans in, 3
Afghanistan, US occupation of, 91
African Americans: Haiti as inspiration to, 78, 107–9, 163, 234n48; rejection of masculinity in, 74–77; slavery and history of, 7–8; terrorist acts against, 210–13
Afro-religious traditions: anti-Haitian portrayals of, 44–45, 56–57; black Dominican identity and, 164–69; *despojo* (cleansing ceremony), 117–18, 161–62, 239n64; Dominicanyork and, 194; *fukú* (Afro-Dominican curse), 83–84; in Haiti, 93–94; historical silence and, 4–5; Liborismo movement and, 65–72, 230n143; Massacre of 1937 in, 117–26; Mateo as symbol of, 67–72; *montarse* (possession) in, 82–92; US marginalization of, 60–64; women's roles in, 222n16
Alcántara, Dominga, 58–64, 66
Alexander, M. Jaqui, 4–5, 81–82, 157
Alexis, Jacques Stéphen, 17, 118–23, 236n75
Alexis, Stéphen, 118–19
Althusser, Louis, 213n18
Álvarez, Julia, 17, 84, 125, 200, 215n14
American Empire, exclusion of Dominican Republic in history of, 2–3
Andújar, Águeda, 50–53, 215n8
Andújar, Ana Francisca, 53

Andújar, Andrés, 24–25, 45, 53–54
Andújar, Marcela, 53
Andújar Murders of 1822, testimony and historical accounts of, 12, 14, 16, 24–27, 45–57
Annexation of Texas, 3
anti-Haitianism: Bosch's condemnation of, 102–9; Dominican Republic independence and, 15, 17, 28–37; in US film, 44–45; Galindo Virgins narrative and, 25–27, 41–49; as global force, 210–13; global war on blackness and, 203–13; Haitian intruder figure in Dominican literature and, 49–57; Hispanophile ideology and, 81–82, 109–17; history of, 6–10, 15, 17; in *Línea fronteriza* video installation, 146–54; linguistic difference and, 149–54; in literature, 15, 44–49; Literature of Compassion as response to, 102–9; Massacre of 1937 and, 94–96; in political and cultural imaginary, 78–82; in post-Trujillo era, 101–9; rayano consciousness and, 131–34; Rueda's poetry and, 139–46; silencing of archive concerning, 109–17
Anzaldúa, Gloria, 4–6, 140, 170, 173, 200, 207
Archive of Dominicanidad, 10; contra-*dictions* in, 12–15; dominicano ausente poetics and, 174–202; Dominican Republic independence and, 30–37; Galindo Virgins narrative and, 25–27, 47–49; Indian affirmation in, 39;

18–19, 170–202; race and borders and, 7–10; rayano consciousness and, 131–34; spiritual possession and, 83–92; terminology of, 213n1, 214n33; whiteness as guardian of, 52–57

dominicanidad ausente, 18–19, 170–202; Dominicanyork and, 192–99; exile and poetics of, 175–80; migration and race and, 186–92; post-Trujillo politics and, 180–86

Dominicanish (performance), 174, 186–92, 196–202

dominicanismos, Penson's dictionary of, 40

dominicano/a ausente, 18–19, 170–202; exile and poetics of, 175–80

dominicano español identity, 34–35, 38–39, 218n57

Dominican Republic: anti-Haitianism in, 15, 17, 28–37, 98–101, 161–69; citizenship exclusion for Haitians in, 203–7; denationalization of Haitians born in, 57, 106–9, 234n44; earthquake in Haiti and, 12, 129–34, 239n2; fictional images of, 38–57; "footnote condition of," 3; foundational myth of, 7–10, 28–30, 49–57; Haitian migration to, 6–10, 12, 14, 77–82, 227n86; independence for, 28–37, 213n6; Massacre of 1937 in, 12, 14, 17; Massacre of 1937 in memory of, 93–96, 231n5; overview of scholarship on, 15–19; post-Trujillo upheaval in, 180–86, 243n25; sexscape images of, 85–92; Spanish re-annexation campaign and, 27, 29, 42, 47–49; US intervention in, 2–3, 6–10, 12, 16, 58–92, 102–9, 116–17, 173–74

Dominican Revolutionary Party (Partido Revolucionario Dominicano) (PRD), 177, 234n40

Dominicanyork, 167–68, 171–202; El Nié and, 192–99; identity of, 4–6; language and, 199–202

dominicanidad: blackness and affirmation of, 39; bolero as allegory in, 183–86; evolution in US of, 1–3; Galindo Virgins narrative and, 26–27, 44–49, 56–57; Haitian role in, 15–16; Mateo's image and, 71–72; poetics of ausente, 18–19, 170–202; race and borders and, 7–10; rayano consciousness and, 131–34; spiritual possession and, 83–92; terminology of, 213n1, 214n33; whiteness as guardian of, 52–57

double-consciousness, 244n55

Douglass, Frederick, 8–9

Duarte, Juan Pablo, 29, 31–37, 39, 42, 164, 241n91

Du Bois, W. E. B., 8, 79, 150, 234n48, 244n55

Durán, Loré, 205, 246n7

Duvalier, Francois, 118–20

earthquake in Haiti, 12, 17–18, 129–34; Haitian-Dominican border and, 144–46, 150–54

East Indian cultural practices, Caribbean identity and, 196–99

El Cable newspaper, 64–66, 79–82, 91, 223n28, 224n38

"El Corte," as euphemism for Massacre of 1937, 95–96, 100–101, 118

El Masacre se pasa a pie (Prestol Castillo), 110–17

El Nié, 4–6, 11; defined, 242n7; dominicano ausentes and, 173–202; Dominicanyork and, 192–99; migration and race in, 186–92

El seno de la esperanza (Milk of Hope) (film), 153–54, 168–69

Emmanuel Methodist Church (Charleston), murders at, 210

embodied memory, Alexander's concept of, 82–92, 224n42

The Emperor Jones (O'Neill), 78–79, 82

Enriquillo (Galván), 38–39, 45, 48–49, 52, 56, 218n68

masculinity: Mateo's projection of, 69–72, 76–77; rejection of black masculinity, 74–77

Massacre of 1937, 12, 14, 17; Afro-religious traditions and, 117–26; Galindo Virgins narrative and, 27, 55–56; Gates's discussion of, 163; global context for, 210–13; in Hernández's "Da pa lo do," 156; historical silence about, 93–96; historiography concerning, 231n7, 238n44; linguistic difference following, 149–54; Literature of Compassion and, 103–9, 125–26; memorial to, 214n40; in Prestol Castillo's work, 109–17; in Rueda's poetry, 138–46; statistics on victims of, 231n3; testimony concerning, 231n5

Mateo, André L., 102

Mateo, Olivorio, 12, 14, 16, 58–60; embodied memory in death of, 83–92; execution of, 64–66, 76–77, 79–82; as religious leader, 67–72, 224n36

Matibag, Eugenio, 121, 231n7, 232n16

Mayes, April, 43

McRuer, Robert, 152

media: anti-Haitian discourse in, 44–45, 79–82; contrasting images of Haiti and Dominican Republic in, 159–60; Dominican censorship of, 223n28; Haitian earthquake coverage in, 130–34; images of Dominicans in, 3; Massacre of 1937 coverage by, 100–101, 233n31; paternalist rhetoric in US occupation coverage, 74–77

Mella, Ramón Matías, 34

Méndez, Danny, 233n39

Méndez, Denny, 200, 241n88

merengue: Trujillo's co-optation of, 182

messianic movements, history in Latin America of, 69–72

mestizaje: Galindo Virgins narrative and, 27, 47–49; Hispanism and, 37; in Latin American fiction, 38–39; race and nationalism and, 7–10, 31–32, 189–90

Mexico, migration to US from, 188–89

middle class, emergence in Dominican Republic of, 68–72, 182–86

Mignolo, Walter, 5

migration: border embodiment and, 4–6; dominicanidad ausente and, 186–92; of Dominicans to Europe, 242n5; of Dominicans to US, 2, 84–92, 167–69; global war on blackness and, 203–7; in post-Trujillo era, 180–86

Minich, Julie, 152

"Mi patria" (Ureña), 25–26, 216n26

Mirabal, Taína, 164, 241n91

Mirabal sisters, martyrdom of, 25, 215n14

Monroe Doctrine, 73–74, 230n140

montarse (possession), 82–92

Montero, Hernando, 217n47

Moraga, Chérrie, 5–6

moreno oscuro (dark brown), 33–34

Morse, George H. Jr. (Captain), 59–60, 62–66, 80–82

Moya Pons, Frank, 191

mulata cabaretera, 194

mulatos (mulataje): colonial exclusion of, 62–64; Dominican concept of, 9, 30–37, 43–44, 52–53, 189–90; in Radical Party, 217n34; whiteness and, 52–57, 216n24

Muñoz, José Esteban, 166–67

mysticism, in Literature of Compassion, 109

Narratives of Migration and Displacement in Dominican Literature (Méndez), 233n39

National City Bank of New York, Dominican finances in, 60

nationalism: disability images and, 150–54; in Dominican literature, 110–17; Dominican Republic independence and, 29–30; Rueda's critique of, 142–46

nationalization, elite support for, 100–101

Nation and Citizen in the Dominican Re-

proletarian literature, 119–26, 236n76

prostitution in Dominican Republic, 87–92, 227n120, 227n123

Puello, Garrido, 67–69, 224n36, 224n38

Puerto Rico: Bosch in, 175–76; Dominican community in, 242n5; Hispanism and, 30–31, 217n39; migration to US from, 189; military bases in, 102–3; revolutionary movement in, 41; transnationalism in, 4

Puri, Shalini, 37, 196

Quiroga, Juan Facundo, 220n105

"Rabia" (photograph), 171, 173–74, 180

race: anti-Haitianism and, 160–69, 210–13; dominicanidad and role of, 1–3; dominicanidad ausente and, 186–92; dominicano ausentes and, 173–202; Dominican Republic independence and, 30–37; eugenics and, 88–89; in Galindo Virgins narratives, 52–57; global war on blackness and, 203–13; Haiti-DR border and, 6–10; Hispanophile ideology and, 98–99; institutionalized racism and, 210–13; rayana identity and, 131–34; rejection of black masculinity and, 74–77. See also black Dominican identity

racexiles: Dominicans as, 173, 186–87, 191, 194, 206–7

Radical Party (Dominican Republic), 28–29, 31, 45, 217n34

Rama, Ángel, 31

Ramírez, Wenceslao (General), 63–64, 222n19

rayanos: consciousness of, 131–46; in dominicanidad discourse, 17–19; Dominican politics and, 42–43; earthquake in Haiti and consciousness of, 130–34; genocide of, 93–96; Haitian-Dominican collaboration and, 205–7; in Hernández's work, 167–69;

Liborismo movement and, 68–72; in Literature of Compassion, 108–9; in Massacre of 1937, 14, 17; in Pérez video installations, 148–54; in Prestol Castillo's writing, 110–17; racialized classification of, 2–3; in Rueda's poetry, 134–46; terminology of, 213n7, 217n27; transborder consciousness of, 155–69

Reconicido (Recognized), 206

Renda, Mary A., 74

Reparations Act (1825), 29

repetition, silencing of history through, 13–14, 25–27, 53

República del Haití Español, 28

Restoration War, 29, 216n27, 246n6

Rivas, Wello, 184

Rivero, Daniel, 206

Robertson, Pat, 159–60

Robles, Frances, 241n90

Rockefeller Group, 60

Rondón, Pura Emeterio, 206

Roosevelt, Franklin D., 77

Roosevelt, Theodore, 73–74

Roosevelt Corollary, 73–74, 158–59, 219n77

Rosario, Nelly, 17, 84–92, 123, 125

Roth, Wendy, 163

Rueda, Manuel, 18, 133–46, 238n31, 238n38; Línea fronteriza video installation and, 146–54

Ruiz, Félix María, 32

Salcedo, Luisa, 87–88

salves: to Mateo, 67–72; possession as theme of, 83–92

Sánchez, Francisco del Rosario, 34

Sánchez, Luis Rafael, 4

San Miguel, Pedro, 14–15, 124–25, 175

Santana, José, 206–7

Santana, Pedro, 29, 42

santera, 117–18

Santo Domingo: "de facto emancipation" in, 33; Hispanophile ideology in,

49; map of, 24; Penson's depictions of, 40–41

Santos-Febres, Mayra, 135

Sarmiento, Domingo Faustino, 36–37, 211, 218n62, 220n105

Schomburg, Arturo, 8, 79, 234n48

sea-border metaphor, in Rueda's poetry, 135

Sentencias de los reos de Galindo, 26

7 Días digital journal, 206

sexualized body of Dominican subject: Andújar Murders of 1822 and, 16, 50–52; Dominicanyork and, 194; US imperialism and, 85–92

Silencing the Past (Trouillot), 14

Silié, Ruben, 136–37

slavery: Dominican abolition of, 33–34; in Galindo Virgins narrative, 45–49; Haitian revolt against, 78–82; Hispaniola independence movements and, 28–29; race and citizenship and history of, 7–10

social realism, in Dominican literature, 102, 109

socioreligious movements, history in Latin America of, 69–72

Solano, Patricia, 206

soledá (loneliness or desolation), 68–72

Soledad (Cruz), 83–84

solidarity, Dominican narratives of, 159

Sólo cenizas hallarás (bolero) (Vergés), 181–86

Sommer, Doris, 14–15, 38, 110, 183

Song of the Water Saints (Rosario), 84–92, 123

sovereignty of Dominican Republic, Haiti as threat to, 41–43, 98–101

Spain: Dominican Republic independence and, 28–30; Hispanophile ideology and, 34–36, 43–44, 156–57; reannexation campaign for Hispaniola by, 27, 29, 42, 47–49

Spanish-American War, 3, 91; Hispanic Caribbean after, 9

Stinchcomb, Dawn F., 10

Suárez, Lucía, 90, 123

sugar industry: corporate ownership of, 60; labor migration in, 77–82; Liborismo movement and, 68–72; in Literature of Compassion, 102–9, 119–26; Massacre of 1937 and, 94–96; workplace conditions in, 232n8

The Sugar Babies (documentary), 232n8

Tapia y Rivera, Alejandro, 31, 217n39

tattoos, 148–49

Taylor, Diana, 14–15, 161

Tejana identity, 4

"Terrible 12," 230n144

textos montados (possessed texts), 84–92, 123

textuality, history of, 11

Thompson, Krista, 85

Tomlinson, Barbara, 211

Torres-Saillant, Silvio, 2, 134, 163, 168, 170, 172–73, 179–80, 190–93

Trabucazo (blunderbuss shot), 28, 30

tradiciones, 219n75

transnationalism: border embodiment and, 4–6; dominicanidad discourse and, 17; in Literature of Compassion, 118–26; Massacre of 1937 and transformation of, 97–101

Treaty of Aranjuez, 136–37

Treaty of Peace, Friendship, and Commerce, 27

Trouillot, Michel, 13–14, 95–96

Trujillo, Rafael Leónidas, 7, 68; antiHaitianism and, 143–44, 233n24; assassination of, 91–92; Bosch and, 175–76; Dominican migration to US during regime of, 84–92; Hispanophile ideology under, 35–37, 48–49, 55–57, 204–7, 233n24; intellectuals' support of, 100–103, 109–10; Massacre of 1937 and, 93–101, 116–17; merengue co-opted by, 182; Rueda and, 140–46;

www.ingramcontent.com/pod-product-compliance
Lightning Source LLC
Chambersburg PA
CBHW071733270326
41928CB00013B/2666